COMPETITIVE STRATEGY FOR MEDIA FIRMS

Strategic and Brand Management in Changing Media Markets

LEA's COMMUNICATION SERIES
Jennings Bryant and Dolf Zillmann, General Editors

For a complete list of titles in LEA's Communication Series, please contact Lawrence Erlbaum Associates, Publishers at www.erlbaum.com

COMPETITIVE STRATEGY FOR MEDIA FIRMS

Strategic and Brand Management in Changing Media Markets

Sylvia M. Chan-Olmsted
University of Florida

LAWRENCE ERLBAUM ASSOCIATES, PUBLISHERS
2006   Mahwah, New Jersey   London

Lawrence Erlbaum Associates, Inc., Publishers
10 Industrial Avenue
Mahwah, New Jersey 07430
www.erlbaum.com

Cover design by Tomai Maridou

Library of Congress Cataloging-in-Publication Data

Chan-Olmsted, Sylvia M.
Competitive strategy for media firms : strategic and brand
    management in changing media markets / Sylvia M.
    Chan-Olmstead.
        p.   cm. — (LEA's communication series)
    Includes bibliographical references and index.
ISBN 0-8058-4812-6 (cloth : alk. paper)
1. Broadcasting—Management.   2. Brand name prod-
    ucts—Management.   3. Brand name products—Marketing.
    I. Title. II. Series
HE8689.4.C43 2006
384.54'068'4—dc22   2005040117
                                                          CIP

Books published by Lawrence Erlbaum Associates are printed
on acid-free paper, and their bindings are chosen for strength
and durability.

Printed in the United States of America
10   9   8   7   6   5   4   3   2   1

This book is dedicated to my heavenly father,
who lavishes me with abundant grace,
and to my dear husband, who is the most
precious blessing in my life.

Contents

Preface

It is my pleasure to present to you this collection of work that addresses the strategic-competition aspect of the electronic media industries as they respond to the arrival of new technologies such as the broadband distribution systems, the Internet, and interactive television. Over the last 15 years, I have devoted much of my time researching the drivers and results of the strategic conducts of many fascinating media companies. I am always curious about the underlying economic factors that shape what we read, listen, and watch every day. I am even more inquisitive about the applicability of various business concepts for analyzing media products. After years of short-form journal article writing, I discovered that all of my work has centered on the topics of strategy, competition, brand management, alliances/mergers and acquisitions, and corporate diversification of media firms. The permeating theme in all these publications is evidently on how media firms compete strategically in a changing environment. With various articles tackling different electronic media industries and applying a mixture of business constructs, I started to see the need to integrate all these interesting subjects and to provide a tool that would help others share my approach to this area of media economics and management studies. With the encouragement of Linda Bathgate, Communications Editor for Lawrence Erlbaum Associates, and the sabbatical leave granted by the University of Florida, I embarked on a writing journey that would survey a relatively new area of investigation in media economics and management—strategy, all in the context of a changing digital media marketplace.

The premise of this book is the need for all media firms to strategize in response to the arrival of new media. The focus not only is timely but also means a more realistic, integrated approach to media industry studies. This book covers all electronic media industries, including both the content providers and distribution systems. It is also the first book to provide overviews of strategic management, branding, and corporate diversification concepts and apply the rich business literature in these areas to media industries. I sincerely hope that you find the end product valuable and even inspiring.

I am grateful to Linda Bathgate, Communications Editor for Lawrence Erlbaum Associates (LEA), and the rest of the staff at LEA for their assistance in the publication of this work. I also appreciate the support from the College of Journalism and Communications at the University of Florida. I am especially indebted to my wonderful research assistants Byeng-Hee Chang and Goro Oba. I don't know how I would ever grow as a researcher without the stimulation and challenges from being an adviser to these exceptionally bright doctoral students.

I would like to also thank my mentor, Dr. Barry Litman of Michigan State University, who opened my eyes to this exciting area of research, and my dear friend, Alan Albarran, who constantly encourages me to climb the next step. Finally, I am most grateful to my parents, who instilled in me the work ethics that carry me through many long, hard days of researching and writing; to my husband, who is always there to take care of "things" when I close my home office door to work; and to my lovely children, Lanya and Wesley, who taught me that life is much more than just being a good teacher or researcher.

—*Sylvia M. Chan-Olmsted*

Chapter 1

Introduction: Enter the Arena of Strategic Media Management

WHY THIS BOOK?

Studies in media and communications have historically been conducted from a "content" perspective with focuses on their effects and roles or approached structurally within a political, legal, or technological context. Although these emphases help us understand and improve the societies we live in, the recent addition of the managerial and economic literatures into this discipline has provided media scholars with a means of comprehending further the critical issues of organizational behavior, business strategy, competition/market concentration, and financial performance that often shape how media firms and industries operate in a society.

It is a fair assessment to say that the fields of media management and economics have evolved tremendously over the last 20 years. The body of literature has grown to include not only basic textbooklike work that reviews general media management and economics concepts and practices (Albarran, 2001; Alexander, Owers, & Carveth, 1993; Doyle, 2002b; Gershon, 2001; Owen & Wildman, 1992; Picard, 1989), but also in-depth writings that survey specific aspects of media industries such as globalization, media ownership, competition, and finance (Albarran & Chan-Olmsted, 1998; Compaine & Gomery, 2000; Dimmick, 2003; Doyle, 2002a; Picard, 2002; Vogel, 2001). The development of various scholarly journals such as The Journal of Media Economics, The International Journal on Media Management, and The Journal of Media Business Studies also offers a platform for both theoretical and empirical work that investigates how media function as an economic institution in a contemporary market environment. In essence, the maturing

1

of media management and economics as a subfield of media and communications studies has been propelled by many scholars' painstaking tasks of laying the fundamental, general framework of how to examine media from various business perspectives and the continuous contribution of scholarly articles that address timely topics such as convergence, consolidation, audience demands of new media, and the evolution of media markets.

So what is the role of this book in the context of the current literary landscape? Compared to the books that offer an overview of management functions such as financial, personnel, and programming management in media organizations, this book attempts to focus more on a subfield of management studies that tackles the subjects of strategic and brand management, with empirical data to illustrate how these concepts influence the decisions and behaviors of media firms. It also holistically integrates the new media context in all chapters and offers both descriptive and analytical discussions. Compared to the books that address general industrial economic issues in media industries, this book is different in that it reviews more micro, firm-related subjects and how these strategic developments shape the media market. In essence, the goal here is to provide empirical contributions coherent to the analytical foundations of a relatively new area of media management and economic literatures.

Outside of the realm of media management and economics, abundant literatures exist in the general business discipline that address the concepts, practices, and issues in strategic or brand management. Although these works are valuable in providing the fundamental analytical frameworks for our studies, we would like to argue that media products have certain inherently unique characteristics that necessitate the revision of some generic concepts derived from nonmedia industries because strategic decisions are often resource dependent and rely on the specificity within a particular industry (Chatterjee & Wernerfelt, 1991). As it is the goal of this book to adopt and appropriately adapt relevant business frameworks and concepts for the analysis of media markets, we now review the major distinctions between media and nonmedia products. Understanding the unique combination of these characteristics is the first step in effectively examining media organizations as an economic institution.

Media products, as a "cultural" output, possess certain qualities that challenge the traditional premise of economic theory. Most notably, the complexity and ambiguity of the objectives of media organizations in a society present a difficult task in assessing economic "efficiency" in the allocation of resources (Doyle, 2002b). Although many media organizations operate to maximize profits and shareholder value, because of their visible role in a society, they also have to respond to the intrinsic cultural identity and value objectives of the society, which might be manifested in a set of regulatory objectives. This set of "official" societal objectives could be further complicated by the fact that a discrepancy might exist between governmental and actual societal media needs. Because the notion of "economic efficiency" is inextricably linked to objectives, the application of conventional economic theory is difficult under such circumstances (Doyle, 2002b).

Media organizations offer dual, complementary products of "content" and "distribution." The content component is intangible and inseparable from a tangible distribution medium. Because intangible, content-based media products may be stored and presented in various formats, media organizations would likely attempt to extend their product lines into related content formats to benefit from content repurposing, marketing know-how, and sharing of production resources. It is also logical for these organizations to acquire or develop distribution products and content products that complement each other. The fact that an existing product may be redistributed to and reused in different outlets, via a "windowing" process, reinforces the advantage of diversifying into multiple related distribution sectors in various geographical markets to increase the product's revenue potential. Such a resource alignment advantage encourages certain expansion strategies (e.g., vertical integration and related diversification) and limits the competitive options of some small, stand-alone firms. Luckily, as a "cultural" good, the value of a content product is dependent on consumers' appreciation of the meaning it expresses. Because each media content creation (not the distribution medium or a duplicated copy) is, by nature, heterogeneous, nonstandardizable, and individually evaluated based on consumers' personal tastes, there are ample opportunities for new-product development based on creativity.

Many media "content" products are also nonexcludable and nondepletable "public goods" whose consumption by one individual does not interfere with their availability to another but adds to the scale economies in production. The public-goods notion magnifies the importance of abundant resources in initial investment (i.e., production of the first copy) and the benefit of appealing to a large audience because of the negligible marginal cost. Nevertheless, media markets are also highly susceptive to technological development and consumer preferences. The advent of digitization, for example, is lowering the initial cost of content production and enhancing product appeals, thus lessening the effect of scale economies. Adding to the complexity of the public-good characteristic, not only are the market boundaries between various types of media products becoming blurred (i.e., the degree of substitutability is increasing) due to technological advances, but also many media firms are dependent on dual revenue sources from consumers and advertisers. The dual-revenue source mechanism, coupled with the public-good nature of media products, tends to encourage the strategy of offering a media content that appeals to the largest possible group of marketable, desirable consumers. Although consumers' content preferences and advertisers' valuation of the preferences are intrinsically linked, without a direct payment from or a price mechanism based on consumers, the responsiveness of product development in reflecting consumers' preferences is less acute and the conventional economic resource allocation theorem is less applicable.

Finally, media products are subject to the cultural preferences and existing communication infrastructure of each geographic market or country and are often subject to more regulatory control because of their pervasive impacts on individual societies. Because of the importance of cultural sensitivity and understanding of the regulatory environment, media firms are more inclined to invest in related products or in related geographic markets to take advantage of their acquired local knowledge and relationships. The dependency on local communication and media infrastructure may also lead to a strategy that is geographically related (i.e., regionalized). This is because geographically clustered markets are often at similar stages of infrastructure development, and clusters of media distribution systems may lead to cost/resource-sharing benefits.

In addition to the aforementioned unique economic properties, today's media markets are competitive, global, and technology-driven and could easily be classified as having an uncertain industry environment. Literatures have suggested that "uncertainty" often leads firms' to active retooling or reinventing of their resources to gain competitive advantages (Landers & Chan-Olmsted, 2004). In other words, managerial decisions concerning the process and content of developing and implementing activities that align a firm's organizational resources with environmental changes (i.e., strategy formulation and implementation) become much more critical. Taking the emergent role of "strategic function" in media markets into consideration, this book is ultimately designed to add to the scholarly work in media management and economics by addressing the "strategy" dimension of media organizations with reviews and empirical investigation of relevant strategic management (including global diversification strategy) and brand management concepts.

HOW IS TODAY'S MEDIA ARENA DIFFERENT?

As mentioned previously, the process of strategy formulation and implementation is basically a firm's careful alignment of its internal resources with the changing environment to develop competitive advantages. The magnitude of this challenge is greater today than it has been historically because the media arena has changed significantly. Not only are there more media and media outlets, there are more ways to package and present media products. Not only have the geographical boundaries of media expanded, the boundaries between different media have become blurry. To set the stage for our discussions in media strategy, branding, and corporate diversification, we first review the major trends that have shaped the competitive arena of today's media markets.

Multicasting and Multiple Distribution Outlets

It is common knowledge that the simple days of the big three broadcast networks are forever gone. Technological advances have enabled the provision of abundant outlets for the exhibition of electronic media content. Because of the multicasting opportunities or the availability of multichannel capacities, media organizations are faced with a changed market landscape that requires careful deliberations of the following realities. First, the increase in exhibition outlets magnifies the importance of a narrowcasting approach, as well as the efforts to build a relationship with a smaller group of audience and to be responsive to what the audience demands. It also means that a certain degree of differentiation is necessary even among the non-narrowcasting content providers (e.g., CNN, a provider of news, a commodity product, needs to be perceived differently than Fox News). Because consumers now have more choices, content product development has become even more essential and scheduling, packaging, and windowing strategies are more critical in determining the total revenues that might be generated from one product. In a way, there are opportunities for new business models and revenues because of the heterogeneity of the environment. On the other hand, organization size becomes a factor as the ownership of multiple outlets grows to be more strategically significant. In essence, with more outlets available, there are either more competitors or different types of competitors (e.g., more consolidated owners). Also, the increase in multiplicity means more chances for content production newcomers and advertising opportunities for better targeted consumers, while, at the same time, this multiplicity translates to a more fragmented and less loyal audience. A successful media organization needs to strategize within this changing market context.

Broadened Pipelines, Digitization, and the Internet

As the impact of technology has reached beyond the facilitation of multiple media outlets and multicasting, we have gradually entered the era of broadband communications, the infrastructure touted as an essential building block of future digital entertainment because its platform enables the fast delivery of digital videos with the personalization and on-demand nature of the Internet. Specifically, broadband systems enhance traditional television with richer graphics, television crossover links to Web sites, electronic mail, chat room activity, and online commerce through a back channel (t-commerce). As the two leading broadband service providers, digital subscriber lines (DSL) and cable modem, continue to expand in this emerging market, we are witnessing a new phase of development for the television medium. Just as the introduction of cable television added the multichannel, narrowcasting capability to broadcast television, the arrival of the Internet and broadband infrastructure brought more enhanced functions such as interactivity and personalization to cable television. Such an expansion of television functions and content varieties means more opportunities for product differentiation in the marketplace and thus more strategic options for market participants. In addition to broadened pipelines, the arrival of digital content production, processing, and distribution also seems to elevate electronic media into an important contender for media supremacy.

The exponential growth of the Internet has changed the rules of competition in many industry sectors. The "reach" and "speed" of the development, coupled with the unique characteristics of interactivity and personalization, amplify the need for innovative business strategies from the competing media incumbents in their attempt to counter or leverage the rising popularity of this new market entrant. In fact, the interactivity and personalization functions enabled by the new broadband, Internet-led, digital media system offer media organizations a unprecedented opportunity of formulating innovative marketing strategies that attract a new audience and build loyalty.

The strategic importance of the Internet is especially evident for the television industry as television and the Internet develop a symbiotic relationship with significant financial implications. Television provides the most desirable marketing communication channels for Internet marketers. With millions of Web sites available on the Net, the Internet is the most cluttered medium in the world. To succeed in marketing an online brand, a marketer most likely will need to distribute messages via a mass medium such as broadcast television to create broad awareness of the product or service, or use a niche medium such as cable television to connect with target markets. On the other hand, the increasingly critical role of the Internet in American media consumers' daily lives has led to a reorientation of business strategy and operations by the leading "mass" medium, the television broadcasters. With the arrival of digital television, many television broadcasters are contemplating the feasibility of Web-enhanced applications such as on-screen links to advertisers' Web addresses, localized news services, late-breaking news, sports statistics, interactive polling, situated documentary presentation, online chat, and links to movie trailers and ticketing services (Nelson, 2001; Pavlik, 2001). All of these changes translate to strategic complexity as well as opportunities.

Changes in Media Value Chains and New Revenue Alternatives

The aforementioned transformation of media products and systems also modifies the existing value chains in media markets. For example, content producers are now capable of delivering products directly to media end users; content media outlets can also participate in e-commerce activities, selling digital media goods along with physical merchandise. The value chain variation is especially evident in the elimination of certain middlemen and the changing functions of packagers and technological facilitators. Specifically, faced with abundant media choices and narrowcasting options, the role of content aggregators/packagers, whose core activities are to assemble contents into packages that appeal to different segments of customers, is becoming strategically significant. Their competencies in accessing popular mass-appeal content, niche content, or narrowcasting distributors; repackaging content for different user segments and/or distribution systems; and having expertise in areas of marketing, brand management, and publicity become critical. In essence, because of the complexity and importance of matching the right product with the right segment of audience in a market full of choices, these media organizations have to develop strategies that enhance their knowledge of consumers, technology know-how, and creative use of information. Brand management expertise would also be essential as the factors of differentiated qualities and brand images are likely to influence consumers' decisions. Technological advances also lifted the role of media product facilitators, which include software developers and hardware manufacturers such as Microsoft and Dell. These organizations add value to the product by providing navigation and interfacing equipment and software programs that enable the easy access of media products. These facilitators influence the media arena in two ways: They might become a major player in a newer-media market segment (e.g., Miscrosoft's MSN TV) and/or they might become important strategic alliance partners for the more traditional media organizations (e.g., the alliance between Motorola and NBC). Note that the modification of the value chain also means new, nonconventional revenue potentials such as the direct sales of digital content and space (e.g., spectrum space rental).

The Three Big C's: Convergence, Consolidation, and Conglomerates

With the continuous integration of the Internet, computing, cable television, and telephone industries and the extraordinary growth of demand for Internet-related products and services, we are witnessing the emergence of a multimedia market that is multilateral and interwoven with previously segmented sectors. Some scholars suggested that there has been a transformation of three vertical industries—media, telecommunication, and information technology—into five horizontal value-adding segments of content, packaging, processing, transmission, and devices. These five segments, rather than the individual industries, characterize more succinctly the emerging multimedia industry (Bane, Bradley, & Collis, 1997). Considering the trend toward such a converging media marketplace, communication technology scholars further asserted that there is a growing importance of "strategic positioning" along the integrating value chains of the Internet and television for the providers of content, distribution, software technology, and hardware manufacturers from the television, computing, and online industries (Thielmann &

Dowling, 1999). Just as the introduction of cable television added the multichannel, narrowcasting capability to broadcast television, the arrival of the Internet and broadband infrastructure brought more enhanced functions such as interactivity and personalization to the television medium. Such an expansion of functions and content varieties means more opportunities for product differentiation in the marketplace and thus more strategic options for the market participants.

While convergence has surfaced as one of the major trends in media markets in the last decade, consolidation and the growth of media conglomerates have been the other hotly debated developments. Resting on the assumptions of market power, internal market efficiency, and synergistic benefit, media organizations have embarked on a journey of mergers and acquisitions. For example, the 1990s produced more than $300 billion in major media transactions including big mergers such as Viacom-Paramount, Disney-ABC, and AOL-Time Warner (Croteau & Hoynes, 2001). The interwoven relationship between media organizations due to converging platforms and/or ownerships amplifies the interdependency of one another's strategic actions. In addition, although consolidation or conglomeration sometimes places firms with limited resources in an unfavorable position, convergence also rewards creative product development and marketing ingenuity. Under such a market environment, the key to competitive advantage seems to be a balance between access to resources and strategic innovativeness.

WHAT DRIVES CHANGE?

What are the forces that propel all these changes in media markets? It is essential for us to look beyond the prominent trends of today and investigate the drivers that will continue to shape the environment in which media organizations will operate tomorrow.

Technology

It is evident that the diffusion of communication technologies has become a critical force in shaping not only a society but also the future of its media industries. New media technologies often have the potential of generating additional revenues or cutting costs; they might also transform the rules of competition in existing media markets. The arrival of the Internet and digitization clearly illustrates the diversity of strategies exhibited by different media firms and the magnitude of change brought about by communication technologies. Nevertheless, media management and economics literature has not adequately explored the subject of technology in the context of firm behavior and the drivers of that behavior. In a sense, technology enables the shifting of the balance of power between different types of media organizations and between media and their consumers. For instance, the advent of multiple media outlets, the Internet, and broadband infrastructure seems to have given consumers more control and benefited media content packagers who have better contacts or knowledge of audience. The essential role of technology in today's media markets means that media organizations need to monitor the types and rates of technological changes and diffusion and develop appropriate strategies to capitalize on that technological development.

Globalization

Another driver for today's complex media environment seems to be the growing global economic, political, and cultural interdependency. Just as in the oil and automotive industries earlier this century, the media industry is going through a profound transformation, moving from a primarily national to a global commercial-media market, and in the process creating a group of powerful global media conglomerates such as Bertelsmann, Time Warner, and Sony. An industry can be defined as global if there is some competitive advantage to integrating activities on a worldwide base. Many of the aforementioned media characteristics (e.g., public goods) certainly contribute to a media firm's tendency of gaining competitive advantages via globalization (e.g., building scale economies). In addition, several environmental developments have fostered a climate for multinational expansions. For example, liberalization, privatization, and a series of international reciprocal agreements that occurred in numerous countries in the last two decades have unleashed many media industries that had been held to traditional boundaries that were nearly a hundred years old. Furthermore, technological advancement, customer demand, and multilateral competition in the new converging market have also promoted the trend of globalization (Jamison, 1999).

Changing Audience

As one of the most critical segments of the general environment, the factor of "audience" sets the range of strategic options available to a media organization. The audience size, ethnic mix, age composition, geographic distribution, income allocation, lifestyles, and media habits all play a role in shaping the type and degree of audience demand for media products. Specifically, over the last two decades, we have seen shifts of population geographically (e.g., to the west and south in the United States), growth of certain ethnic and age groups (e.g., the Hispanic segment and baby boomers), change in workforce diversity (e.g., women in the workforce), increase in dual-career couples, a faster-paced lifestyle but fewer physical activities, shorter attention spans, and new composition of media mix (e.g., viewing television and using computer at the same time). The implication of these changes is that, amid the increasing cost of doing business and numbers of stakeholders to answer to, media organizations need to scan, monitor, forecast, and assess the audience segment of the market environment even more diligently because media audiences now have more product choices as well as control over how they consume the media.

WHAT IS THIS BOOK ALL ABOUT?

This book is a collection of work that addresses the strategic competition aspect of the electronic media industries as they respond to the arrival of new technologies such as broadband distribution systems, the Internet, interactive television, and others. Under the premise of a changing media marketplace, this book provides an overview of strategic management concepts and the application of these concepts in the media industries, and examines brand management components, structures, and programs in the context of media products. Finally, this book empirically reviews the phenomenon of global media conglomerates and applies the rich business literature in corporate diversification to media industries.

This book is composed of two sections. The first part offers a primer of the important concepts and theoretical frameworks in brand management, general strategic management, and specific corporate-level strategies and how these concepts and frameworks might be adapted to reflect the unique characteristics of media products. The second part provides empirical examinations of broadcasting, multichannel video, interactive television, and broadband industries following an analytical framework devised for each of the markets. The goal of this work is to survey a relatively new area of study in media economics and management—strategy—and to begin the necessary empirical discussions of many strategy constructs in media industries.

Specifically, chapter 1 presents the rationale for this book, discusses the major trends in various electronic media industries, and establishes the essentiality of "strategy" in today's changing media market. Chapter 2 examines major strategic management concepts and frameworks such as the industrial organization approach and resource-based view of strategy, strategic decision making, leadership, agency theory, strategic entrepreneurship, and competitiveness dynamics theories; discusses how these concepts and frameworks might be applicable to media products in the context of a changing marketplace; and provides examples of strategic management concepts in media industries. Chapter 3 describes major corporate strategies and relevant theories in areas of diversification, mergers and acquisition, strategic networks, and international strategies, and discusses how these strategic approaches and theories might be applicable to media products in the context of a changing marketplace. Chapter 4 reviews major brand management concepts and theoretical frameworks such as brand knowledge structures and brand equity measurement, discusses how these concepts and frameworks might be applicable to media products in the context of a changing marketplace, and provides examples of brand management practices in media industries.

In the second half of the book, chapter 5 first considers the changes in the market environment of the broadcast industry and examines each of the external factors that shape or limit the strategic practices of broadcasters. It then reviews the competitive dynamics in the broadcast industry using Porter's industry analysis framework. It also empirically addresses the issues of strategic alliances, mergers and acquisitions (M&A), Internet business models, and brand management in the new broadcast industry. Chapter 6 also begins with discussions of the changes in the market environment of the multichannel video industry (aka multichannel video programming distribution industry or MVPD) and examines each of the external factors that shape or limit the strategic practices of MVPD firms. It then reviews the competitive dynamics in the MVPD industry using the same framework of analysis. This chapter ends with a review of the issues of strategic alliances, M&A, strategic groups, and a new-media value chain. Chapter 7 first discusses the development of enhanced television. It then examines the drivers, ventures, and the strategic implications of enhanced television as well as the major media firms' enhanced television strategies. The chapter concludes with a proposed strategic architecture for the enhanced television market. Chapter 8 offers a review of the development and competition of the broadband telecommunications industry. It then examines the strategic network strategies of broadband firms and the video ventures of the telephone companies. The chapter ends with a comparison of the strategic differences between cable and telephone broadband firms. Chapter 9 begins with some international business concepts relevant to the global media business. It continues with a review of the world media landscape from the perspectives of media market multiplicity, diffusion, openness, and new-media potential. It also examines the diversification patterns of the leading global media conglomerates and the effect of these strategies on performance. The chapter concludes with an analysis of the top 10 global media conglomerates' current media holdings and a proposed framework for exploring these firms' diversification approaches. Finally, chapter 10 summarizes the concepts essential to the strategy studies of media industries, compares the strategic trends in various industries, and discusses the implications of the similarities and differences. It also addresses the strategic opportunities and challenges for media firms considering the trend toward the development of a digital media marketplace that is characterized by consolidated ownership and fragmented audiences. The chapter ends with a discussion of the important issues concerning the research methods, theories, and topics in the studies of strategic management, brand management, and global diversification as applied in the context of media markets.

REFERENCES

Albarran, A. B. (2001). *Management of electronic media.*Belmont, CA: Wadsworth/Thompson Learning.

Albarran, A. B., & Chan-Olmsted, S. M. (1998). *Global media economics: Commercialization, concentration and integration of world media markets.* Ames: Iowa State University Press.

Alexander, A., Owers, J., & Carveth, R. (1993). *Media economics: Theory and practice.*Hillsdale: Lawrence Erlbaum Associates.

Bane, P. W., Bradley, S. P., & Collis, D. (1997). Winners and losers: Industry structure in the converging world of telecommunications, computing, and entertainment. In D. B. Yoffie (Ed.), *Competing in the age of digital convergence*(pp. 227–246). Boston: Harvard Business School Press.

Chatterjee, S., & Wernerfelt, B. (1991). The link between resources and type of diversification: Theory and evidence. *Strategic Management Journal, 12*(1), 33–48.

Compaine, B. M., & Gomery, D. (2000). *Who owns the media?*Mahwah, NJ: Lawrence Erlbaum Associates.

Croteau, D., & Hoynes, W. (2001). *The business of media: Corporate media and the public interest.*Thousand Oaks, CA: Sage.

Dimmick, J. (2003). *Media competition and coexistence: The theory of niche.*Mahwah, NJ: Lawrence Erlbaum Associates.

Doyle, G. (2002a). *Media ownership: The economics and politics of convergence and concentration in the UK and European media.*Thousand Oaks, CA: Sage.

Doyle, G. (2002b). *Understanding media economics.*London: Sage.

Gershon, R. A. (2001). *Telecommunications management: Industry structures and planning strategies.*Mahwah, NJ: Lawrence Erlbaum Associates.

Jamison, M. A. (1999). *Industry structure and pricing: The new rivalry in infrastructure.*Boston: Kluwer Academic.

Landers, D., & Chan-Olmsted, S. M. (2004). Assessing the changing network television market: A resource-based analysis of broadcast television networks. *The Journal of Media Business Studies, 1*(1), 1–26.

Nelson, K. (2001, March 19). Cable show put new technology on front burner. *Electronic Media, 20*(12), pp. 13.

Owen, B. M., & Wildman, S. S. (1992). Video economics.Cambridge, MA: Harvard University Press.

Pavlik, J. (2001). *Journalism and new media.*New York: Columbia University Press.

Picard, R. G. (1989). *Media economics: Concepts and issues.*Newbury Park, CA: Sage.

Picard, R. G. (2002). *Media firms: Structures, operations and performance.*Mahwah, NJ: Lawrence Erlbaum Associates.

Thielmann, B., & Dowling, M. (1999). Convergence and innovation strategy for service provision in emerging Web-TV markets. *The International Journal of Media Management, 1*(1), 4–9.

Vogel, H. L. (2001). *Entertainment industry economics: A guide for financial analysis.*New York: Cambridge University Press.

Chapter 2

A Primer in Strategic Management for Media Firms

The goals of gaining a competitive advantage and increasing profitability are quite challenging for media firms, which constantly have to wrestle with their social responsibilities, regulatory concerns, technological advances, and changing consumer preferences. Historically, these media firms' attempts to analyze, plan, and implement strategies in response to environmental changes have been largely presented descriptively in media management literature. For example, most have acknowledged that terrestrial radio stations have started delivering programming products online, but few have investigated the drivers behind these strategic decisions. It is also well documented that nearly all television networks have invested in joint ventures with Internet-based firms, but what factors contributed to such alliances and what kind of partnerships produce a sustainable competitive advantage? Many of these managerial decisions are a result of the dynamic relationship between a media organization, its environment, and its attempt to develop and implement activities that align its organizational resources with environmental changes. And how our media environment has changed in the last 20 years! The previous chapter depicted this magnitude of change with discussions on the additions of new media, media outlets, and distribution systems; trends in consolidation and convergence; and alternative business models in today's media marketplace. Under such a dynamic environment, media managers have to be proactive, anticipate change, and continually refine their strategies to stay competitive. Accordingly, it is essential for media scholars to go beyond the mere synthesis of current industry practices and examine the antecedents and predictors of certain firm conducts. Such an emphasis on developing and testing theory-based propositions offers a better contextual explanation of the firm and the linkage between strategy and superior performance in this particular sector.

Nevertheless, moving from anecdotal, descriptive studies to analytical, prescriptive research of media firms requires a sound understanding of various economics and management concepts in firm behavior. The current chapter offers a primer of some relevant frameworks and constructs in "strategic management" because this field of study addresses the process and content of a firm's efforts in aligning its resources with the changing environment, the premise as well as focus of this book. In this context, strategic management offers valuable insights about the nature of mass media as business entities at the firm level, complementing existing media economics research that often provides the normative view of resource allocation of media goods. Furthermore, strategic management highlights the importance of traditional decision-making research; the critical process of strategic planning; the tug of war between environment and resources; the fluidity of competitive dynamics; and the many market phenomena we witness daily in media industries such as mergers and acquisitions, corporate diversification, and strategic alliances. Given the broad and diverse nature of strategy research, our goal here is not to provide a comprehensive review of all streams of strategic management literature. Instead, after briefly reviewing some key strategic management concepts and frameworks such as strategic decision making, value creation, the resource-based view (RBV), and competitive dynamics theories, this chapter focuses on how these concepts and frameworks might be applicable to media products in the context of a changing marketplace.

WHAT IS A STRATEGY?

The term *strategy* can be defined and subsequently studied from two distinctive perspectives: "process" and "content"; that is, "how" a strategy is formulated and implemented and "what" the strategy is. Integrating both perspectives, strategy involves a range of a firm's decisions and activities that are enacted to fulfill the firm's strategic missions and goals through the effective use of skills and resources, considering the opportunities and threats in its market environment. For example, a media strategy study may encompass the examination of one or more aspects of the financial, marketing, operation, and personnel functions that lead to the sustainable competitive advantage (SCA) of a firm or a group of firms in media industries. Consequently, strategic management is generally defined as the "analysis," "decisions," and "actions" an organization takes to create and sustain competitive advantages. Task-wise, strategic analysis generally involves the examinations of organizational objectives, the external and internal environments, and a firm's intellectual assets; strategic decisions include the formulation of business, corporate, international, and Internet strategies; and strategic actions entail the implementation of strategic control and corporate governance, effective organizational designs and structures, and ongoing activities that aim to achieve organizational excellence, ethical behavior, and entrepreneurship (Dess, Lumpkin, & Taylor, 2004).

DEVELOPMENT OF STRATEGIC MANAGEMENT STUDIES

The history of the strategic management discipline is rooted between the economic and behavioral/organizational perspectives and reflected by a variety of prior theories such as industrial organization (IO) economics, game theory, leadership, human resource management, Penrose's theory of the growth of firms, evolutionary theory, organizational learning, and cognitive models (Sanchez & Heene, 2004). Methodologically, most of the early studies were carried out by profiling of actual managerial decisions and thus were more descriptive and anecdotal. In addition, the focus on the "strategy" component of a firm or a group of firms actually began in the general capstone courses offered in many master of business administration (MBA) programs in the United States. Such an origin has significant implications for the initial direction of strategic management as an academic field of inquiry. For instance, the emphasis on integrating disciplines and practical applications translated into limited theory construction during its early stage of development, with a focus on models and typologies of various approaches to strategy formulation rather than synthesis of multiple, integrated theoretical perspectives (Hoskisson, Hitt, Wan, & Yiu, 1999).

Because of the complexity and breadth of this subject, many different theories on the studies and practice of strategic management eventually emerged. They may be summarized in two main approaches: the prescriptive and the evolutionary. Although the two basic approaches share the same commonalities, the prescriptive approach stresses that the practice of strategic management is a rational and linear process with well-defined and -developed elements before the strategy begins. By comparison, the evolutionary view does not present a clear, final objective for its strategy as proponents believe that strategy emerges, adapts, and evolves over time (Lynch, 1997). Chaffee (1985) further suggests that strategy can be studied from three distinct approaches: linear strategy, which focuses on planning and forecasting; adaptive strategy, which emphasizes the concept of "fit" and is most related to "strategic management"; and interpretive strategy, which sees strategy as a metaphor and thus views it in qualitative terms. After analyzing contemporary research and taking into consideration the historical perspectives in this area, Mintzberg, Ahlstrand, and Lampel (1998) identified 10 "schools" of strategy research that have developed since strategic management emerged as a field of study during the 1960s. These scholars proposed that the "design schools" see strategy as a process of conception, the "planning schools" treat strategy as a formal process, the "positioning schools" view strategy as an analytical process, the "entrepreneurial schools" regard strategy as a visionary process, the "cognitive schools" see strategy as a mental process, the "learning schools" treat strategy as an emergent process, the "power schools" view strategy as a process of negotiation, the "cultural schools" regard strategy as a collective process, the "environmental schools" see strategy as a reactive process, and the "configuration schools" treat strategy as a process of transformation. The contrasting definitions of the 10 emphases clearly show that the studies of strategy or strategic management have evolved tremendously over time.

THEORETICAL FOUNDATIONS IN STRATEGIC MANAGEMENT

To establish a base on which applicable frameworks and propositions might be suggested for media products, this chapter first reviews some major theoretical foundations in strategy studies.

The Essence of Strategic Thinking

Fundamental to the development of strategy literature and the practice of strategic management, "strategic thinking" is a particular mode of thinking with specific characteristics (Liedtka, 2001). Mintzberg (1994) stressed that, unlike strategic planning, which is preoccupied with following preprogramming rules, strategic thinking involves synthesis, intuition, creativity, and exploration, which results in an integrated perspective for reaching organizational goals. Liedtka succinctly identified five elements that define "strategic thinking." Specifically, strategic thinking is built on a systems perspective, under which the interrelationships between a firm and its external business ecosystem have to be seen as interdependent and evaluated as an end-to-end system of value creation. Strategic thinking is intent focused with a directed organizational energy toward the intended goals. Strategic thinking also includes intelligent opportunism. This means that the intention should be flexible enough to allow for unanticipated opportunities and the emergence of new, alternative strategies for a changing environment. Strategic thinking also stresses time continuity in that it takes into account institutional memory and historical context in working toward its intended goals. Finally, strategic thinking is a hypothesis-driven process in that it formulates hypotheses and analytically tests the hypotheses. Applications of strategic management in media industries, consequently, first need to be consistent with these principles.

Strategic Decision-Making, Agency Theory, and Strategic Leadership

Within the strategic thinking context, research in decision making focuses on determining how decisions are made in organizations to best develop a competitive advantage and how to improve such processes for the best outcome. Through either the descriptive approach by observing firm behaviors or the prescriptive approach by testing theories, scholars in this area have addressed personality topics such as risk propensity, uncertainty tolerance, creativity, decision styles, need for control, and experience; system factors such as domains of action, types of decisions, and authority structures; and organizational issues such as firm types, communications, and power. Notably, scholars have empirically pro- filed decision making in many corporations to identify the typical activ- ities and steps of decision making. From the early study by Mintzberg, Raisinghani, and Theoret (1976), which more simplistically categorized decision-making phases (e.g., identification, development, selection, and authorization), to later studies that attempted to uncover the ante- cedents and contexts of effective decisions (Dean & Sharfman, 1996; Sharfman & Dean, 1998), literatures in this area are rich in anecdotal discussions of typological managerial decisions. For example, Mintzberg and Westley (2001) suggested that managers can rely on "logic," "vision," or "action" in making decisions and the outcome of the different approaches is often dependent on the context in which the deci- sion is made. Nevertheless, Nutt (2001) argued that most strategic deci- sion-making studies are still behavioral in nature because of the missing empirical linkages between decisions, actions, measures of key contex- tual factors, and decision consequences.

Another strategy-related theoretical perspective that involves the role of managers is the traditional economics model of agency relation- ships in firm governance. The agency theory in strategic management deals primarily with the topics of corporate governance, compensation, firm performance, as well as diversification, mergers, and acquisition strategies. Microeconomists use agency theory to study the problems of motivating and controlling cooperative action. The primary focus here is the situation in which one party, the risk-neutral principal (e.g., shareholders, board of directors), seeks some outcome but requires the assistance of a risk-averse agent (e.g., managers) to carry out the neces- sary activities. It is assumed that both parties are motivated by self-in- terest. As a result, conflicts might arise because their goals might not be congruent. The assumptions are that although there are ways of miti- gating this problem of conflicts, it cannot be totally eliminated. Agency problems may include overcompensation (chief executive officer [CEO] salaries), empire building (unprofitable growth strategy), executive per- quisites, and CEO duality (CEO on board of directors). Unfortunately, agents usually know more about the tasks than the principals, but prin- cipals, unable to observe agents' actions directly, can attempt to control in a variety of ways (e.g., inspection, evaluation, and incentive systems) (Alchian & Demsetz, 1972; Eisenhardt, 1989). In essence, agency theory stresses the importance of organizational incentives to induce effective, coordinated, and cooperative work and the control of managerial be- havior for the benefit of the corporation. Considering the importance of agents as resources and strategy formulators and implementers and the importance of principals in resource acquisition and development (Chatterjee & Harrison, 2001), agency theory is a significant area of discipline for strategic media management scholars to venture into.

Finally, approaching the agent factor from a leadership angle in the context of strategic management, Hitt, Ireland, and Hoskisson (2001) proposed that top-level managers are an important resource for firms seeking to formulate and implement effective strategies and that strategic leadership is the essential managerial ability of anticipating, envisioning, maintaining flexibility, and empowering others to create strategic change as needed. Hitt et al. also suggested that the domain of strategic leadership involves five sets of activities: (a) determination of strategic direction, (b) exploitation and maintenance of core competencies, (c) development of human capital, (d) emphasis of ethical practices, and (e) establishment of balanced organizational controls. In summary, effective strategic leadership is necessary for a successful strategic management process, and strategic leaders can be a basis of competitive advantage.

Moving to a discussion of more macro, systematic explanations of strategic behavior and competitive advantage, two main perspectives that theorize the persistent firm performance differences in the field of strategic management, the industrial organization and the resource-based view of strategy, are presented next.

The Industrial Organization (IO) View of Strategy

As mentioned earlier, the study of strategic management has its roots in industrial economics. Based primarily on industrial organization concepts, the discipline has traditionally focused on the linkage between a firm's strategy and its external environment. Such a linkage is especially evident in the structure-conduct-performance (SCP) paradigm proposed by Bain (1968) and popularized with a strategic emphasis by Porter (1985). Specifically, the foundation of strategic management as a field may be traced to Chandler's definition of strategy as a set of managerial goals and choices, distinct from a structure, and the allocation of resources necessary to carry out these goals (Chandler, 1962). In a sense, the industry structure in which a firm chooses to compete determines the state of competition, the context for strategies, and thus the resulting performance of the strategies (Collis & Montgomery, 1995; Grant, 1991). Process-wise, the IO approach to developing competitive advantage begins with examining the external environment, followed by locating an industry with a high potential for above-average returns. A strategy is then formulated to benefit from the exogenous factors, and assets and skills are developed to effectively implement the chosen strategy (Hitt et al., 2001).

As the foundational theory of antitrust applications, the IO view of strategy was initially derived from its implications for social policy, which denote the undesirability of a less than perfectly competitive industry structure because it allows for conduct options that lead to superior performance of firms and thus reduction of social welfare. The SCP paradigm, which aims at developing competitive advantage and thus better performance, basically turned the antitrust notion on its head by suggesting that firms should seek to enter markets with the best environment (i.e., structure) that allows for strategic options to obtain persistent superior performance.

Some have argued that one of the most significant contributions to the development of strategic management came from industrial economics paradigms, especially the work of Michael Porter. His SCP model and the notion of strategic groups, where firms are clustered into groups of firms with strategic similarity within and differences across groups, have established a foundation for research on competitive dynamics (Hoskisson et al., 1999). As economics scholars gradually adopt other theories such as "game theory," "transaction costs economics," and "agency theory," strategic management research moves closer to firm-level and competitive dynamics (Hoskisson et al., 1999). Beginning in the late 1980s, business scholars, seeking to explain the impact of firm attributes and behavior, such as diversification, vertical integration, and technological experience, on performance (Lockett & Thompson, 2001), started investigating an "inside-out," resource-based view of strategy.

The Resource-Based View of Strategy

Emphasizing the critical value of the internal resources of a firm and the firm's abilities to manage them, the RBV assumes that each firm is a collection of unique resources that provide the foundation for its strategy and lead to the differences in each firm's performance (Hitt et al., 2001; Peteraf, 1993; Wernerfelt, 1984). The RBV literature also stresses that a firm's heterogeneous resources are the foremost factors influencing performance and sustainable competitive advantage. Historically, the RBV drew its rationales from four theoretical sources: (a) the traditional notion of distinctive competencies, which regards general managers and institutional leaders as distinctive competencies that critically impact a firm's strategy and final performance, (b) Ricardian economics, which proposes that certain resources used by firms are inelastic in supply and are possible sources of economic rents through proper exploitations (Barney & Arikan, 2001), (c) Penrosian economics, which stresses firms' heterogeneity, and (d) the IO-based theories of antitrust, which stimulated the RBV's counterargument of firm competency as the source of superior performance instead of the presumed anticompetitive activities.

The RBV theory has several assumptions. First, as in many other economics theories, RBV assumes that managers are generally rational and firms aim to maximize profits. Second, resource heterogeneity exists in industries because different firms might have different combinations of resources. Third, resource immobility exists in industries because firms' resource differences may persist (Barney & Arikan, 2001). According to the RBV, four specific attributes—value, rareness, nonsubstitutability, and inimitability—must work in tandem to increase performance. Valuable resources "exploit opportunities and/or neutralize threats in a firm's environment" (Barney, 1991, p. 105). A rare resource is one that is not easily located and implemented, moving firms beyond the "competitive parity" that is associated with common resources. Similarly, a nonsubstitutable resource has no strategic equivalents that perform the same function. The final factor, imperfect imitability, virtually guarantees a firm's sustainable competitive advantage, but it must work jointly with the aforementioned characteristics. That is, although a resource may be valuable, rare, and not easily substituted, it must be inimitable to bestow the firm with a sustained competitive advantage. Imperfect imitability may be the result of three factors: unique historical conditions, causal ambiguity, and social complexity (Barney, 1991). That is, competitors may not be able to capture and re-create the historical conditions that have led the firm to experience success. They may not be able to understand the linkages between the firm's resources and its competitive advantage, or they may be unable to unravel the complex interactions among resources. In sum, the concurrent interactions between these four resource attributes form the basis of a firm's superior performance.

Process-wise, an RBV approach begins with identifying and assessing a firm's resources and capabilities, locating an attractive industry in which the firm's resources and capabilities can be exploited, and finally selecting a strategy that best utilizes the firm's resources and capabilities relative to opportunities in that industry (Hitt et al., 2001). Scholars, such as McGahan and Porter (1997), have examined the relationship between the comparative impact of firm (an RBV approach) and industry (an IO approach) attributes on firm performance and concluded that firm-related factors seem to carry more weight in influencing performance.

As a theoretical framework of investigation, the RBV approach has become more popular among strategic management scholars since the 1990s after the initial dominance of the IO approach. There seems to be an interesting parallel in such a progression between the general studies of strategic management and strategy studies in the context of media economics. As some media scholars have pointed out, historically, there has been an overreliance on industrial organization studies in media economics (Picard, 2002); examinations of the exogenous factors (i.e., the IO framework) that influence firm conduct have been the primary focus of many media industry studies. As we move toward the study of media firms, the RBV investigative approach might provide more insight into explaining the different performances of individual media firms and various clusters of media firms.

The IO and RBV perspectives of strategic management establish the basic approaches for investigating media firms' strategic postures and their relationships to superior performance. Four more areas of research—strategic and resource taxonomy, value creation, competitive dynamics, and strategic entrepreneurship—have also made a substantial contribution to the strategic management literature and are reviewed next. These supporting constructs may offer a rich theoretical base to inspire more investigations of media products within a strategic management perspective. Note that other relevant concepts in the field of corporate strategy such as strategic networks, diversification, mergers, and acquisitions are examined in chapter 3. However, strategy-related organizational topics such as organizational design and structure, human resources management, organizational learning, and strategic leadership and stewardship are not discussed in this chapter because of the extensiveness of these issues and our focus on the RBV perspective of the strategic formulation phase of strategic management.

Strategic and Resource Taxonomy

Classification of strategy types offers the utility of comparative analysis and systematic assessment of the relationship between different strategic postures and market performance. To this end, the strategy typologies proposed by Miles and Snow (1978) and Porter (1980) are perhaps the most popular frameworks used by strategic management researchers for analyzing business strategy (Slater & Olson, 2000). Whereas Porter proposed that most business strategies fall under one of three strategic types—"focus," "differentiation," and "low-cost leadership"—Miles and Snow developed a framework for defining firms' approaches in product market development, structures, and processes. The notion is that different types of firms have different strategic preferences. Though firms in the same category might have a similar strategic tendency, they could achieve various levels of performance due to different implementations of the strategy. Miles and Snow classified firms into four groups: (a) prospectors, who continuously seek and exploit new products and market opportunities and are often the first to market with new products and services, (b) defenders, who focus on occupying a market segment to develop a stable set of products and customers, (c) analyzers, who have an intermediate position between prospectors and defenders by cautiously following the prospectors while at the same time monitoring and protecting a stable set of products and customers, and (d) reactors, who do not have a consistent product–market orientation but act or respond to competition with a more short-term focus (Zahra & Pearce, 1990).

Despite the differences in strategic aggressiveness, empirical studies have found that except for the reactors, the other three groups of firms achieve equal performance on average (Zahra & Pearce, 1990). The implication is that the implementation of the strategy is most critical to the performance variation within each strategy type. Strategic taxonomy might be applied in the media industries to empirically assess how organization factors and activities contribute to the effective implementation of different strategies. For example, how have different types of television stations, with their various organizational resources and capabilities, implemented their Internet-related strategies? The taxonomy approach also provides a useful framework for analyzing cross-media competition in an increasingly converged media world. For example, instead of investigating media corporations by sectors, which is becoming increasingly meaningless, one might use the Miles and Snow (1978) typology to examine these firms by analyzing their strategic preferences toward different media sectors.

In examining a firm's strategy, the relationship between strategy and resources, and the link between strategy and performance, strategy scholars have also developed a number of resource categorization systems in an attempt to assess the different contributions of various resources to performance in different market environments. Hofer and Schendel (1978) suggested that resources can be classified into six categories: financial, physical, human, technological, reputation, and organizational. Barney (1991) placed firm resources into three groups: physical capital, human capital, and organizational. Porter (1996) maintained that resources are of three types: activities, skills/routines, and external assets such as reputations and relationships. Black and Boal (1994) further argued that resources are best classified as operating in bundles—or network configurations—of two types: contained and system, based on the complexity of the network to which the resource belongs. Habann (2000), from a different perspective, divided firm resources into two sets according to their contents: competence, which refers to firm-specific capabilities, and strategic assets, which refer to tangible and intangible assets of strategic importance.

Nonetheless, Miller and Shamsie (1996) and Das and Teng (2000) maintained that the classification of resources is theoretically sound only when incorporated into the aforementioned characteristics of value, rareness, nonsubstitutability, and inimitability. Specifically, because the basis of a sustainable competitive advantage lies mainly in the inimitability of a resource, categorization of resources therefore must incorporate this notion of imperfect imitability. Resources thus may be classified into two broad categories: property based and knowledge based, each based on the inimitability of property rights or knowledge barriers, respectively. Miller and Shamsie (1996) further incorporated Black and Boal's (1994) concept of resource configurations, thus subclassifying property- and knowledge-based resources into discrete or systemic resources. That is, both property- and knowledge-based resources may stand alone or compose part of a network of resources.

Specifically, property-based resources are inimitable due to the protection afforded by property rights. A firm may secure a competitive advantage based on the length of the protection, thus proscribing competitors from imitation and appropriation of the resource (Miller & Shamsie, 1996). Contractual agreements form the foundation of the two types of property-based resources. Discrete property-based resources, for example, "take the form of ownership rights or legal agreements that give an organization control over scarce and valuable inputs, facilities, locations, or patents" (Miller & Shamsie, 1996, p. 524). Disney, for example, has "international rights to about 853 feature films, 671 cartoon shorts and animated features, and tens of thousands of television productions" (Hollywood wired, 2001). Systemic property-based resources include configurations of physical facilities and equipment whose inimitability lies in the complexity of the network configurations. Viacom's television station group, which consists of 34 owned and operated (O&O) stations, is an example of systemic property-based resources (Viacom, 2003).

Knowledge-based resources refer to a firm's intangible know-how and skills, which cannot be imitated because they are protected by knowledge barriers. Competitors do not have the know-how to imitate a firm's processed resources, such as technical and managerial skill (Hall, 1992). McEvily and Chakravarthy (2002) attributed uncertain imitability to complexity, tacitness, and specificity of knowledge. Like property-based resources, knowledge-based resources are composed of discrete and systemic resources. Discrete knowledge-based resources, such as technical, creative, and functional skills, stand alone. The management experience of specific media subsidiaries is an example of discrete knowledge-based resources. Systemic knowledge-based resources, on the other hand, "may take the form of integrative or coordinative skills required for multidisciplinary teamwork" (Miller & Shamsie, 1996, p. 527). Increasing attention in the strategy literature within the RBV framework has centered on the factor of "knowledge." Many studies have focused on how firms generate, leverage, transfer, integrate, and protect knowledge (Wright, Dunford, & Snell, 2001). Some have gone even further, arguing for a "knowledge-based" theory of the firm under the notion that firms exist because they can better integrate, apply, and protect knowledge than can markets (Grant, 1991; Liebeskind, 1996). In recent years, knowledge-based competition has become a popular area of study among strategic management scholars and practitioners. Some researchers claim that knowledge is the most important source of sustainable competitive advantage and performance (McEvily & Chakravarthy, 2002). Because media content products are intangible and largely rely on knowledge-based resources for both production and marketing, this is another fruitful ground for further application of strategic management constructs of media products.

Value Creation

To better understand the activities through which a firm develops competitive advantages, it is useful to separate its business system into a series of value-generating activities referred to as the value chain. The value chain categorizes the generic value-adding activities of an organization and serves as an analysis tool for strategic planning. The ultimate goal is to maximize value creating while minimizing costs in this process. Porter's (1998) model of the value chain is perhaps the most well known value-creating system (Sanchez & Heene, 2004). Porter proposed that a firm's value-creating activities can be divided into primary and support activities. Whereas the primary activities include those that are directly concerned with creating and delivering a product such as outbound logistics, inbound logistics, operations, sales, marketing, and service, support activities involve those that are not directly connected to the production function but may increase the efficiency or effectiveness of the process such as infrastructure, human resource management, technology development, and procurement (Porter, 1998). Value chain analysis is critical in strategic management because a firm might outperform its competitors by capturing value through cost reduction or differentiation in a specific segment of the chain, better coordination of connected chain activities, or even the creation of new business models that modify these value chain activities. The value chain concept has also been extended beyond individual organizations. It can be applied to the whole value creation system in an industry. Thus, the delivery of a product or service to the end customer (i.e., the extended industry value chain) would involve different parts of a value system such as the supplier value chain, channel value chain, organization value chain, and customer value chain, each managing its own value chain while interconnecting to others (Porter, 1998). The value creation/value chain concept, though in need of modifications to apply to certain media products (e.g., intangible content product), is useful for identifying the vital activities that might lead to competitive advantages, optimizing the linkage between different activities, and identifying possible cost reduction opportunities in a rapidly changing media marketplace.

Competitive Dynamics

Competitive dynamics may be defined as a series of competitive actions and counter responses among firms pursuing superior performance in an industry. Thus, the study of competitive dynamics is the study of how a firm's moves affect its competitors' countermoves, competitive advantage, and performance (Smith, Ferrier, & Ndofor, 2001). Considering the changing competitive landscape today—infused by technological advances, a global market, and changing competitive relationships (e.g., increasing use of alliance strategy)—an understanding of this topic seems to be even more critical. In essence, strategies are formulated to exploit the competitive asymmetries due to different firms' different resources, capabilities, core competences, and external opportunities and threats in the environments (Hitt et al., 2001).

Research on competitive dynamics began in the 1980s; many studies investigated competitor response timing/orders, antecedents, predictors, consequences of competitive moves and countermoves, and relationships between different kinds of rivalry and performance (Smith et al., 2001). Various models have been proposed to explain the competitive dynamics between firms. Most have examined the following components: the actor (i.e., the move initiator), the action, the responder, the response, drivers for competitive behavior, and the competitive environment of the industry. In researching the dynamic rivalry, one may examine the market commonality and resource similarity between the actor and responder; the awareness, capability, and motivation for competitive moves; the organizational characteristics of movers (e.g., reputations, dependence on the market, resource availability, size, speed, and innovativeness); likelihood of moves and countermoves by types of actions; types of environment in inducing certain rivalries (e.g., slow-, standard-, or fast-cycle market); and the sustainability of competitive advantage as a result of action or response. In general, studies in this area suggest the following (Chen & Hambrick, 1995; Dimmick, 2003; Hitt et al., 2001; Smith et al., 2001):

1. Firms' awareness of the competitive environment, the resource similarities, and relative characteristics between competitors is linked to the timing, actions, and reactions of the rivalry.
2. The magnitude, scope, and threat of an action is related to the speed and likelihood of response.
3. Organizational characteristics such as size, age, and reputation play a role in rivalry timing and initiation (e.g., smaller firms are more likely to initiate moves and do them quickly).
4. There might be less rivalry when firms compete against one another in several product or geographic markets (i.e., multipoint competition or multimarket contact) because of fear of mutual retaliation.
5. The timing and magnitude of a response is linked to a competitor's reliance on a particular market.
6. Degrees of rivalry are negatively related to industry characteristics such as conditions of demand, concentration, and barriers to entry.
7. Because markets evolve over time, competitive dynamics may be examined as evolutionary interactions longitudinally.

Considering the asymmetric resources between many different types of media firms, the necessity of multimarket contact and competition between media conglomerates, and the changing market environment due to technological development, one might garner additional insight by examining the strategies of media firms by applying the perspective of competitive dynamics.

Strategic Entrepreneurship

Today's organizations are in a new landscape filled with threats to existing ways of competition, new opportunities due to innovations, and temporary competitive advantages. Such an environment offers revolutionaries (i.e., entrepreneurs) the potential to capture market shares, develop new markets, and develop innovative resources and capabilities (Hitt, Ireland, Camp, & Sexton, 2002). In other words, entrepreneurial strategies are vital for success in today's media landscape. In fact, media industries are fundamentally shaped by many entrepreneurs who took the risks required to introduce a media product in response to opportunities presented by environmental changes. From Disney to CNN to the DISH Network, media entrepreneurs such as Walt Disney, Ted Turner, Charlie Ergen, and many more have offered new products and/or developed new markets. In a sense, strategic entrepreneurship offers an excellent framework for investigating how media products evolve and develop over time.

Entrepreneurship is a well-established disciplinary area that is increasingly regarded as highly complementary to the study of strategic management. This is because both are primarily concerned with growth and wealth creation, albeit with slightly different emphases (Ireland, Hitt, & Sirmon, 2003). Whereas strategic management is based mostly on the theories of competitive advantage, entrepreneurship often concentrates on the theories of organizational creativity, innovation, and opportunity recognition and exploitation. Empirically, whereas entrepreneurship has mostly examined small businesses, strategic management focuses on large businesses (Meyer, Neck, & Meeks, 2002). Integrating entrepreneurial activities with strategic perspectives, strategic entrepreneurship may be defined as the strategic management and deployment of resources for identifying and exploiting opportunities to form competitive advantages and thus superior performance in established firms or new ventures. In fact, entrepreneurial and strategic actions are complementary and likely achieve the best results when integrated (Hitt et al., 2002).

Scholars have presented various models or frameworks for examining entrepreneurship in a strategic setting. Specifically, Johnson and Van de Ven (2002) suggested that one might utilize the theories in population ecology to study market opportunity recognition, new institutionalism models to examine the establishment of legitimacy for entrepreneurs, organizational evolution theories to consider the subjects of adaptability and fitness of entrepreneurs, and industrial communities notions to explore the issues involved in constructing an industrial infrastructure that facilitates entrepreneurship. Ireland, Hitt, and Sirmon (2003) suggested four dimensions of strategic entrepreneurship for investigation: entrepreneurial mindset, entrepreneurial culture and leadership, the strategic management of resources, and the development of creativity and innovation. Specifically, the entrepreneurial mindset is defined as a way of approaching business with a focus on uncertainty in order to capture the benefits of uncertainty (McGrath & MacMillan, 2000). Such a mindset enables a firm to proactively and cognitively handle environmental risk and ambiguity because it is oriented toward growth opportunities and promotion of flexibility, creativity, and renewal. Entrepreneurial culture is defined as a set of shared entrepreneurial values that shape the behavioral norms and actions of a firm (and its members). The value system might include expectations of creativity, risk taking, occasional failure, learning and innovation, and continuous change. A related concept, entrepreneurial leadership, is the ability to influence others, nurture the aforementioned culture, and manage resources to both exploit opportunities and sustain competitive advantages. Strategic management of resources in this context includes the functions of structuring, integrating, and leveraging financial, human, and social capital to enhance entrepreneurial activities. Finally, the development of creativity and innovation involves the process of bisociation (i.e., the combining of previously unrelated information or skills) (Koestler, 1964) and results in either disruptive (brand-new) innovation or sustaining (improved) innovation (Ireland et al., 2003).

Scholars have suggested that strategic entrepreneurship manifests itself differently in established firms than in smaller firms or new ventures (Ireland et al., 2003). Although established firms are more skilled at developing sustainable competitive advantages, they are often less able to effectively identify new market opportunities. On the other hand, smaller firms or new ventures often excel at recognizing and exploiting new market opportunities, but they are often less capable of sustaining competitive advantages. Nevertheless, entrepreneurial attitudes and conduct are important for firms of all sizes to survive and prosper in competitive environments (Barringer & Bluedorn, 1999). The subfield of how large established firms can become entrepreneurial through integration of strategic and entrepreneurial actions is referred to as corporate entrepreneurship.

Hoskisson and Busenitz (2002) linked market entry modes to degrees of market uncertainty and learning distance, recommending entry modes from joint venture, to internal venture, to acquisition for markets with high to low uncertainty and learning distance. Because alliances and joint ventures have been a staple strategy in media industries, it would also be fruitful to investigate strategic entrepreneurship in the context of such strategies, especially the topic of alliance proactiveness, which might create access relationships to resources and capabilities that contribute to the exploitation of opportunities (Sarkar, Echambadi, & Harrison, 2001). Another concept that is especially suitable to incorporate in a media context is entrepreneurial intensity. Scholars have found that firms in turbulent environments tend to be more innovative, risk taking, and proactive (Naman & Slevin, 1993). As the media environment continues to be infused with new technologies such as content digitization and the Internet, it would be interesting to examine how strategic entrepreneurship in the media sectors is influenced by external contexts, in both intensity and approaches (e.g., attitudes and activities).

EMPIRICAL STUDIES IN STRATEGIC MANAGEMENT

To test the main propositions in strategic management, such as firm effects in determining performance; immobile, valuable resources in influencing performance; and the impact of certain corporate strategies (e.g., global/product diversification, mergers, and acquisitions) on performance, many empirical studies have been conducted. In general, these studies confirmed that:

1. Firm effects are relatively more important in determining performance.
2. Many firm resources such as innovativeness, corporate culture, a firm's history, and employee know-how are effective in influencing firm performance.
3. Only diversification strategies based on valuable, rare, and costly-to-imitate resources generate superior performance.
4. There is a noticeable impact of national differences on firm capabilities.
5. Certain resources and combinations of resources produce better performance for alliances.
6. There are no rules for garnering "persistent" superior performance (Barney & Arikan, 2001).

Although many empirical methods of investigation have been adopted for these studies, strategic management researchers have found it challenging to develop ways to empirically test the resource-based view of a firm because valuable resources, by nature, are less observable (Godfrey & Hill, 1995). As previously stated, the resources and capabilities that create sustainable competitive advantages are valuable, rare, not substitutable, and imperfectly imitable. Such a definition seems to be fundamentally tautological and presents difficulties in strategy measurement and thus causality examination. It becomes even more challenging when intangible, knowledge-based assets are considered. Lockett and Thompson (2001) concluded that causal ambiguity and firm-specific opportunity sets have been the greatest challenges for empirical testing in such studies.

In response to such measurement challenges, early scholars focused on examining strategies using in-depth case studies, especially in instances in which less tangible resources are involved (Hoskisson et al., 1999). Although one might review a firm or a group of firms in their market context, by adopting detailed field-based case studies that incorporate both archival and interview data, the lack of large data sets to test theory and apply multivariate statistical tools creates significant challenges for strategic management researchers. It also makes it more difficult for media strategy studies to become a more mature, respected scholarly field of study. Finally, because it is difficult to measure many intangible resources, proxy variables such as awards (e.g., Emmys) and salaries (e.g., CEO's compensation) have been used as measures of many intangible resources (Landers & Chan-Olmsted, 2002; Miller & Shamsie, 1996). Some strategic management researchers have expressed reservations that proxies may not be valid measures for many underlying constructs (Godfrey & Hill, 1995).

In response to such empirical challenges, some strategy researchers have tried combining quantitative questionnaires and qualitative interviews to increase the validity and reliability of their measures (Henderson & Cockburn, 1994). Some have suggested a step-by-step approach: First, identify a potential resource; second, examine its properties theoretically based on previous research; third measure the effect of the resource on performance (Deephouse, 2000). Because of the multiplicity of methods needed to identify, measure, and understand firm characteristics, strategy might be best researched as a dynamic or evolutionary phenomenon and empirically approached with a combination of longitudinal, in-depth case studies and other quantitative measures.

In terms of the application of statistical techniques, cluster analysis, which groups observations into similar segments, has been used frequently in strategic management research since the 1970s. This multivariate technique is often used because the variables in strategy studies are complex and multidimensional. As a result, researchers need some way to identify sets of firms that share commonalities among a set of variables and to find configurations that capture the complexity of organizational reality (Ketchen & Shook, 1996). Nevertheless, cluster analysis has been heavily criticized by scholars in recent years because of its extensive reliance on researcher judgment and its lack of test statistics for hypothesis testing. In fact, many empirical studies in strategic management have failed to find links between group membership and performance. As a result, strategic management scholars recommend limited use of this statistical technique and stress the importance of selecting variables inductively. When using this technique, researchers should also pay extra attention to determining and validating the number of clusters (Ketchen & Shook, 1996).

APPLICATIONS OF STRATEGIC MANAGEMENT CONCEPTS TO MEDIA PRODUCTS

The strategic management frameworks and constructs discussed thus far present a fertile ground for both theoretical propositions and empirical investigations from media management and economics scholars who are interested in studying firm behavior and performance. Considering the economic properties reviewed in chapter 1, although some of the concepts might be applicable, some would need to be modified. For instance, "intangible," "content-based" media products may be stored and presented in various formats. A strategy of "related product diversification," which extends a media firm's product lines into related content formats (e.g., print and online content), typically benefits firms by enabling content repurposing, marketing know-how, and sharing of production resources and thus is likely to be preferred over many manufactured tangible products. It is also logical for media firms to seek out distribution products and content products that complement each other because the two are inseparable in consumption. Furthermore, because of the importance of cultural sensitivity and understanding of the regulatory environment, media firms are more inclined to diversify into related product and geographic markets to take advantage of their acquired local knowledge and relationships. The dependency on local communication and media infrastructure may also lead to a strategy that is geographically related (i.e., regionalized). This is because geographically clustered markets are often at similar stages of infrastructure development, and clusters of media distribution systems may lead to cost- and resource-sharing benefits. The dual-revenue source mechanism and the public-goods characteristic of media content products also drive firms to offer media content that appeals to the largest possible group of marketable consumers. This is because a larger number of subscribers or bigger audience adds to the value of advertising spots or space with minimal incremental costs for the firms. On the other hand, because of the heterogeneous, nonstandardizable, creative characteristic of media content products, intangible resources become especially essential in building competitive advantages. As a result, small firms that do not have access to a mass audience but that possess unique creative resources still have the opportunity to achieve superior performance. Next, some examples of applying strategic management concepts on media products are presented.

Resource Typology in Media Industries

The property–knowledge resource typology presents a meaningful system for classifying and analyzing media firms' resources because knowledge-related resources are particularly important in developing competitive advantages in a media industry where the end product is mostly in the form of "intangible content," where "creativity" and "industry knowledge" remain the essential elements in the production of the content product, and where "content" is often seen as the key to success in any media distribution system. Furthermore, because of the fact that today's media industries are entering a period of unprecedented changes brought about by emerging new technologies such as the Internet and digitization, examinations of knowledge-based resources for media firms are becoming more critical. For example, applying the property–knowledge resource typology, Landers and Chan-Olmsted (2002) studied the broadcast television networks' changing strategies longitudinally as the broadcast market becomes less stable due to many technological developments. The notion of market uncertainty might be another important factor to investigate. As Miller and Shamsie (1996) discovered in their study of Hollywood film studios, both discrete and systemic property-based resources led to superior performance in the stable environment, whereas knowledge-based resources led to superior performance in the uncertain environment.

Landers and Chan-Olmsted (2002) suggested that resources such as affiliate contracts (or franchise agreements for cable television), station ownership, top content or news properties, and content or product copyright might be considered property-based resources, whereas technology management, audience expertise, talent pools, and content multipurposing expertise might be viewed as knowledge-based resources. Logically, the list of resources would be somewhat different depending on the nature and the value chain of the particular media market. For example, for the newspaper sector, distribution and printing properties represent essential property-based resources. Note that knowledge is a difficult resource to measure because of its fluidity. Most strategy studies have used proxies for knowledge-related variables under the assumption that firms acquire more knowledge about activities they invest or engage in to a greater extent (McEvily & Chakravarthy, 2002). In the case of media industries, film and television program awards as well as managers' average tenures have been used as proxy measures for such a variable (Landers & Chan-Olmsted, 2002).

Media Product Taxonomy

As discussed earlier, technological development is constantly changing the degree of substitutability between different types of media products. For example, the increasing application of digitization is blurring radio product consumption patterns as more and more audiences begin listening to radio stations on the Internet. As a result, it might be fruitful to examine the audio product or the providers of the product from the perspective of the consumer rather than of the radio industry. In other words, as technology shifts more control and power to consumers, media strategies and "competitive dynamics" may be evaluated based on consumer rather than industry factors or definitions.

One example would be to review the relative positions of different media firms using consumer-based concepts such as "risk involved" (i.e., time and cost invested) and "degree of involvement." Chan-Olmsted (2006) proposed such a media product taxonomy. Media products like the Internet, broadcast radio and television, cable television, books, and magazines are classified based on how involved a typical consumer might be with the specific media product and how much time and cost are required to consume the product (see Fig. 2.1). These factors influence consumers' perceived risk and thus their assessment of the value of that product. For instance, whereas the Internet, by nature,

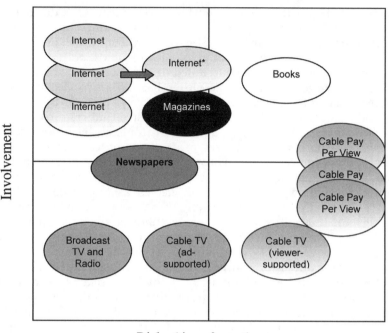

FIG. 2.1. A proposed media product taxonomy. *This might be paid or personalized online content in which the audience has invested money and/or relatively more time.

is a relatively more involved product than broadcast television, pay cable is often perceived to involve more risks and is, therefore, subject to different value scales than the mostly free Internet content product. On the other hand, paid Internet content product is evaluated differently as it moves to the right on the "risks" scale. The taxonomy may be used to assess the competitive dynamics of various firms in a particular media market or a mixture of media markets. It may also be used as a tool for analyzing corporate strategy portfolios. The integrated factors of risks and involvement are only one example of a consumer-based framework for analyzing media products and firms. As technology continues to reshape the media landscape, strategy scholars need to construct more theoretically sound taxonomies to reflect the changing nature of media products and to take into consideration the factor of consumer choice and consumers' changing degree of control over the media products they consume.

A Media Strategy Research Framework

Incorporating both the IO and RBV concepts, Chan–Olmsted (2006) proposed a system of factors that might affect the formulation and implementation of strategy in the media industries. This analytical framework integrates both exogenous and endogenous variables and serves as a beginning point to stimulate more media strategy inquiries (see Fig. 2.2). Theoretically, a media firm's strategy (formulation) and its ability to execute that strategy (implementation) are influenced by a combination of external characteristics relating to the general environment and a particular media market in which the media firm operates. General exogenous factors, such as the economy and technological advancement, affect the interplay of the six forces present in a specific media industry (i.e., audience preferences, substitutability between different media products, supplier–buyer relationship, in-market competition, and threats from potential entrants), ultimately impacting the strategic behavior of a media firm. The environmental complexity is further complicated by a series of firm capabilities and resources at the business and corporate level, which shape the firm's strategy. Either property or knowledge based, a media firm's corporate structure (e.g., its degree of vertical and horizontal integration with other media properties, its product and geographical diversification, and its windowing and resource alignment corporate capabilities) along with its specific business unit resources and capabilities (e.g., cross-media integration and marketing) directly determine the type of strategy formulated and implemented. Adding the essential factors of strategic leadership and entrepreneurship, along with the consideration of competitive dynamics in an industry, the framework presents a useful starting point for analyzing the antecedents of strategic behavior and predictors of performance.

FINAL THOUGHTS

This chapter has examined an array of strategic management theories for further applications to media products. For research ideas, media management and economics researchers may also want to survey the scholarly work published in the top strategy research academic journals: *Strategic Management Journal, Academy of Management Journal, Academy*

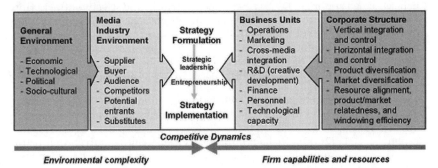

FIG. 2.2. A system of factors that affect strategy formulation and implementation.

of Management Review, the *Journal of Management,* and the *Journal of Management Studies* (Park & Gordon, 1996). The fluidity of media industries, due to the continuous changes in communication technology, creative development, and audience preferences, encourages the introduction, incorporation, and testing of new paradigms. In fact, we believe that a multiplicity of theories is needed in this area of study because media management and economics, by nature, are multidimensional disciplines. Chapters 5 to 9 empirically showcase some additional applications of the concepts discussed here in a media industry setting.

REFERENCES

Alchian, A. A., & Demsetz, H. (1972). Production, information costs, and economic organization. *American Economic Review, 62*(5), 777–795.

Bain, J. S. (1968). *Industrial organization.* New York: Wiley.

Barney, J. (1991). Firm resources and sustained competitive advantage. *Journal of Management, 17*(1), 99–120.

Barney, J. B., & Arikan, A. M. (2001). The resource-based view: Origins and implications. In M. A. Hitt, R. E. Freeman, & J. Harrison (Eds.), *The Blackwell handbook of strategic management* (pp. 124–188). Oxford, England: Blackwell.

Barringer, B. R., & Bluedorn, A. C. (1999). The relationship between corporate enterpreneurship and strategic management. *Strategic Management Journal, 20*(5), 421–444.

Black, J. A., & Boal, K. B. (1994). Strategic resources: Traits, configurations and paths to sustainable competitive advantage. *Strategic Management Journal, 15*(special issue), 131–148.

Chaffee, E. (1985). Three models of strategy. *Academy of Management Review, 10*(1), 89–98.

Chandler, A. (1962). *Strategy and structure.* Cambridge, MA: MIT Press.

Chan-Olmsted, S. M. (2006). Issues in strategic management. In A. B. Albarran, S. M. Chan-Olmsted, & M. O. Wirth (Eds.), *Handbook of media management and economics* (pp. 161–180). Mahwah, NJ: Lawrence Erlbaum Associates.

Chatterjee, S., & Harrison, J. (2001). Corporate governance. In M. A. Hitt, R. E. Freeman, & J. Harrison (Eds.), *The Blackwell handbook of strategic management* (pp. 23–46). Oxford, England: Blackwell.

Chen, M. J., & Hambrick, D. C. (1995). Speed, stealth, and selective attack: How small firms differ from large firms in competitive behavior. *Academy of Management Journal, 38*(2), 453–482.

Collis, D. J., & Montgomery, C. A. (1995). Competing on resources: Strategy in the 1990s. *Harvard Business Review, 73*(4), 118–129.

Das, T. K., & Teng, B. (2000). A resource-based theory of strategic alliances. *Journal of Management, 26*(1), 31–61.

Dean, J. W., Jr., & Sharfman, M. P. (1996). Does decision making matter: A study of strategic decision making effectiveness. *Academy of Management Journal, 39*(2), 368–396.

Deephouse, D. L. (2000). Media reputation as a strategic resource: An integration of mass communication and resource-based theories. *Journal of Management, 26*(6), 1091–1113.

Dess, G. G., Lumpkin, G. T., & Taylor, M. (2004). *Strategic management: Creating competitive advantages.* Maidenhead, England: McGraw-Hill Education.

Dimmick, J. (2003). *Media competition and coexistence: The theory of niche.* Mahwah, NJ: Lawrence Erlbaum Associates.

Eisenhardt, K. M. (1989). Agency theory: An assessment and review. *Academy of Management Review, 14*(1), 57–74.

Godfrey, P. C., & Hill, C. W. (1995). The problem of unobservables in strategic management research. *Strategic Management Journal, 16*(7), 519–535.

Grant, R. M. (1991). The resource-based theory of competitive advantage: Implications for strategy formulation. *California Management Review, 33*(3), 114–135.

Habann, F. (2000). Management of core resources: The case of media enterprises. *International Journal on Media Management, 2*(1), 14–24.

Hall, R. (1992). The strategic analysis of intangible resources. *Strategic Management Journal, 13*(2), 135–144.

Henderson, R., & Cockburn, I. (1994). Measuring competence? Exploring firm effects in pharmaceutical research. *Strategic Management Journal, 15*(special issue), 63–84.

Hitt, M. A., Ireland, R. D., Camp, S. M., & Sexton, D. L. (Eds.). (2002). *Strategic entrepreneurship: Creating a new integrated mindset.* Oxford, England: Blackwell.

Hitt, M. A., Ireland, R. D., & Hoskisson, R. E. (2001). *Strategic management: Competitiveness and globalization.* Cincinnati, OH: South-Western College.

Hofer, C. W., & Schendel, D. (1978). *Strategy formulation: Analytical concepts.* St. Paul, MN: West.

Hollywood wired. (2001, January). *Multichannel News International.* Retrieved June 21, 2002, from http://www.onesource.com

Hoskisson, R. E., & Busenitz, L. W. (2002). Market uncertainty and learning distance in corporate entrepreneurship entry mode choice. In M. A. Hitt, R. D. Ireland, S. M. Camp, & D. L. Sexton (Eds.), *Strategic entrepreneurship: Creating a new integrated mindset* (pp. 151–172). Oxford, England: Blackwell.

Hoskisson, R. E., Hitt, M. A., Wan, W. P., & Yiu, D. (1999). Theory and research in strategic management: Swings of a pendulum. *Journal of Management, 25*(3), 417–456.

Ireland, R. D., Hitt, M. A., & Sirmon, D. G. (2003). A model of strategic entrepreneurship: The construct and its dimensions. *Journal of Management, 29*(6), 963–989.

Johnson, S., & Van de Ven, A. (2002). A framework for entrepreneurial strategy. In M. A. Hitt, R. D. Ireland, & S. M. Camp (Eds.), *Integrating strategy and entrepreneurship perspectives* (pp. 66–85). New York: Wiley.

Ketchen, D. J., & Shook, C. L. (1996). The application of cluster analysis in strategic management research. *Strategic Management Journal, 17*(6), 441–458.

Koestler, A. (1964). *The act of creation.* New York: Dell.

Landers, D., & Chan-Olmsted, S. M. (2002, April). *Assessing the changing network television market: A resource-based analysis of broadcast television networks.* Paper presented at the meeting of the Media Management and Sales Division of the Broadcast Education Association, Las Vegas, NV.

Liebeskind, J. P. (1996). Knowledge, strategy, and the theory of the firm. *Strategic Management Journal, 17*(special issue), 93–109.

Liedtka, J. M. (2001). Strategy formulation: The roles of conversation and design. In M. A. Hitt, R. E. Freeman, & J. Harrison (Eds.), *The Blackwell handbook of strategic management* (pp. 70–94). Oxford, England: Blackwell.

Lockett, A., & Thompson, S. (2001). The resource-based view and economics. *Journal of Management, 27*(6), 723–755.

Lynch, R. (1997). *Corporate strategy*. London: Pitman.

McEvily, S. K., & Chakravarthy, B. (2002). The persistence of knowledge-based advantage: An empirical test for product performance and technological knowledge. *Strategic Management Journal, 23*(4), 285–305.

McGahan, A. M., & Porter, M. E. (1997). How much does industry matter, really? *Strategic Management Journal, 18*(special issue), 15–31.

McGrath, R., & MacMillan, I. C. (2000). *The enterpreneurial mindset*. Boston: Harvard Business School Press.

Meyer, G. D., Neck, H. M., & Meeks, M. D. (2002). The entrepreneurship: Strategic management interface. In M. A. Hitt, R. D. Ireland, S. M. Camp, & D. L. Sexton (Eds.), *Strategic entrepreneurship: Creating a new integrated mindset* (pp. 19–44). Oxford, England: Blackwell.

Miles, R. E., & Snow, C. C. (1978). *Organizational strategy, structure, and process*. New York: McGraw-Hill.

Miller, D., & Shamsie, J. (1996). The resource-based view of the firm in two environments: The Hollywood firm studios from 1936 to 1965. *Academy of Management Journal, 39*(3), 519–543.

Mintzberg, H. (1994). The fall and rise of strategic planning. *Harvard Business Review, 72*(1), 107–114.

Mintzberg, H., Ahlstrand, B., & Lampel, J. (1998). *Strategy safari: A guided tour through the wilds of strategic management*. New York: The Free Press.

Mintzberg, H., Raisinghani, D., & Theoret, A. (1976). The structure of unstructured decision process. *Administrative Science Quarterly, 21*(2), 246–275.

Mintzberg, H., & Westley, F. (2001). Decision making: It is not what you think. *MIT Sloan Management Review, 42*(3), 89–93.

Naman, J., & Slevin, D. (1993). Enterpreneurship and the scope of fit: A model and empirical tests. *Strategic Management Journal, 14*(2), 137–153.

Nutt, P. C. (2001). Strategic decision-making. In M. A. Hitt, R. E. Freeman, & J. Harrison (Eds.), *The Blackwell handbook of strategic management* (pp. 35–69). Oxford, England: Blackwell.

Park, S. H., & Gordon, M. E. (1996). Publication records and tenure decisions in the field of strategic management. *Strategic Management Journal, 17*(2), 109–128.

Peteraf, M. A. (1993). The cornerstones of competitive advantage: A resource-based view. *Strategic Management Journal, 14*(3), 179–190.

Picard, R. G. (2002). *Media firms: Structures, operations and performance*. Mahwah, NJ: Lawrence Erlbaum Associates.

Porter, M. (1980). *Competitive strategy*. New York: The Free Press.

Porter, M. (1985). *Competitive advantage: Creating and sustaining superior performance*. New York: The Free Press.

Porter, M. (1996). Toward a dynamic theory of strategy. In R. P. Rumelt, D. E. Schendel, & D. J. Teece (Eds.), *Fundamental issues in strategy: A research agenda* (pp. 423–461). Cambridge, MA: Harvard Business School Press.

Porter, M. E. (1998). *On competition*. Boston: Harvard Business School Press.

Sanchez, R., & Heene, A. (2004). *The new strategic management: Organization, competition, and competence*. New York: Wiley.

Sarkar, M., Echambadi, R., & Harrison, J. S. (2001). Alliance enterpreneurship and firm market performance. *Strategic Management Journal, 22*(6/7), 701–711.

Sharfman, M. P., & Dean, J. W., Jr. (1998). The effects of context on strategic decision making processes and outcomes. In V. Papadakis & P. Barwise (Eds.), *Strategic decisions* (pp. 179–203). Boston: Kluwer Academic.

Slater, S. F., & Olson, E. M. (2000). Strategy type and performance: The influence of sales force management. *Strategic Management Journal, 21*(8), 813–829.

Smith, K., Ferrier, W., & Ndofor, H. (2001). Competitive dynamics research: Critique and future directions. In M. A. Hitt, R. E. Freeman, & J. Harrison (Eds.), *The Blackwell handbook of strategic management* (pp. 315–361). Oxford, England: Blackwell.

Viacom Television Stations Group. (2003). Available from http://www.viacom/prodbyunit.tin

Wernerfelt, B. (1984). A resource-based view of the firm. *Strategic Management Journal, 5*(2), 171–180.

Wright, P. M., Dunford, B. B., & Snell, S. A. (2001). Human resources and the resource based view of the firm. *Journal of Management, 27*(6), 701–723.

Zahra, S. A., & Pearce, J. (1990). Research evidence on the Miles–Snow typology. *Journal of Management, 16*(4), 751–768.

Chapter 3

A Primer in Corporate and International Strategy for Media Firms

In pursuing competitive advantages, a media firm goes through the stages of strategy analysis, formulation, and implementation (Dess, Lumpkin, & Taylor, 2004). These strategic actions involve different levels of complexity as well as resource commitments, ranging from microlevel, functional strategies like an advertising campaign; to business-level strategies that are mainly concerned with developing core competencies in a specific product market (e.g., a differentiation or cost leadership strategy); to corporate strategies that deal with how a media corporation diversifies its business units, allocates resources, and manages its portfolio. Although each business unit of a diversified firm has to analyze and align the external and internal environment of its product market with the unit's business mission and intent to exploit competitive advantages in a particular market (e.g., ABC in the network TV market), a diversified corporation such as Disney, the corporate parent of ABC, also has the challenging tasks of finding the best combination of resources and business environments in which the overall company can be competitive in multiple markets. Hitt, Ireland, and Hoskisson (2001) suggested that a company may adopt among five generic business-level strategies: cost leadership, differentiation, focused cost leadership, focused differentiation, and integrated cost leadership/differentiation. Compared to these single-market business-level strategies, corporate strategies tackle more multidimensional issues such as mergers and acquisitions as well as product and geographical diversification that are heavily dependent on the conditions of a firm's external environment and have substantial implications for the development and appropriation of its resources. Along the same line, considering the popularity of strategic alliances in the media industries and the emergence of numerous global media conglomerates, a media firm's cooperative strategies that exploit pooled competitive advantages and international strategies that aim at capitalizing on the technological, political, societal, and economic changes in the global marketplace have also become critical corporate decisions that impact a media firm's competitiveness in the marketplace. Thus, to supplement the general strategic management concepts discussed in chapter 2, this chapter further reviews relevant theories in areas of diversification, M&A, strategic alliances and networks, and international strategy. It also discusses how these strategic approaches and theories might be applicable to media products in the context of a changing media marketplace. Note that whereas diversification, M&A, and cooperative strategies such as strategic alliances are examined in the context of an international marketplace, additional concepts in international expansion are discussed separately.

DIVERSIFICATION

Diversification is the dominant topic in the studies of corporate strategy—the strategic management of organizations with multiple business units in search of synergistic competitive advantages. Various reasons have been cited as the drivers for diversification. These rationales might be grouped into six categories: growth, market power, market efficiency, financial-performance improvement, profit stability, and synergy effects. In fact, diversification is simply a "faster" way to grow, especially via the means of acquisitions. Unlike natural internal expansion, which takes time for planning, developing, and implementing, an acquisition or merger can be achieved fairly quickly and new resources and customers become immediately available. For example, most leading cable television multiple system operators (MSOs) have grown tremendously in the last decade through acquisitions of clustered systems rather than through building new systems. Scholars have noted that a diversified firm may acquire market power that is unavailable to its undiversified counterparts (Caves, 1981; Hitt et al., 2001; McCutcheon, 1991; Scherer, 1980; Sobel, 1984). For instance, a vertically integrated diversifier may gain market power through reciprocal buying and selling (Grant, 1998). A diversified firm can make use of efficiencies that are unavailable to its single-business-unit (SBU) counterparts by owning sharable, transferable resources and thus leading to scale/scope economies. A diversifier can also generate cash from its core, successful business unit to invest in other ventures for additional profits. Television networks and movie studios have long used the cash they garner from blockbusters to invest in new content or technology projects. Furthermore, diversification into new businesses can reduce risks and variations in corporate profits by expanding the firm's lines of business.

NBC's entry into the cable market with its MSNBC and CNBC properties has helped boost its advertising sales amid declining broadcast TV audiences. Finally, a diversified firm may benefit from synergy—the added value created by business units working together.

Sanchez and Heene (2004) suggested that corporate synergies might be achieved as a result of cost reductions through a combination of economies of scale, scope, learning, and substitution (i.e., resource substitution) enabled by a firm's business portfolio; or as a result of improved products or processes through better control of key inputs and supply/distribution relationships with vertical integration, leveraging of technology and intangible assets such as brands, and sharing of knowledge and capabilities. Such synergistic effects have also frequently been cited as a driver for media firms' diversification (Jung & Chan-Olmsted, in press). For instance, media conglomerates have placed more emphasis on the promotion of their own subsidiaries' products such as television programs or movies. The result is that these conglomerates, with their enormous resources and diverse holdings, have been very successful in developing and promoting content products in ways their stand-alone counterparts cannot match (Jung, 2001, 2002; McAllister, 2000; D. Williams, 2002).

Diversification involves either geographic or product market expansions (see Fig. 3.1). Sanchez and Heene (2004) suggested that an SBU typically grows geographically in a domestic market before expanding internationally or beginning horizontal integration with acquisitions of business units in its domestic market. Very often, domestic or even international vertical integration with businesses upstream or downstream from the distribution channel is the last step. In fact, the media industry is going through a phase of transformation, moving from a national to an international marketplace as many media conglomerates also become multinational corporations. The strategy of international diversification

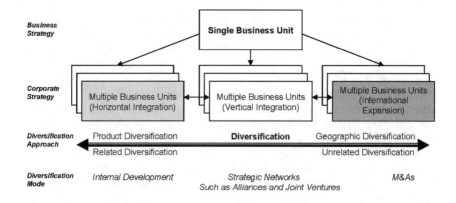

FIG. 3.1.   Types of corporate and international strategies.

by media firms has indeed generated heated debates among policymakers, consumer advocates, and scholars (Croteau & Hoynes, 2001; S. Davis, 1999; C. Davis & Craft, 2000; Demers, 1999; Teinowitz, 2001). Some have suggested that a media firm is inclined to diversify internationally to increase the size of its potential market. It is a particularly attractive option for those located in developed countries with limited continuous domestic growth opportunities. For example, some U.S. cable television firms are venturing into South American and Asian cable markets as demands for cable television services in the United States are saturated (Chan-Olmsted & Albarran, 1998). Access to local talent and to knowledge of local preferences for culture-sensitive content product is another unique driver for media diversification. Gershon (1997) further identified another motive for the international diversification of media firms—empire building. For instance, News Corporation's Rupert Murdoch has been characterized as an empire builder in the tradition of the 19th-century press barons (Smith, 1991). Bagdikian (2000) also referred to the current generation of media businessmen as the "Lords of the Global Village." Transnational media owners are risk takers who often measure success by business gamesmanship and the art of deal making (Gershon, 1997).

Approaches to Diversification

There are various approaches to diversification strategies. For analytical purposes, diversification strategies may be classified as concentric, vertically integrated, or conglomerate. Whereas concentric diversification refers to a firm's branching into business units in related markets, vertical integration is the linking of businesses that have a buyer–supplier relationship or represent stages of production. Conglomerate diversification is the expansion of a corporation into new, unrelated lines of business. A diversification can again be viewed as either "related" or "unrelated." Related diversification enables a firm to benefit from economies of scope and scale through the leveraging of core competencies and sharing of activities and information. Related diversification also offers a firm the advantages of pooled negotiation power and access to, as well as control over, production materials and product flows through vertical integration. Unrelated diversification, on the other hand, may derive benefits from the possible synergies created by leveraging corporate restructuring and general management capabilities, learning "best practices" in other business units, improving capital allocations by forming an internal capital market, and reducing financial risk through a diversified business portfolio (Dess et al., 2004; Sanchez & Heene, 2004).

Diversification Strategy and Performance

So do diversifiers generally outperform nondiversifiers? The empirical results on the linkage between diversification and performance seem to suggest that a "moderate" diversification strategy is the key to success. Grant, Jammine, and Thomas (1988) found managerial difficulties as a firm tries to manage an increasingly disparate portfolio of businesses. Markides (1992) discovered many hidden costs such as coordination costs and other diseconomies related to the organizational inefficiencies of conflicting "dominant logics" between businesses and internal capital market inefficiencies. In essence, studies put forward that moderate levels of product diversification yield higher levels of performance than either limited or extensive diversification. In fact, an inverted-U curvilinear model wherein performance increases as firms shift from single-business strategies to related diversification but performance decreases as firms change from related diversification to unrelated diversification was generally supported by empirical findings (Geringer, Tallman, & Olsen, 2000; Grant et al., 1988; W. C. Kim, Hwang, & Burgers, 1989; Palepu, 1985; Palich, Cardinal, & C. C. Miller, 2000; Palich, Carini, & Seaman, 2000; Sambharya, 1995).

Researchers have also found that international diversification increases the stability of a firm's revenues and that geographic scope is positively related to firm performance in the analysis of U.S. corporations (Geringer, Beamish, & daCosta, 1989; Grant, 1987; Grant et al., 1988; Hitt, Hoskisson, & H. Kim, 1997; W.C. Kim et al., 1989; Tallman & Li, 1996). The positive relationship between international diversification and firm performance was supported in the context of other countries outside of the United States as well (Bengtsson, 2000; Buhner, 1987). However, some studies have argued that as firms diversified internationally, the costs associated with geographic dispersion began escalating. Thus, profit margins erode after a certain hurdle point (Chen, 1998; Geringer et al., 2000; Hitt et al., 1997).

Some research has shown that the interaction between international and product diversification leads to a substantial increase in firm performance (Sambharya, 1995). Hitt et al. (1997) found that geographical diversification improves performance in firms that are highly diversified in terms of product markets. In fact, W. C. Kim et al. (1989) concluded that the performance of related and unrelated product diversification strategies depends on the degree of international diversification. Nevertheless, another group of studies has also indicated an inverse relationship between product and international diversification (Buhner, 1987; Madura & Rose, 1987). As both types of diversification involve substantial risks, it is unlikely that a firm would take on both strategies simultaneously (Sambharya, 1995). In sum, geographic and product diversifications interact with one another and, individually and collectively, influence different performances among firms (Grant, 1987; Palepu, 1985).

Research in Diversification

Diversification has had a rich tradition as a topic of research since the late 1950s (Ansoff, 1958; Chandler, 1962; Gort, 1962). Salter and Weinhold

(1979) proposed three general but related models in the discussion of corporate diversification strategies. The product/market-portfolio model emphasizes the attractiveness of the target market in terms of attributes such as market size, growth rate, and profitability. The strategy model stresses the interrelationship between the core-business market and the target market. The third approach, the risk/return model, derives mainly from financial theories and reflects the concern and interest of investors. Studies of diversification have generally focused on one or more of the three aspects of diversification: (a) the "extent" (i.e., less or more diversification), (b) the "directions" (i.e., related or unrelated diversification), and (c) the "mode" (i.e., diversification via internal expansion, M&A, or choices of M&A strategy) of diversification (Qian, 1997; Sambharya, 1995). Diversification strategy may be studied from either the "product" or "geographic" perspective. More recent studies in product diversification often investigate the directions of diversification as related or unrelated (Qian, 1997; Rumelt, 1984). Some have argued that related diversification might exploit economies of scope, product knowledge, and other relevant experience, thus reducing transaction costs and improving performance (Grant, 1988; Williamson, 1981). Others have found no differences or the opposite (Grant & Jammine, 1988; Michel & Shaked, 1984). In general, the RBV of strategic management strongly argues for strategic relatedness within a conglomerate when it comes to diversification strategy (Chatterjee & Wernerfelt, 1991).

Diversification has gradually become a topic of interest in media management and economics research as well. Dimmick and Wallschlaeger (1986), in one of the initial diversification endeavors, examined the level of diversification of television network parent companies and found that the least diversified parent companies were most active in new media ventures. Albarran and Porco (1990), applying Dimmick and Wallschlaeger's measures, studied the diversification strategy of pay cable and concluded that these firms appeared to utilize diversification as a means to limit resource dependency and ensure organizational survival. Picard and Rimmer (1999) further explored whether the degree of product and geographical diversification affected the financial performance of newspaper firms during the economic downturn. Whereas Albarran and Moellinger (2002) examined 6 leading media conglomerates' structure, conduct, and performance following the IO model, Powers and Pang (2002) reviewed the diversification and performance of 11 media conglomerates before and after the Telecommunications Act of 1996. The trend of research in this area continued as Shaver and Shaver (2003) investigated the activities of 11 companies over a 10-year period and concluded that operating margins were significantly and negatively correlated to the degree of business diversity. Peltier (2002) further suggested that although there is no positive correlation between a media conglomerate's presence in multiple businesses and its economic performance, the internationalization rate of a firm appears to be positively correlated with its economic performance. Adopting a strategic management perspective, Chan-Olmsted and Chang (2003) studied the diversification patterns of seven leading media companies in the product/international dimension and proposed an analytical framework for examining the factors influencing these strategic choices. They also explained how the medium diversifiers yielded the best financial performance. Finally, Kranenburg (2004) proposed a series of useful indicators to measure the international diversification of publishing companies and discovered that the publishing companies have preferred related diversification.

It is our belief that the embedded characteristics of media products (see chap. 1) would lead to a market environment in which related product and geographic diversification are likely to be the preferred diversification strategy. For example, as the "intangible," "content-based" media product may be stored and presented in various formats (e.g., print vs. electronic media), related product diversification that extends a diversifier's product lines into related content formats (e.g., owning a magazine and an online content site) would likely benefit the corporation by enabling content repurposing, marketing know-how, and sharing of production resources, thus leading to superior performance. It is also likely for a media diversifier to seek out distribution products that complement its own content products and vice versa. The fact that an existing product may be redistributed to and reused in different outlets via a windowing process again reinforces the advantage of diversifying into multiple related distribution sectors in various international markets to increase the revenue potential for such a product.

The dual-revenue source mechanism would likely lead to related diversification as the larger aggregated number of subscribers or audience enhances a media firm's ability to offer promotional outlets to multinational corporations more efficiently and acquired marketing knowledge about the customers more effectively. In addition, because of the importance of cultural sensitivity and the understanding of a country's regulatory environment, global media corporations are more inclined to diversify into related product and geographic markets to take advantage of the acquired local knowledge and relationships. The dependency on local communications and media infrastructure may also lead to a diversification strategy that is geographically related (i.e., regionalized) because geographically clustered countries are often at similar stages of infrastructure development and clusters of media systems may lead to cost- and resource-sharing benefits.

MERGERS AND ACQUISITIONS

The strategy of M&A is closely related to the previous topic. It is, in fact, a main means to achieve diversification. There are subtle differences between the terms *mergers*, *acquisitions*, and *takeovers*. According to Hitt et al. (2001), strategically, a merger is a balanced integration of two firms' operations to combine resources and capabilities for creating a stronger competitive advantage, whereas an acquisition is the purchase of a target firm as a subsidiary business with the intent of enhancing a core competency of the acquirer. When the target firm did not solicit the acquisition, it is called a takeover.

Many rationales have been suggested as the drivers for M&A. Assuming a rational managerial approach, thus excluding the motives of "empire building" and "risk reduction" for maximizing a manager's personal utility, a primary reason for M&A might be to achieve greater "market power" (Haspeslagh, 1999). Market power exists when a firm is able to sell its goods or services above competitive levels or when the costs of its primary or support activities are below those of the competitors (Hitt et al., 2001). Many media companies may have attractive core competencies such as the ownership of valuable content or talents and distribution outlets, but lack the size to benefit from these unique resources and capabilities. M&As offer an opportunity to achieve greater market power through the increase of firm size (e.g., mergers of MSOs). An attempt to reduce barriers to entry might be another driver for the formation of M&As. For example, market barriers may arise when well-established competitors are able to enjoy significant scale economies and/or brand loyalty. Facing these barriers, a new entrant may find the acquisition of an established company to be more effective than an attempt to enter the market as a competitor offering a good or service that is unfamiliar to current buyers (Hitt et al., 2001; e.g., GE's acquisition of NBC). In addition, because developing new products internally and successfully introducing them into the marketplace often requires significant investments of a firm's resources and makes it difficult to earn a profitable return quickly (Shank & Govindarajan, 1992), M&As are another means through which a firm can gain access to new products and to current products that are new to the firm. Compared to internal development processes, M&As provide a more predictable return and faster market entry (McCardle & Viswanathan, 1994; Rappaport & Sirower, 1999) (e.g., the merger between AOL and Time Warner gave Time Warner immediate access to many Internet subscribers). Again, because it is harder for companies to develop products that differ from their current lines for new geographical markets in which they lack experience, a firm is more likely to use M&A rather than internal development as a strategy when engaging in international product diversification (Hitt, Hoskisson, & Ireland, 1990; Hitt, Hoskisson, Ireland, & J. S. Harrison, 1991; e.g., News Corp.'s acquisition of DirecTV via Hughes gave News Corp. a presence in the U.S. direct broadcast satellite [DBS] market). Finally, a firm may use M&A as a way to restrict its dependence on a single or a few products or markets, thus reducing its reliance on the financial performance of individual sectors (e.g., NBC's merger with Universal gave NBC the important access to a major studio).

Various issues have been pointed out as potential problems for the strategies of mergers and acquisitions. Hitt et al. (2001) specifically identified seven pitfalls to watch for: integration difficulties, inadequate evaluation of target firms, large or extraordinary debt, inability to achieve synergy, overdiversification, excessive focus on acquisitions by management, and oversized corporations. The high-profile restructuring efforts of AOL Time Warner and AT&T illustrate some of these post-M&A challenges.

STRATEGIC NETWORKS AND ALLIANCES

Media industries are among the top sectors for seeking out strategic alliances or network relationships with other firms. This alliance or network orientation might be attributed to media content's public-goods nature, the media industries' need to be responsive to audience preferences and technological changes, and the symbiotic connection between media distribution and content (Chan-Olmsted, 2006). For the rest of the chapter, the term *strategic networks* is used to denote various cooperative agreements, including strategic alliances.

What Is a Strategic Network?

Strategic networks may be defined as the "stable inter-organizational relationships that are strategically important to participating firms" (Amit & Zott, 2001, p. 498). These ties may take the form of joint ventures, alliances, and even long-term buyer–supplier partnerships (Amit & Zott, 2001). Specifically, alliances can also take a variety of forms such as joint firms, minority equity alliances, joint production, joint marketing and promotion, enhanced supplier partnerships, distribution agreements, and licensing agreements (Yoshino & Rangan, 1995). Furthermore, an alliance can be examined by its structure—equity alliances, which involve the creation of new entities or ownership transfer of existing entities, and nonequity alliances, which do not (Das & Teng, 2000; Gulati, 1995). Finally, equity alliances involve equity joint firms and minority equity alliances, whereas nonequity alliances refer to all other cooperative arrangements that do not involve equity exchange and can be grouped into either unilateral or bilateral contract-based alliances (Mowery, Oxley, & Silverman, 1998).

Why Create a Strategic Network?

Firms might seek out such interorganizational partnerships to gain access to information, resources, and restricted markets; reduce costs and share risks; improve competitive position (e.g., competition reduction and leadership maintenance); generate scale and scope economies; share knowledge and facilitate learning; develop industry standards; align resources for large-scale projects; and increase speed in product development or market entry (Bailey & Shan, 1995; Gulati, Nohria, & Zaheer, 2000; Hitt et al., 2001; Kale, Singh, & Perlmutter, 2000; Stuart, 2000; J. R. Williams, 1992, 1998). For instance, in media industries, an alliance with a movie studio would provide its partner the critical access to "content" resources; an equity joint venture would allow a media firm to enter a new country or market that has ownership quota regulations for its media products. Parise and Henderson (2001) further suggested that technological advances also tend to induce strategic alliances as firms strive to acquire technology complementarity, reduce the time span for innovation, lessen uncertainty in terms of emerging technologies, and assist firms to position themselves where there is a convergence of several industry segments. The technological driver is especially applicable in the context of an emerging digital media marketplace.

Theoretically, transaction cost economics provides the principal rationale for explaining strategic network formation and development (Ramanathan, Seth, & Thomas, 1997), though various theories such as agency theory, game theory, RBV, social exchange theory, power-dependence theory, and organizational learning have also been applied to explain the factors influencing the formation and dynamics of strategic networks (Das & Teng, 2000; Robson, Leonidou, & Katsikeas, 2002). The RBV approach of analyzing strategic alliances seems to be especially fruitful in explicating the choice of certain alliance strategies. For instance, linking strategic alliance formats to RBV, Das and Teng argued that the types of resources contributed by the alliance partners are the key determinants of the structural preference in an alliance. Das and Teng proposed that a firm will prefer an equity joint firm if it primarily contributes property-based resources, and its partner primarily contributes knowledge-based resources; a firm will prefer a minority equity alliance if it primarily contributes knowledge-based resources, and its partner primarily contributes property-based resources; a firm will prefer a bilateral contract-based alliance if both partner firms primarily contribute knowledge-based resources; and a firm will prefer a unilateral contract-based alliance if both partner firms primarily contribute property-based resources. In essence, RBV scholars suggest that firms seek partners that have resources complementary to their own and alliances that allow them to acquire new capabilities (Eisenhardt & Schoonhoven, 1996; H. M. Harrison, Hoskisson, & Ireland, 2001). The RBV has been applied in some empirical studies of media markets (Chan-Olmsted, 1998; D. Miller & Shamsie, 1996). Chan-Olmsted used the RBV framework to study the strategic alliances of broadcasting, cable television, and telephone services in the telecommunication industry. Miller and Shamsie applied the RBV approach to study the property-based and knowledge-based resources' role in determining the U.S. film studios' performance in two different environments, one uncertain and one predictable.

Studies of Strategic Networks

Research in strategic networks often addresses questions that deal with such factors as the drivers and processes of strategic network formation, the type of interfirm relationships that help participating firms compete, the sources of value creation in these networks, and the linkage between performance and participating firms' different network positions and relationships (Amit & Zott, 2001). In general, studies in cooperative strategy may be grouped into three bodies of research: (a) those that focus on the reasons why alliances are formed, (b) those that emphasize how collaborative agreements should be managed to be successful, and (c) those that examine the evolution of the interpartner relationship (Ariño & García-Pont, 1998).

The most evident strategic network forms in the media industry are joint ventures and alliances. Many media firms have attractive core competencies such as the ownership of valuable content, talent, or distribution outlets but lack the size, access, or expertise to benefit from these unique resources and capabilities. Strategic networks not only offer an opportunity for access to a greater combination of competencies but also reduce barriers to entry (e.g., scale economies and brand loyalty) in newer, technology-driven media markets such as the Internet and broadband sectors. Many recent studies in media industries have found alliances to be a preferred method of entering the Internet, broadband, and wireless markets (Chan-Olmsted & Chang, 2003; Chan-Olmsted & Kang, 2003; Fang & Chan-Olmsted, 2003). The network strategy may also serve as a precursor for the essential M&A strategy. For example, local marketing agreements (LMAs), which exist in many local television markets, offer participating stations access to expanded sales and marketing resources while at the same time reducing competition.

The notion of strategic networks also complements the strategic taxonomy research framework. Examination of firm resources and resource typology for media products are especially appropriate because of the tendency of media firms to adopt alliance strategies that enhance the value of a content product through content repurposing, cross-promotion, and product windowing, and to pool resources together to compete in a fast-changing information technology environment. In a sense, the RBV theory of strategic management provides the fundamental rationale for many alliance studies (Barney, 1986; Zahra, Ireland, Gutierrez, & Hitt, 2000). By the same token, RBV and the corresponding resource typology studies present an excellent opportunity for media scholars to examine alliances in the media industries with a more theory-driven framework. For example, Liu and Chan-Olmsted (2002) examined the strategic alliances between the U.S. broadcast television networks and Internet firms in the context of convergence using the aforementioned knowledge–property resource typology.

Scholars have also begun investigating cooperative agreements in an international context. Alliance strategies became popular between multinational corporations beginning in the 1980s (Ariño & García-Pont, 1998); however, recent studies have found that American multinational firms increasingly organize their foreign business operations as wholly owned ventures rather than strategic networks such as joint ventures, mainly due to difficulties in coordinating business operations (Desai, Foley, & Hines, 2001). Regarding the performance of international strategic networks, it was suggested that business relatedness, partner rivalry, previous network experience, equity ownership, firm size, level of political risks, and similarity between partners' national cultures were important determinants. Nevertheless, researchers also found no significant performance differences in the American firms' international networks with partners from developed versus developing countries (Merchant, 2000).

INTERNATIONAL STRATEGY

As discussed earlier, international diversification is a popular corporate strategy of growth. Media firms such as Time Warner now operate in more than 60 countries. Multinational industrial giants such as Vivendi Universal (before the sale of Universal) and Bertelsmann have turned to the communication sectors by acquiring U.S.-based media companies and either divesting or packaging their industrial assets into separate publicly traded companies (Goldsmith, 2000). There is also evidence of oligopolistic, interdependent behavior as we began to see many strategic alliances between the same leading media conglomerates. Several drivers have contributed to the growth of a global media market. Most evidently, the progress in communications technology enables the provision of entertainment and information in a faster, more efficient manner and actually makes many media industries more attractive sectors for capital investment, which is necessary for a move toward global expansion. Also because of the technological changes, many countries are revamping their existing media policies. We are seeing more liberalization and privatization of media industries. This, of course, fosters the growth of an international media market. Furthermore, there has been a decreasing dominance of the U.S.-based media companies in the international marketplace during the last decade. Many high-profile M&As brought about the development of non-U.S.-based global media conglomerates such as News Corporation and Bertelsmann. The importance of the international market is further magnified by the fact that the demand for certain media products in the United States, such as broadcasting and cable television, is saturated. Also because of technological advances, the lifestyle differences between individual societies are now less pronounced. The traditional market segmentation approach by demographics like age and location is not as practical with the rise of information-based attitude groups that share similar consumption patterns. This is an important factor for a product like media content, which is associated with pop cultures. This lifestyle parallelism provides further incentives for the globalization of media companies. Finally, as a result of increasingly blurry industry boundaries and the growth of global multimedia conglomerates, there is a tendency to compete multilaterally in several media sectors and multiple countries at the same time. In other words, to compete successfully with a growing number of firms that have international holdings of multiple media products, a media company would have to do the same, which again leads to a trend toward internationalization.

Conceptually, various theories of internationalization have been proposed to explain why firms expand internationally or why they should do so. The product life cycle theory of internationalization postulated that as a product loses its competitiveness (i.e., started to decline in its life cycle) in an existing market within more developed economies, it will need to be progressively exported to markets in less-developed economies where it could start new cycles till it reaches the end of its commercial lifetime (Vernon, 1966). The opportunistic growth theory of international expansion regards internationalization as opportunities presented by changing environments that a firm encounters and pursues rather than as a result of systematic rational analyses. The economics of transaction costs also provides extensive literature in the area of foreign direct investment to explain a firm's international expansion choices based on its ability to define, specify, and contract for various kinds of economic activities in an international setting (Sanchez & Heene, 2004).

Many of the studies in international strategies seem to fall into two main categories: research that tackles a firm's entry mode strategies in international expansion and research that investigates an internationally diversified firm's choice of a global, multidomestic, or transnational management approach. In terms of market entry modes, a firm has many options when it decides to expand internationally. The modes of foreign entry range from export, license, franchise, strategic alliance, and joint venture, to wholly owned subsidiary, with increasing ownership and control as well as investment and risk. (Dess et al., 2004). Thus, the entry mode strategy has significant performance consequences. Hitt et al. (2001) suggested that a firm's entry mode decision is likely to be influenced by the industry's competitive conditions; the firm's unique set of resources, capabilities, and core competencies; and the country's situation and government policies. Traditionally, media firms have followed the option continuum sequentially beginning with exports and continuing with strategic alliances and joint ventures. There seems to be less green-field investment with the establishment of wholly owned subsidiaries in this industry, perhaps due to the diversity of local environments (e.g., regulation and infrastructure) and preferences in regards to media products.

Another major area of international corporate-level strategy is the balance between centralized and localized managerial control, considering the opposing pressures of reducing costs and expenses in adaptation to local markets. A firm might adopt a multidomestic strategy in which local responsiveness is the priority and strategic decisions are decentralized to the business unit in each country. On the other hand, a firm might adopt a global strategy in which global integration and standardization is the priority and the headquarters is often in charge of formulating the competitive strategies. A third option, a transnational strategy, aims to obtain both global efficiency and local responsiveness through shared vision, flexible coordination, and an integrated network of domestic resources. Nevertheless, it is difficult to carry out a transnational strategy in reality (Hitt et al., 2001). Dess et al. (2004) suggested that the existence of a global product; the potential for economies of scale, learning, and scope; and limited availability of an essential resource would likely tip the scale toward a global strategic approach, whereas differential local market preferences, high transportation and distribution costs, widely available resources, regulations, and speed in providing customer support would encourage a more localized, multidomestic strategy. For example, Hollywood studios are likely to adopt a more global strategy because their "content" products are globally attractive; contain locally unavailable resources such as internationally recognizable talent and sophisticated production studios; have a potential for scale, scope, and learning economies; and require minimal distribution costs.

FINAL THOUGHTS

Corporate strategies such as diversification approaches, M&A, and strategic networks, along with international strategies like foreign entry modes and global versus localized management design, play a significant role in shaping today's media industries as multinational media corporations such as Time Warner, Disney, Sony, and Bertelsmann continue to expand their holdings in both product and geographic markets and the SBU mom-and-pop media firms gradually disappear. As media firms continue to respond to environmental opportunities and contemplate their capabilities and competencies in formulating expansion strategies, the aforementioned media-specific characteristics such as the complementary nature of content and distribution and the windowing process for media content products matter in this process. In other words, there is a tendency for media firms to diversify, acquire, collaborate, and internationalize in a certain fashion. In essence, media industries today are infused with digital technologies and converging platforms. Consequentially, media firms are faced with an increasing need to be less reliant on traditional business models (e.g., advertising revenues), to develop attractive new-media services, and to compete multilaterally (i.e., multipoint competition in different product and geographic markets). In this complex market environment of abundant potentials as well as risks, corporate-level strategies, with the utilities of improving efficiency, spreading risk, and sharing resources, are indispensable tools in the race to develop competitive advantages.

REFERENCES

Albarran, A. B., & Moellinger, T. (2002). The top six communication industry firms: Structure, performance, and strategy. In R. G. Picard (Ed.), Media firms: Structures, operations, and performance (pp. 103–122). Mahwah, NJ: Lawrence Erlbaum Associates.

Albarran, A. B., & Porco, J. F. (1990). Measuring and analyzing diversification of corporations involved in pay cable. *Journal of Media Economics, 3*(3), 3–14.

Amit, R., & Zott, C. (2001). Value creation in e-business. *Strategic Management Journal, 22*(6/7), 493–520.

Ansoff, H. I. (1958). A model for diversification. *Management Science, 4*(4), 392–414.

Ariño, A., & García-Pont, C. (1998). Strategic alliances and blocks: Cooperative behavior as a driving force for their evolution. In M. A. Hitt, J. E. Ricart I Costa, & R. D. Nixon (Eds.), *Managing strategically in an interconnected world*(pp. 281–300). New York: Wiley.

Bagdikian, B. (2000). *The media monopoly.* Boston: Beacon.

Bailey, E. E., & Shan, W. (1995). Sustainable competitive advantage through alliances. In E. Bowman & B. Kogut (Eds.), *Redesigning the firm* (pp. 132–156). New York: Oxford University Press.

Barney, J. (1986). Types of competition and the theory of strategy: Toward an integrative framework. *The Academy of Management Review, 11*(4), 791–800.

Bengtsson, L. (2000). Corporate strategy in a small open economy: Reducing product diversification while increasing international diversification. *European Management Journal, 18*(4), 444–453.

Buhner, R. (1987). Assessing international diversification of West German corporations. *Strategic Management Journal, 8*(1), 25–37.

Caves, R. E. (1981). Diversification and seller concentration: evidence from change, 1963–1972. *Review of Economics and Statistics, 63*(2), 289–293.

Chan-Olmsted, S. M. (1998). Mergers, acquisitions, and convergence: the strategic alliances of broadcasting, cable television, and telephone services. *Journal of Media Economics, 11*(3), 33–46.

Chan-Olmsted, S. M. (2006). Issues in strategic management. In A. Albarran, S. M. Chan-Olmsted, & M. Wirth (Eds.), *Media management and economics handbook* (pp. 161–180). Mahwah, NJ: Lawrence Erlbaum Associates.

Chan-Olmsted, S. M., & Albarran, A. B. (1998). The global media economic patterns and issues. In A. B. Albarran & S. M. Chan-Olmsted (Eds.), *Global media economics: Commercialization, concentration and integration of world media markets* (pp. 331–339). Ames: Iowa State University Press.

Chan-Olmsted, S. M., & Chang, B. (2003). Diversification strategy of global media conglomerates: Examining its patterns and drivers. *Journal of Media Economics, 16*(4), 213–233.

Chan-Olmsted, S. M., & Kang, J. (2003). The emerging broadband television market in the United States: Assessing the strategic differences between cable television and telephone firms. *Journal of Interactive Advertising, 4.* Retrieved May 18, 2004, from http://jiad.org

Chandler, A. D. (1962). *Strategy and structure: Chapters in the history of American industrial enterprise.* Cambridge, MA: MIT Press.

Chatterjee, S., & Wernerfelt, B. (1991). The link between resources and type of diversification: Theory and evidence. *Strategic Management Journal, 12*(1), 33–48.

Chen, C. (1998). *Exploration into firm diversification: Performance effects of product, international market and international operations diversification.* Unpublished doctoral dissertation, University of Texas at Dallas.

Croteau, D., & Hoynes, W. (2001). *The business of media: Corporate media and the public interest.* Thousand Oaks, CA: Sage.

Das, T. K., & Teng, B. (2000). A resource-based theory of strategic alliances. *Journal of Management, 26*(1), 31–61.

Davis, C., & Craft, S. (2000). New media synergy: Emergence of institutional conflicts of interest. *Journal of Mass Media Ethics, 15*(4), 219–231.

Davis, S. (1999). Space jam: Media conglomerates build the entertainment city. *European Journal of Communication, 14*(4), 435–459.

Demers, D. P. (1999). *Global media: Menace or messiah?* Cresskill, NJ: Hampton.

Desai, M., Foley, C. F., & Hines, J. R. (2001). *International joint ventures and the boundaries of the firm.* Unpublished manuscript.

Dess, G. G., Lumpkin, G. T., & Taylor, M. (2004). *Strategic management: Creating competitive advantages.* Maidenhead, England: McGraw-Hill Education.

Dimmick, J., & Wallschlaeger, M. (1986). Measuring corporate diversification: A case study of new media ventures by television network parent companies. *Journal of Broadcasting & Electronic Media, 30*(1), 1–14.

Eisenhardt, K. M., & Schoonhoven, C. B. (1996). Resource-based view of strategic alliance formation: Strategic and social effects of entrepreneurial firms. *Organization Science, 7*(2), 136–150.

Fang, L., & Chan-Olmsted, S. M. (2003). Partnerships between the old and the new: Examining the strategic alliances between broadcast television networks and Internet firms in the context of convergence. *International Journal on Media Management, 5*(1), 47–56.

Geringer, J. M., Beamish, P. W., & daCosta, R. C. (1989). Diversification strategy and internationalization: Implications for MNE performance. *Strategic Management Journal, 10*(2), 109–119.

Geringer, J. M., Tallman, S., & Olsen, D. M. (2000). Product and international diversification among Japanese multinational firms. *Strategic Management Journal, 21*(1), 51–80.

Gershon, R. A. (1997). *The transnational media corporation: Global messages and free market competition.* Mahwah, NJ: Lawrence Erlbaum Associates.

Goldsmith, J. (2000, December 17). Congloms & showbiz: An uneasy alliance. *Variety, 381*(4), 3.

Gort, M. (1962). *Diversification and integration in American industry.* Princeton, NJ: Princeton University Press.

Grant, R. M. (1987). Multinationality and performance among British manufacturing companies. *Journal of International Business Studies, 18*(3), 79–89.

Grant, R. M. (1988). On dominant logic, relatedness and the link between diversity and performance. *Strategic Management Journal, 9*(6), 639–642.

Grant, R. M. (1998). *Contemporary strategy analysis.* Oxford, England: Backwell.

Grant, R. M., & Jammine, A. P. (1988). Performance differences between the Wrigley/Rumelt strategic categories. *Strategic Management Journal, 9*(4), 333–346.

Grant, R. M., Jammine, A. P., & Thomas, H. (1988). Diversity, diversification, and profitability among British manufacturing companies. *Academy of Management Journal, 31*(4), 771–801.

Gulati, R. (1995). Does familiarity breed trust? The implications of repeated ties for contractual choice in alliances. *Academy of Management Journal, 38*(1), 85–112.

Gulati, R., Nohria, N., & Zaheer, A. (2000). Strategic networks. *Strategic Management Journal, 21*(3), 203–215.

Harrison, H. M., Hoskisson, R. E., & Ireland, R. D. (2001). Resource complementarity in business combinations: Extending the logic to organization alliances. *Journal of Management, 27*(6), 679–690.

Haspeslagh, P. (1999, April 7). Managing the matching dance in equal mergers. *Financial Times,* pp. 14–15.

Hitt, M. A., Hoskisson, R. E., & Ireland, R. D. (1990). Mergers and acquisitions and managerial commitment to innovation in M-form firms. *Strategic Management Journal, 11*(5), 29–47.

Hitt, M. A., Hoskisson, R. E., Ireland, R. D., & Harrison, J. S. (1991). Effects of acquisitions on R&D inputs and outputs. *Academy of Management Journal, 34*(3), 693–706.

Hitt, M. A., Hoskisson, R. E., & Kim, H. (1997). International diversification: Effects on innovation firm performance in product-diversified firms. *Academy of Management Journal, 40*(4), 767–798.

Hitt, M. A., Ireland, R. D., & Hoskisson, R. E. (2001). *Strategic management: Competitiveness and globalization* (4th ed.). Cincinnati, OH: South-Western College.

Jung, J. (2001, August). *The influence of media ownership on news coverage: The case of CNN's coverage of movies.* Paper presented at the meeting of the Association for Education in Journalism and Mass Communication, Washington, DC.

Jung, J. (2002). How magazines covered media companies' mergers: The case of the evolution of Time Inc. *Journalism & Mass Communication Quarterly, 79*(3), 681–696.

Jung, J., & Chan-Olmsted, S. M. (in press). Global media diversification strategy and performance: Assessing the relationship between dual diversification and firm performance in media industries. *Journal of Media Economics.*

Kale, P., Singh, H., & Perlmutter, H. (2000). Learning and protection of proprietary assets in strategic alliances: Building rational capital. *Strategic Management Journal, 21*(3), 217–237.

Kim, W. C., Hwang, P., & Burgers, W. P. (1989). Global diversification strategy and corporate performance. *Strategic Management Journal, 10*(1), 45–57.

Kranenburg, H. L. (2004, May). *Diversification strategy, diversity and performance among publishing companies.* Paper presented at the 6th World Media Economics Conference, Montreal, Canada.

Liu, F., & Chan-Olmsted, S. M. (2002, April). *Partners between the old and the new: Examining the strategic alliances between broadcast television networks and internet firms in the context of convergence.* Paper presented at the meeting of the Media Management and Sales Division of the Broadcast Education Association, Las Vegas.

Madura, J., & Rose, L. C. (1987). Are product specialization and international diversification strategies compatible? *Management International Review, 27*(3), 38–44.

Markides, C. C. (1992). Consequence of corporate refocusing: Ex ante evidence. *Academy of Management Journal, 35*(2), 398–412.

McAllister, M. P. (2000). From flick to flack: The increased emphasis on marketing by media entertainment corporations. In R. Anderson & L. Strate (Eds.), *Critical studies in media commercialism* (pp. 101–122). New York: Oxford University Press.

McCardle, K. F., & Viswanathan, S. (1994). The direct entry versus takeover decision and stock price performance around takeovers. *Journal of Business, 67*(1), 1–43.

McCutcheon, B. J. (1991). *What caused conglomerate formation? An examination of managerial behavior and internal capital markets in the 1960s conglomerates.* Unpublished doctoral dissertation, University of Chicago.

Merchant, H. (2000). Configurations of international joint ventures. *Management International Review, 20*(2), 107–140.

Michel, A., & Shaked, I. (1984). Does business diversification affect performance? *Financial Management, 13*(4), 18–25.

Miller, D., & Shamsie, J. (1996). The resource-based view of the firm in two environments: The Hollywood firm studios from 1936 to 1965. *Academy of Management Journal, 39*(3), 519–543.

Mowery, D. C., Oxley, J. E., & Silverman, B. S. (1998). Technological overlap and interfirm cooperation: Implications for the resource-based view of the firm. *Research Policy, 27*(5), 507–523.

Palepu, K. (1985). Diversification strategy, profit performance, and the entropy measure. *Strategic Management Journal, 6*(3), 239–255.

Palich, L. E., Cardinal, L. B., & Miller, C. C. (2000). Curvilinearity in the diversification–performance linkage: An examination of over three decades of research. *Strategic Management Journal, 21*(2), 155–174.

Palich, L. E., Carini, G. R., & Seaman, S. L. (2000). The impact of internationalization on the diversification-performance relationship: A replication and extension of prior research. *Journal of Business Research, 48*(1), 43–54.

Parise, S., & Henderson, J. C. (2001). Knowledge resource exchange in strategic alliance. *IBM Systems Journal, 40*(4), 908–925.

Peltier, S. (2002, May). *Mergers & acquisitions in the media industries: A preliminary study of the impact on performance.* Paper presented at the 5th World Media Economics Conference, Turku, Finland.

Picard, R. G., & Rimmer, T. (1999). Weathering a recession effects of size and diversification on newspaper companies. *Journal of Media Economics, 12*(1), 1–18.

Powers, A., & Pang, I. (2002, May). *Media diversification: Is bigger better after all?* Paper presented at the 5th World Media Economics Conference, Turku, Finland.

Qian, G. (1997). Assessing product-market diversification of U.S. firms. *Management International Review, 37*(2), 127–149.

Ramanathan, K., Seth, A., & Thomas, H. (1997). Explaining joint ventures. In P. W. Beamish & J. P. Killings (Eds.), *Cooperative strategies: North American perspective* (pp. 51–85). San Francisco: New Lexington Press.

Rappaport, A., & Sirower, M. L. (1999). Stock or crash. *Harvard Business Review, 77*(6), 147–158.

Robson, M., Leonidou, L. D., & Katsikeas, C. S. (2002). Factors influencing international joint venture performance: Theoretical perspectives, assessment, and future directions. *Management International Review, 42*(4), 385–418.

Rumelt, R. (1984). Toward a strategic theory of the firm. In R. Lamb (Ed.), *Competitive strategic management* (pp. 556–570). Englewood Cliffs, NJ: Prentice-Hall.

Salter, M. S., & Weinhold, W. S. (1979). *Diversification through acquisition.* New York: The Free Press.

Sambharya, R. B. (1995). The combined effect of international diversification and product diversification strategies on the performance of U.S.-based multinational corporations. *Management International Review, 35*(3), 197–218.

Sanchez, R., & Heene, A. (2004). *The new strategic management: Organization, competition, and competence.* New York: Wiley.

Scherer, F. M. (1980). *Industrial market structure and economic performance*. Chicago: Rand McNally.

Shank, J. K., & Govindarajan, V. (1992). Strategic cost analysis of technological investments. *MIT Sloan Management Review, 34*(1), 39–51.

Shaver, D., & Shaver, M. A. (2003). The impact of concentration and convergence on managerial efficiencies of time and cost. In A. B. Albarran & A. Arress (Eds.), *Time and media markets* (pp. 61–79). Mahwah, NJ: Lawrence Erlbaum Associates.

Smith, A. (1991). *The age of behemoths: The globalization of mass media firms*. New York: Priority Press.

Sobel, R. (1984). *The rise and fall of the conglomerates kings*. New York: Stein & Day.

Stuart, T. E. (2000). Interorganizational alliances and the performance of firms: A study of growth and innovation rates in a high-technology industry. *Strategic Management Journal, 21*(8), 791–811.

Tallman, S., & Li, J. (1996). Effects of international diversity and product diversity on the performance of multinational firms. *Academy of Management Journal, 39*(1), 179–196.

Teinowitz, I. (2001, July 23). Senate eyes media mergers. *Advertising Age*, p. 31.

Vernon, R. (1966). International investment and international trade in the product cycle. *Quarterly Journal of Economics, 80*(2), 190–207.

Williams, D. (2002). Synergy bias: Conglomerates and promotion in the news. *Journal of Broadcasting & Electronic Media, 46*(3), 453–472.

Williams, J. R. (1992). How sustainable is your competitive advantage? *California Management Review, 34*(3), 29–51.

Williams, J. R. (1998). *Renewable advantage: Crafting strategy through economic time*. New York: The Free Press.

Williamson, O. E. (1981). The economics of organization: The transaction cost approach. *American Journal of Sociology, 87*(3), 548–577.

Yoshino, M. Y., & Rangan, U. S. (1995). *Strategic alliances: An entrepreneurial approach to globalization*. Boston: Harvard Business School Press.

Zahra, S. A., Ireland, R. D., Gutierrez, I., & Hitt, M. A. (2000). Privatization and entrepreneurial transformation: Emerging issues and a reseach agenda. *Academy of Management Review, 25*, 509–524

Chapter 4

A Primer in Brand Management for Media Firms

Moving from strategic management to "brands," this chapter reviews major brand management concepts and theoretical frameworks such as brand knowledge and brand equity, discusses how these concepts and frameworks might apply to media products in the context of a changing marketplace, and provides examples of brand management practices in media industries. By now we know that business activities such as strategic planning are essential for gaining competitive advantages, but why is brand management important? What has changed in our media environment that makes a traditional consumer goods management tool and construct applicable to media products?

In principle, the most essential driver for a branding strategy is the element of "competition" in a market. When consumers are faced with choices in products, they need a way to identify the one that will best satisfy their needs, so suppliers must create identities for their offerings to avoid confusion and reach the target consumers in the marketplace. The tremendous proliferation of media outlets and the continuous fragmentation of audiences during the last two decades have created an increasingly competitive media marketplace. The same element of "competition" that propelled the introduction of branding practices in consumer goods industries is now facilitating the application of brand management in many media industries as media firms race to establish clear and memorable brand images in a growingly complicated marketplace filled with infinite content offered by broadcasters, cablecasters, Internet, telcos, and DBS. In fact, the branding process is consistent with the "experience good" characteristic of media products: It is difficult for consumers to estimate the quality of a new media product such as movies or television series before they actually experience it. In order to avoid risks (e.g., money

57

and time) related to purchasing and consuming these products, consumers may depend on brands and their associated images and expectations as one of the initial decision factors (Chang, 2004).

WHAT IS BRANDING?

Fundamentally, a brand is a name, term, sign, symbol, package design, or combination of these elements intended to identify and distinguish a product or service from its competitors. A "brand" is different from a "product" because, although it is designed to satisfy the same basic need as an unbranded product, it also adds certain rational, tangible and/or emotional, intangible attributes to a product so it is perceived to be different from an unbranded product in its expected performance and benefits. In essence, these brand-related elements are supposed to communicate thoughts and feelings that enhance the value of a product beyond its product category and basic functional value. For instance, the brand *New York Times* represents a certain level of news reporting and editorial quality that distinguishes it from its competitors.

Why are brands valuable? Keller (1998) succinctly listed a number of reasons why brands matter to both consumers and producers. He suggested that brands help consumers identify the source of a product, assign responsibility to product makers, reduce risk and search cost, signal quality, form relationships between consumers and product makers, and serve as a symbolic device. Brands also provide producers a means of identification to simplify handling or tracing, a way to legally protect unique features, a tool to signal "quality" levels, a means to endow products with special associations, and a source of competitive advantages and thus the final financial returns. All of these benefits are applicable in the context of media products. For example, the brand name "PBS" is strongly associated with the images of "trust" and "quality" in the mind of television audiences (Chan-Olmsted & Y. Kim, 2002). The brand name "Discovery" has been used by its corporate owner in the introduction of various new cable channels and even retail learning products.

There are various strategic aspects that a firm can pursue to engage competitors: marketing, production, financial, technological, and managerial. Whereas the topics in strategic management discussed in earlier chapters mainly dealt with managerial competition strategies, the development and maintenance of brands are traditionally a part of a marketing program. Because a brand is built over time, branding is also a continuous process of marketing activities that should be designed to reflect the changing life cycle of a product and its environment. Various marketing researchers have tried to explain the nature of brands and branding activities. Donahue (1995) suggested that a valuable brand has to be relevant and distinctive and brand-building activities may include demonstrations, seminars, shows, effective service material, public relations, advertising, direct marketing, and promotions that extend positioning. Murphy (1987) indicated that branding consists of the development and maintenance of sets of product attributes and values that are coherent, appropriate, distinctive, protectable, and appealing to consumers. Cowley (1991) also stated that sources of added value in branding include a guarantee of authenticity, the promise of performance, the value of reassurance, and the transformation of experience (the subjective experience of using a brand, and differentiation or brand personality). The value of authenticity and promise of positive experience seem to be especially important for media content providers in an increasingly crowded marketplace. In fact, Davis (1995) suggested that brand management should be viewed as a strategic management process to maximize the long-term value of a brand. The role of branding is often misunderstood by companies that have not had a traditional marketing focus. Many companies hire senior-level packaged goods marketers and expect quick fixes (Bissell, 1998). Branding is seen simply as a new "design and control" function to quickly clean up corporate identity and wrap an existing product or service into a nice, neat package. Bissell reiterated the importance of management commitment in treating branding as part of a firm's fundamental strategic process and daily tactical operations.

On the surface, the branding and brand management notions appear to be less applicable to media industries due to many media products' intangible, nonpreservable nature, the possibility of group consumption, the selection of a content product based on the merits of individual units (e.g., movies), the lack of actual purchasing action (and risk) for advertising-supported content products, and the absence of easily identifiable product logos. In addition, prior to the 1990s, most media markets were relatively uncompetitive; media products were based on distinct technologies consumed in separate markets with distinctive consumer behaviors (McDowell, 2006). Nevertheless, the landscape of media industries has changed dramatically. We now have a converging media marketplace enabled by digital technologies and new network conduits such as the Internet; the potential for providing additional new media services; and a fragmented, multitasking audience. These environmental developments present an unprecedented need for differentiation using all possible means. With varying degrees, branding or brand management can enhance a media consumer's association, perception, and expectation of a media product. For example, a radio station that has established a family-friendly brand may increase its chance of being selected by a certain segment of the audience. And a signature local news program can easily become a proprietary brand asset for a TV station.

Although branding offers media firms opportunities for differentiation, the aforementioned media characteristics still present some challenges in this process. In addition, there are general obstacles associated with the branding approach. For example, the essence of branding as developing something of value often conflicts with the current accounting system, which treats a brand as an expense rather than asset. The necessary long-term orientation of brand building also conflicts with the generally high personnel turnover in businesses. Finally, the integrated nature of brand building (i.e., the involvement of production, sales, marketing, etc.) often conflicts with the reality of a segmented organizational structure and single-dimension advertising focuses (Kapferer, 1992).

BRAND MANAGEMENT CONCEPTS

Brand management has become a major subfield within the marketing discipline over the years, infusing it with various theoretical constructs and analytical frameworks. Many of these conceptual building blocks are useful for analyzing media products and thus are reviewed next.

Brand Identity

Brand identity encompasses two dimensions: one that indicates the outward expression of a brand, including the tangible elements such as names, symbols, logos, slogans, and packaging that can be used to recognize a brand; and the other that symbolizes the brand's differentiated characteristics, including the unique set of associations that represent what the brand stands for and would do for customers. The process is the linking of differentiated features and attributes of a product or service to anticipated perceived benefits based on customers' values and beliefs. In a way, brand identity is like clothing to a product in that it can set one apart in a crowd as well as say something about the person who chooses the brand. It is important to note that brand identity is something that is formulated and worked on by the firm, whereas another relevant concept, brand image, is based on consumer perception (i.e., formulated by the consumer). In other words, image is the result of how consumers interpret the brand identity put forth by a firm, amid noises and personal circumstances. Time can also change the identity of a brand as it gradually acquires other meanings from associations with things that are both intended and unintended by its firm.

So how does a firm successfully develop a brand identity for a product? Kapferer (1992) suggested that brand identities should be formulated on the basis of three qualities: durability, coherence, and realism (as opposed to idealism or opportunism). Keller (1998) listed five criteria in choosing brand elements to form a brand identity: memorability, meaningfulness, transferability (both culturally and geographically), adaptability, and protectability (both legally and competitively). Cable networks offer some excellent examples of establishing and modifying a media brand over time. For example, Discovery Communications Inc.'s TLC channel began as an education network that offered foreign-language instruction, an SAT review course, and other adult personal-enrichment series with the name of "The Learning Channel" (Eastman, 1993). With the success of its reality-based series such as *Trading Spaces* and its continuous programming transformation to this particular genre, it is now renamed as "TLC" with a "Life Unscripted" slogan and logo. Finally, a firm may look to various sources to define a brand's identity. Kapferer also suggested some sources of identities: (a) the actual product or service through which the brand may display its uniqueness (e.g., NASA Television), (b) a brand name through which the brand may convey its characteristics (e.g., The Cartoon Network), (c) brand characters and symbols through which the brand may represent its traits and features in the etymological sense (e.g., PBS and its logo), (d) trademarks and logos through which a brand may reflect its personality and value (e.g., Playboy TV Networks), (e) geographical and historical roots through which a brand may paint its individuality and competence (e.g., BBC America cable channel), and (f) advertising through which a brand may develop or reinvent identities as conceived by its firm (e.g., TLC cable channel).

Brand Knowledge: Awareness, Association, and Image

Although a brand identity may be the strategic goal for a brand, the resultant brand image of what actually resides in the minds of consumers about the brand could be very different from that goal. According to Keller (1998), such a discrepancy is due to the differential brand knowledge structures of individual consumers as reflected by the levels of brand awareness and brand image (i.e., the strength, favorability, and uniqueness of brand associations) of that product.

Creating "brand awareness" is often considered the first step of branding. Brand awareness can be defined as the degree to which a target audience is able to identify a brand among others and even recall its promise. As a typical measure of marketing communications effectiveness, awareness may be assessed unaidedly or aidedly (i.e., when a brand name is recognized among others that are listed or identified). Conceptually, brand awareness is hierarchical. Keller (1993) suggested that brand awareness consists of brand recognition, which communicates consumers' ability to verify prior exposure to the brand when given the brand as a cue, and brand recall, which relates consumers' ability to retrieve the brand from memory when given cues such as benefits, usage/purchase situations, or product categories. Another related concept is "top-of-the-mind" awareness, which denotes the highest level of brand awareness for a brand because the brand is the first to come to mind when consumers recall a brand relating to a certain quality. It is evident that brand awareness is fundamental to a brand's success. For example, by increasing the brand awareness of HBO On Demand (a video-on-demand programming service offered by HBO), HBO raises the potential that an audience might include this service in his or her viewing consideration list. By increasing the brand awareness of Movielink.Com (a broadband movie download service), Movielink raises the probability that an audience might choose this service because it is perceived to be more established and familiar. This power of awareness is especially significant for new media products that consumers have not experienced or have no prior knowledge to relate to. Finally, by increasing the brand awareness of Bravo Cable Network, its owner, NBC, would have an easier time cultivating the associations that make up Bravo's brand image.

As indicated previously, brand image rests in the consumers' minds and is developed through brand associations. Consequently, brand image may be defined as a unique set of associations within the target customers' minds that characterizes what the brand stands for and implies the brand's promise to them. For users of the brand, the image is also influenced by their experience with the brand. For nonusers, the image is largely shaped by their impressions of the brand amid personal beliefs and attitudes. Keller (1998) identified three main types of brand associations with increasing abstraction: attributes (product related or nonproduct related such as price and usage imagery), benefits (functional, symbolic, or experiential), and attitudes formed on the basis of beliefs about a product's attributes and benefits. Note that a brand image is influenced not only by the types of associations but also by the strength, uniqueness, and favorability of the associations (Keller, 1998). For instance, Fox News has established relatively strong and unique brand associations based on certain attributes and benefits (e.g., conservative commentaries such as the *O'Reilly Factor* program). The value of its brand image, however, is largely dependent on an audience segment's favorability or desirability toward those associations.

Brand Attitudes

Another consumer-based concept, brand attitudes, is an important subject in traditional consumer behavior, marketing, and advertising disciplines (Gardner, 1985; Mitchell & Olsen, 1981). Many studies in advertising effectiveness have focused on investigating the relationships between brand attitudes, attitudes toward advertising, and purchase intention (Heath & Gaeth, 1994; Kalwani & Silk, 1982; MacKenzie & Lutz, 1989). Brand attitudes can be defined as consumers' overall evaluations of a brand, which can be influenced by experience as well as marketing programs (Wilkie, 1990). Ajzen and Fishbein (1980) examined brand attitudes as a predisposition to respond in a consistently favorable or unfavorable manner to a particular brand.

Understandably, such a definition implies significant consequences for both consumers' formation of brand image and purchasing behavior. Katz (1960) proposed that consumers actually form brand attitudes based on what the brands can do to help them achieve what they desire. He listed four major functions that consumers often seek from a product: to satisfy their needs, to allow them to express themselves, to simplify decision making, or to eliminate threats or insecurity. Here we are dealing with the multiplicative result of both the functions that are perceived to be embedded in a product and personal beliefs of the importance of these functions. To capture the meaning of these abstract attitudinal concepts in a marketing context, Fishbein and Ajzen (1975) proposed a famous expectancy-value model to assess brand attitudes. They stated that brand attitudes are a function of (a) salient beliefs about the attitude object, defined as the subjective probability that the attitude object has each attribute (i.e., strength of association between the brand and the salient attributes or benefits), and (b) the evaluative aspect of these beliefs, defined as the evaluation of each attribute (i.e., the favorability of the salient attributes or benefits). It was also suggested that brand attitudes that were formed based on direct behavior or experience are often more influential in the purchasing decision process (Farquhar, 1989).

How does the concept of brand attitudes work in the context of media products? The functional theory of attitudes proposed by Katz (1960) is useful to explain the dynamics of consumption choices for media products. In fact, it is similar to the utility notions as suggested by the uses and gratification theory in mass communication. A media brand may seek to create associations with certain product–related attributes such as the extensive amount of information offered (e.g., Discovery), non-product-related attributes such as a user (audience) imagery of being young and hip (e.g., MTV), functional benefits such as knowledge obtainment (e.g., PBS), symbolic benefits such as being socially visible and accepted (e.g., ESPN), and experiential benefits such as high sensory entertainment (e.g., a digital cable service). By investigating the functions desired by a target audience and how the product delivers that function as perceived by the group, a media firm can assess the effectiveness of its product offering and marketing programs in associating the attributes and benefits with its brand.

Brand Extension, Hierarchy, and Portfolio

When a brand has acquired a strong, favorable brand image, it is logical that its firm will want to extend the brand's value to its other businesses. Brand extension is defined as the use of an established brand name for a new product to capitalize on the equity of the existing brand name. Successful brand extensions require marketing strategies that reasonably establish a connection between the new and the old product and transfer the perceived benefit from the old to the new in a meaningful continuation of brand identity. Note that established brands are most valuable in those extensions where the perceptions of brand identity are relevant to the potential consumer of the new product. For instance, NBC's extensions to the cable network business, MSNBC and CNBC, seem to provide the consistent content images (upscale and urban) that appeal to the core audience of NBC. Nevertheless, overextensions or wrong extensions of a successful brand can also damage the existing brand. Research has shown that a brand extension strategy may lead to cannibalization or dilution of the parent brand (Chakravarti, MacInnis, & Nakamoto, 1990; John, Loken, & Joiner, 1998; Loken & John, 1993).

Brand extensions can be grouped into two different categories: line extensions, which extend a brand name vertically by introducing a new product of modifying features (e.g., different attributes, pricing points, or qualities) into the same product category as the parent brand, and category extensions, which extend a brand name horizontally by introducing a new product into a product category different from that of the parent brand (Kirmani, Sood, & Bridges, 1999). For example, it is a line extension when the Discovery Channel set up another cable network, Discovery Health, whereas it is a category extension when Discovery entered the magazine-publishing business by introducing its *Discovery* magazine.

Several factors have been suggested to motivate line extension strategies: customer segmentation, consumer desires, pricing breadth and flexibility (e.g., encouraging customers to trade up to premium products), excess capacity, competitive intensity, trade pressure, and short-term sales gain. Kapferer (1992) suggested that the high cost of advertising, a main-brand building tool, has prevented many firms from launching new brands and to opt for brand maintenance instead. In general, a firm may adopt a brand extension strategy to facilitate new-product acceptance and/or provide feedback benefits to the parent brand (Quelch & Kenny, 1999). Specifically, brand extensions may reduce risk perceived by customers, increase the probability of gaining distribution and trial, increase promotional efficiency, reduce costs of marketing programs, avoid cost of developing a new brand, allow for packaging and labeling efficiencies, and permit consumer variety seeking. From the perspective of the parent brand, brand extensions can clarify brand meaning, enhance the parent brand image, revitalize the brand, bring new customers into the brand franchise and increase market coverage, and permit subsequent extensions (Keller, 1998).

There are various problems that might be associated with line extensions, including lower brand loyalty, oversegmentation (i.e., weaker lines), underexploited product ideas (i.e., the product might warrant a new brand), stagnant category demand, more opportunities for competitors, increased costs, and poorer trade relations (Quelch & Kenny, 1999). Keller (1998) also suggested that brand extensions can confuse or frustrate consumers, encounter retailer resistance, hurt the parent brand image, cannibalize sales of the parent brand, diminish identification with any one product category, dilute brand meaning, or cause the firm to forgo the chance to develop a new, profitable brand.

Many studies in this area have focused on finding the factors contributing to successful brand extensions (e.g., Aaker & Keller, 1990; Barwise, 1993; Keller & Aaker, 1992; Rangaswamy, Burke, & Oliva, 1993; Shocker,

Srivastava, & Ruekert, 1994; Sunde & Brodie, 1993; Uncles, 1996). Generally, past research related to the role of the parent brand seems to indicate that the number of products associated to a brand, the variability among product types represented by a brand name (brand breadth), and the quality variance of products associated to a brand are major explanatory variables regarding brand extension evaluations (Chang, 2005). There are also studies that emphasize the aspect of the parent-extended brand relationship. It was found that the more common and fewer distinctive associations that exist, the greater the perception of overall similarity between the parent and extended brands. Although these similarity judgments could be based on product-related attributes or benefits as well as non-product-related attributes or benefits, they also provide the foundation for value transfer from the parent brand to the extended brand (MacInnis & Nakamoto, 1990).

Brand extension is an increasingly popular branding strategy in media industries. Beginning with the practices of movie sequels (e.g., *Home Alone 2*, the *Star Wars* trilogy), it is also widely applied in television programming development and cable network expansions. For example, the success of the program *Law and Order* prompted the introductions of *Law and Order: Special Victims Unit* and *Law and Order: Criminal Intent*. HBO, the Discovery Channel, CNN, and ESPN all have adopted both line and category brand extension strategies. In fact, studies have shown that in 2004, among the 312 cable television networks, approximately 37% of them were brand extensions. In addition, it was found that the use of the brand extension strategy has become very popular since the mid-1990s (Chang, 2005). In essence, the deregulatory environment as well as technological advances have enabled the growth of multiple media outlets (both content and distribution), which offers the opportunity of additional brand development. As advertising costs continue to escalate and consumers are bombarded by proliferated media choices, brand extensions seem to be an effective strategy of expansion for many media firms.

Brand hierarchy refers to the graphical ordering of brands to examine the number and nature of common and distinctive brand components across a firm's products, thus identifying the branding relationships and corporate brand portfolios. A brand hierarchy may be composed of a corporate brand (e.g., Time Warner), family brand (e.g., Turner Broadcasting), individual brand (CNN), and modifier (individual item or model; e.g., CNNfn). A number of factors need to be contemplated while designing a brand hierarchy. A firm has to find the best combination of hierarchy levels, the similarities and distinctions between brands, and how these brands should be related so a new brand might leverage the associations with more established brands in the hierarchy while also creating its own meanings (Keller, 1998).

Another relevant concept to brand extension is brand portfolio. Similar to corporate strategies, a brand portfolio is a set of brands that a firm offers to consumers in a product category or in the overall market.

Brand portfolio strategy is closely related to the type and size of consumer segments available in a market. The management of a brand portfolio encompasses the development and monitoring of a firm's brand holdings over time along a conceptual matrix to achieve the best overall profitability for its stakeholders. Matrix analytical frameworks utilizing aspects such as market share, sales volume, and brand images to map the trends of an individual brand's positions and thus its subsequent resource commitments are often adopted in this process. Aaker (2004) stated that a brand portfolio strategy should create relevance, clarity, differentiation, energy, and leverage. Nevertheless, Kumar (2003) argued that companies can often achieve greater economies of scale, corporate growth, and profitability by reducing the number of brands in their portfolios because once any unprofitable brands have been killed off, companies are left with more freedom to invest in the growth of their remaining brands. In the context of media products, the brand portfolio concept is another valuable tool for analyzing the strategies of media conglomerates because digitization increasingly offers more expansion opportunities for these media firms.

THE VALUE OF BRANDING

Brand Equity

The goal of branding is to create something of value that would otherwise be unattainable. Brand equity is typically the "value" that a firm aims to generate with its marketing programs for a brand. Brand equity is therefore defined as the accrued marketing and financial value, both tangible and intangible, that a brand adds to a product or service as a result of a combination of factors such as the awareness, loyalty, perceived quality, images, and emotions that consumers associate with the brand name. Keller (1991) provided a conceptual framework of what brands mean to consumers and what this implies for marketing strategies. He conceptualized brand equity from the perspective of the individual consumer. This customer-based brand equity occurs when the consumer is familiar with the brand and holds some favorable, strong, and unique brand associations in memory. Keller proposed that brand equity is closely related to two dimensions of a brand: brand awareness or familiarity, which includes brand recall and brand recognition; and brand image, which is a combination of the types of brand association and favorability, strength, and uniqueness of brand associations. To clarify the nature of branding, Aaker (1991) also stressed that brand equity can go both ways because it is a set of brand assets and liabilities linked to a brand and its name and symbol that adds to or subtracts from the value provided by a product or service to a customer. The assets and liabilities can be classified into five categories: brand loyalty, name awareness, perceived quality, brand associations, and other proprietary brand assets such as patents and trademarks.

Brand equity brings forth a variety of values. First of all, it allows a brand to charge a premium price compared to competitors with less brand equity, thus contributing to profitability. Brand equity also maintains higher awareness of the product, reduces perceived risk, simplifies the decision process for low-involvement products, helps brand extension efforts, increases the probability of being included in a consumer's set of brand considerations, and offers a strong defense against new products and new competitors. For example, the strong brand equity of the *Wall Street Journal* has contributed to its financial performance, subscription rates, and defense against new financial news competitors. The fact that the Discovery Channel was ranked as the top brand for overall quality by the EquiTrend brand study for eight consecutive years since 1997 may explain some of Discovery's expansions into retailing and additional cable networks.

Brand equity has been the focus of marketing research and advertising research since the early 1990s (Aaker, 1991; Aaker & Biel, 1992; Aaker & Jacobson, 1994; Cobb-Walgren, Ruble, & Donthu, 1995). In general, the topic of brand equity is investigated from either a customer- or firm-based perspective. Whereas customer-based brand equity studies examine the theories and practices that address how consumers develop their brand awareness and knowledge, how different marketing programs impact these consumer mindsets, and the relationship between brand awareness/image and behavior, firm-based equity studies emphasize the relationship between marketing programs and equity, the management of brand portfolios or hierarchy, and the evaluation of brand equity with financial valuation such as return on investment (ROI). As discussed earlier, the financial evaluation of brands is a difficult subject because of the current accounting practices that regard brands as expenses rather than assets. The typical financial reporting principle is also inconsistent with the sometimes subjective evaluations of brand value, which are inherently rooted in brand concepts such as identities and images. Nevertheless, Kapferer (1992) suggested that financial evaluations of brands can be based on costs, comparable market value, or potential earnings. Specifically, a brand's value may be determined by (a) historical costs, which include all developments, marketing, advertising, and other communication costs, and (b) replacement costs, which are the estimated costs of re-creating the brand of focus. As we can see, there are a lot of assumptions that would have to be made on the sources of brand value and performance with such an approach. The market value method, on the other hand, determines the value of a brand in reference to the value of similar brands up for purchase. Although it might be a useful way of gauging a media brand's value given that there are many mergers and acquisitions of media properties nowadays, it is important to note that the purchase value is not really the current value of the brand but the anticipated value of the brand when the purchaser uses it. In terms of valuating by potential earnings, Kapferer explained that a firm would have to first isolate the net revenue brought in by the brand and then predict its future cash flows. Because of the difficulties of evaluating brand equity using these firm-based approaches, the value of most media brands are assessed from a customer-based perspective such as the evaluation of brand knowledge (brand awareness and/or image)(e.g., radio stations' perceptual/positioning studies), brand attitude (e.g., focus group assessment of attitudes), or even the resultant brand behavior (e.g., ratings).

THE PROCESS OF BRAND MANAGEMENT

Now that the essential characteristics of branding and the value a firm may garner from branding have been laid out, how does a media firm actually put these abstract concepts in action? How can we study the process and outcome of such practices to understand the dynamics of these concepts? This section discusses the various approaches of developing and monitoring brands in a market context, including how a firm may attach meanings to brands, nurture the brands' images, formulate a program to manage brands, and adapt its brand strategies to respond to changes.

Branding Through Associations

A firm can develop a brand's identity through three basic procedures: (a) the selection of a brand's tangible elements such as its brand name, logo, packaging, and slogan; (b) the association of certain intangible, desirable qualities to the brand; and (c) the execution of a marketing program that presents to target consumers the brand elements and intended associations. Although the selected brand elements may directly produce certain primary associations to the product (e.g., the explicit brand name Animal Planet quickly associates itself with the identity of the animal-related programming cable channel), a firm may also utilize the so-called secondary associations to transfer and thus leverage certain benefits from other entities of the brand, given an effective marketing communication program to deliver the association messages. In other words, the process of brand associations is fundamental to a firm's efforts to establish brand identities.

Direct, primary associations typically link a brand to product, pricing, distribution, or other marketing communications–related elements. In the context of media products, primary associations may take the forms of content approach (e.g., The Weather Channel), brand name (e.g., Netzero.com), logo (e.g., Disney), delivery system (e.g., DISH Network), and marketing communication campaigns (e.g., AOL—You've Got Mail). In addition to or in place of such direct associations based on "own" product-related elements, a firm may attempt to indirectly link its brand to certain entities with established equities. Keller (1998) suggested eight different means of secondary brand associations: companies (e.g., via branding strategies), countries or other geographical areas (e.g., via identification of product origin), channels of distribution (e.g., via channels strategy), other brands (e.g., via cobranding or ingredient branding), characters (e.g., via licensing), spokesperson (e.g., via endorsements), events (e.g., via sponsorship), and other third-party sources (e.g., via awards or reviews). For instance, all Pixar's theatrical products are strategically associated with the Pixar corporate name, the cable channel BBC America is linked to its product origin, celebrity casts or contributors (i.e., an ingredient in a content product) are often used to give a content product an identity (e.g., *Bill O'Reilly* of the Fox News Channel), and awards such as the Emmy's are now being associated with HBO's image of quality original programming. Note that there are certain premises for the effective transfer of equity through association with entities other than the product itself. First, the target consumers must have a certain degree of familiarity with or knowledge of the entity. It would be fruitless to associate a new children's magazine with an educator that the target segment (children) has never heard of. Second, there must be some meaningful connection between the brand and the associated entity. The secondary association of a basketball player with a sports cable channel would make much more sense than with a business news channel. Finally, the associations must be transferable in the context of the associated brand because certain meanings may not remain strong, favorable, and unique when supplanted from one entity to another. The corporate image of Disney may not be as effective when associated with broadband access services as with a children's cable network.

Brand Management Programs

The formulation and implementation of brand elements, associations, and marketing communications strategies are an ongoing process that needs the commitment of institutional resources. Brand management also involves various marketing activities in a larger context. In fact, the traditional marketing mix of product, price, distribution, and promotion shapes the equity potential of a brand. Thus, marketing programs can be designed to build the desirable brand image. For example, product strategies directly impact brand identity development and the consumption experience, which also shape a brand's image. Pricing and channel strategies again influence consumers' perception of a brand's quality and the associated status. Finally, marketing communications programs that utilize advertising, public relations, sales promotion, personal selling, and/or event sponsorship to communicate with target consumers provide the key to leverage both primary and secondary associations for a brand.

In essence, brand management programs involve organizing, planning, monitoring, and evaluating the tangible and intangible aspects of a brand. Specifically, brand managers create and communicate to the target consumers about a brand, direct and structure the brand, manage the brand organization, audit the strength of the brand, develop relationships with customers, configure brand portfolios and hierarchy, assess the financial value of the brand, and leverage the equity of established brands through brand extensions.

Unfortunately, in many media industries, brand management often materializes as tactical sales promotional programs. Chan-Olmsted and Y. Kim (2002) found that most broadcast television managers considered branding a promotional, tactical function (promoting a station and/or its news), rather than a strategic managerial process or asset management. The reason that media brand management is simplified as a tangible identity-building tactic may be attributed to the fact that the concept of media as brands was first introduced only in 1993 (Bender, 1993). In addition, there are some significant differences between branding conventional consumer goods and media products (McDowell, 2006). The first dissimilarity is related to the marketing element of pricing. Most media brands are not price sensitive because many of them are distributed via an advertising-based business model, wherein the only real "cost" is consumers' time and attention. The pricing issue also means that the consumption process lacks risk. In other words, consumers are less likely to depend on familiar brands to reduce the risk of bad purchases, thus reducing the utility of media brands. Another distinction is the accessibility of competing brands. For most consumer goods, brand trials require time and effort. On the contrary, consumers can sample competitive media brands easily, with a remote control in some cases. McDowell again suggested that the most significant disparities between consumer goods and media product branding perhaps lies in two characteristics of media brands: (a) essentially all benefits from media brands are intangible associations ranging from attributes to attitudinal evaluations and (b) media products are themselves communication tools capable of self-branding.

The distinctions made thus far point to a few considerations when designing a brand management program for media products. First, pricing is not an important association entity for most media products. Second, the relevancy of channel strategies varies because of the diversity of media products. For most print media, distribution and access methods do not add value to a brand. For electronic media, packager (e.g., CBS or Lifetime) and retailer-exhibitor (e.g., Cox Cable or a local television station) brands might sometimes contribute to or inhibit the building of brand identities or even limit the access to certain brands. Note that the development of digital media distribution systems also increasingly enables a direct channel of content distribution to consumers, which may require adjustments in some existing branding strategies. Third, product strategies are the core of building media brands. Special attention should be directed to creating intangible primary and secondary associations as well as designing coherent brand hierarchy and corporate portfolios that leverage the equity of successful content brands (e.g., *Time* magazine brand). Finally, media firms should utilize their own marketing communications channels to efficiently carry out self-branding activities.

MEDIA BRAND RESEARCH

Although brand management has been a staple marketing concept in the consumer goods industries for a long time, it has become a term that media firms refer to only in recent years. It was argued that, as a newly introduced business concept (or a newly revised concept that approaches existing marketing practices differently), the branding emphasis in media industries is expected to be at the level of tactical application in its early stage (Gordon, 1991). That is, media firms would tend to invest their marketing energy and financial resources in more visible, tangible differentiation efforts such as logo designs and brand slogans, which are more comparable with their historical promotional practices but represent a more short-term design and control function than long-term strategic managerial commitment.

Although media firms have initially regarded branding activities as more tangible promotional tactics, they have in fact long practiced a concept relevant to branding—positioning. As Ries and Trout (1993, 1997) proposed in their popular positioning series, the objective of positioning was to place products, companies, services, or institutions in the minds of potential customers in a way that differentiated them from the clutter and confusion of the marketplace. Moving from advertising superlatives to marketing comparatives, positioning actually accented ideas that already existed in the prospect's mind because it is easier and more cost-effective to promote product benefits consumers already believe and accept in a noisy, overcommunicating marketplace. In comparison, branding—which involves multiple components such as brand awareness, brand association, brand position, brand assets, perceived quality, and the name, symbol, and slogan in which the brand is marketed—is closely related to but broader and more strategic in nature than positioning as it is historically defined. Specifically, positioning resembles two areas of branding discussed in brand-marketing literature, brand position and brand association, which refer to anything mentally linked to the brand that affects recall, establishes a point of differentiation, creates positive attitudes and feelings, and provides a reason to buy (Nykiel, 1997). As for differences, whereas the goal of branding is to eventually build brand equity, positioning is relatively a more short-term strategic means to build differential competitive advantages. In addition, positioning focuses on what a marketer does to the "mind" of the prospect rather than to the product itself, which comes under the territory of branding. In reality, a packaged goods brand manager may restage a faltering brand by adding an ingredient or changing the package, while maintaining or refining the product's position.

The early studies of media brands did not really investigate the characteristics of media brands but simply identified media as "brands" among other products. Owen (1993) noted that NBC was one of the top brands among adults. Based on Young & Rubicon's brand equity study, Aaker (1996) showed that CNN ranked second and PBS ranked eighth in brand strength compared to all measured brands. Later on, media scholars began to contemplate the effects of strong brands on programming practices in electronic media industries. McDowell and Sutherland (2000) found that television program brand equity is revealed in the differential rating response of a program to its direct competitors and to its lead-in programming. Adopting a more macro approach, the next phase of media brand research turns to the strategic value of branding. Chan-Olmsted and Jung (2001) discussed how television networks use the Internet in order to strengthen their brand images. McGovern (2001) stressed the uniqueness of online branding with an information and logic emphasis. Chan-Olmsted and Y. Kim (2001, 2002) investigated the perceptions of branding among television station managers and later compared the PBS brand with cable brands. J. Kim, Sharma, and Setzekorn (2002) provided a conceptual framework for building brand equity on the Internet using a consumer-based model. There are also a growing number of studies exploring the applicability of brand extensions in programming and in the cable network market (Chang, 2005; Ha & Chan-Olmsted, 2001; Landers, 2004).

FINAL THOUGHTS

Brand management concepts provide a fertile ground for theory development in and analyses of media firms' market practices. As competition heats up among media firms in an increasingly fragmented and converging marketplace, the nourishing of brand equity, sensible extension of successful brands, and thoughtful management of brand portfolio present excellent strategic avenues for media firms to create competitive advantages and eventually superior financial returns. Also considering the gradual changes in audience behaviors (e.g., time shifting, active, asynchronized, and multitasking media consumption) and access technologies (e.g., wireless and digital access), media firms need a marketing system that enables them to connect with target consumers so to anticipate perceptual and behavior changes continuously. However, the branding of media products are challenging because of their diversity, intangibility, and sometimes individuality (e.g., individual programming products). Consequently, many brand constructs may need to be modified conceptually for applications in media industries or measured creatively in empirical studies of media products. The development of a media product taxonomy in a brand context may be the first step of tackling these challenges. For instance, using a firm-based approach, an analysis of typical marketing programs by types of media products would shed light in branding applicability by media characteristics. From the perspective of consumers, investigations of the brand knowledge structures of different media products may provide more realistic parameters for selecting media brand elements and associations. In summary, while there is an urgency to practice branding in today's media marketplace, there are also ample research opportunities to study the branding of media products as a subfield of media management and economics.

REFERENCES

Aaker, D. A. (1991). *Managing brand equity.* New York: The Free Press.

Aaker, D. A. (1996). Measuring brand equity across products and markets. *California Management Review, 38*(3), 102–120.

Aaker, D. A. (2004, March 8). Strategic thinking here's how to meet the challenge of creating focus and clarity in a brand portfolio. *Brandweek, 45,* 36–40.

Aaker, D. A., & Biel, A. (Eds.). (1992). *Building strong brands.* Hillsdale, NJ: Lawrence Erlbaum Associates.

Aaker, D. A., & Jacobson, R. (1994). The financial information content of perceived quality. *Journal of Marketing Research, 31*(2), 191–202.

Aaker, D. A., & Keller, K. L. (1990). Consumer evaluations of brand extensions. *Journal of Marketing, 54*(1), 27–41.

Ajzen, I., & Fishbein, M. (1980). *Understanding attitudes and predicting social behaviour.* Englewood Cliffs, NJ: Prentice-Hall.

Barwise, P. (1993). Introduction to the special issue on brand equity. *International Journal of Research in Marketing, 10*(1), 3–8.

Bender, D. C. (1993, March). *Media as brands.* Paper presented at the Advertising Research Foundation 39th Annual Conference, New York.

Bissell, J. (1998, January 19). Brand outsiders make a difference. *Brandweek,* p. 16.

Chakravarti, D., MacInnis, D., & Nakamoto, K. (1990). Product category perceptions, elaborative processing and brand name extension strategies. *Advances in Consumer Research, 17*(1), 910–917.

Chan-Olmsted, S. M., & Jung, J. (2001). Strategizing the net business: How television networks compete in the age of the Internet. *International Journal on Media Management, 3.* Retrieved August 3, 2002, from http://www.mediamanagement.orgmodules/pubview.php/mediajournal-57

Chan-Olmsted, S. M., & Kim, Y. (2001). Perception of branding among television station managers: An explanatory analysis. *Journal of Broadcasting and Electronic Media, 45*(1), 75–91.

Chan-Olmsted, S. M., & Kim, Y. (2002). The PBS brand versus cable brands: Assessing the brand equity of public television in a multi-channel environment. *Journal of Broadcasting & Electronic Media, 46*(2), 300–320.

Chang, B. (2005). *Brand extension of cable networks.* Unpublished doctoral dissertation, University of Florida, Gainesville.

Cobb-Walgren, C. J., Ruble, C. A., & Donthu, N. (1995). Brand equity, brand preference, and purchase intent. *Journal of Advertising, 24*(3), 25–40.

Cowley, D. (1991). *Understanding brands: By 10 people who do.* London: Kogan Page.

Davis, S. M. (1995). *Brand asset management for the 21st century.* Chicago: Kuczmarski & Associates.

Donahue, M. D. (1995). *Translating vision into a meaningful identity: Brand loyalty marketing.* New York: Advertising Research Foundation.

Eastman, S. T. (1993). *Broadcast/cable programming: Strategies and practices* (4th ed.). Belmont, CA: Wadsworth.

Farquhar, P. (1989). Managing brand equity. *Marketing Research, 1*(3), 24–33.

Fishbein, M., & Ajzen, I. (1975). *Belief, attitude, intention and behavior: An introduction to theory and research.* Reading, MA: Addison-Welsey.

Gardner, M. P. (1985). Does attitude toward the ad affect brand attitude under a brand evaluation set? *Journal of Marketing Research, 22*(2), 192–198.

Gordon, W. (1991). Accessing the brand through research. In D. Cowley (Ed.), *Understanding brands: By 10 people who do* (pp. 31–56). London: Kogan Page.

Ha, L., & Chan-Olmsted, S. M. (2001). Enhanced television as brand extension: TV viewers' perception of enhanced TV features and TV commerce on broadcast networks' web sites. *International Journal on Media Management, 3*(4), 202–213.

Heath, T. B., & Gaeth, G. J. (1994). Theory and method in the study of ad and brand attitudes: Toward a systemic model. In E. M. Clark, T. W. Brock, & D. W. Stewart (Eds.), *Attention, attitude and affect in response to advertising.* Hillsdale, NJ: Lawrence Erlbaum Associates.

John, D. R., Loken, B., & Joiner, C. (1998). The negative impact of extension: Can flagship products be diluted? *Journal of Marketing, 62*(1), 19–32.

Kalwani, M. U., & Silk, A. J. (1982). On the reliability and predictive validity of purchase intention measures. *Marketing Science, 1*(3), 243–286.

Kapferer, J. N. (1992). *Strategic brand management: New approaches to creating and evaluating brand equity.* London: Kogan Page.

Katz, D. (1960). The functional approach to the study of attitudes. *Public Opinion Quarterly, 24*(2), 163–204.

Keller, K. L. (1991). *Conceptualizing, measuring, and managing customer-based brand equity.* Cambridge, MA: Marketing Science Institute.

Keller, K. L. (1993). Conceptualizing, measuring, and managing customer-based brand equity. *Journal of Marketing, 57*(1), 1–22.

Keller, K. L. (1998). *Strategic brand management: Building, measuring, and managing brand equity.* Upper Saddle River, NJ: Prentice-Hall.

Keller, K. L., & Aaker, D. A. (1992). The effects of sequential introduction of brand extensions. *Journal of Marketing Research, 29*(1), 35–50.

Kim, J., Sharma, S., & Setzekorn, K. (2002). A framework of building brand equity online for pure-play B2C retailers and services. *International Journal on Media Management, 4*(2), 123–133.

Kirmani, A., Sood, S., & Bridges, S. (1999). The ownership effect in consumer responses to brand line stretches. *Journal of Marketing, 63*(1), 88–101.

Kumar, R. S. (2003). Branding strategies in a changing marketing environment. *The Journal of Brand Management, 11*(1), 48–62.

Landers, D. E. (2004, August). *Programming spin-offs as brand extensions: Capitalizing on the brand equity of network television hit series.* Paper presented at the meeting of the Association for Education in Journalism and Mass Communication, Toronto, Canada.

Loken, B., & John, D. R. (1993). Diluting brand beliefs: When do brand extensions have a negative impact? *Journal of Marketing, 57*(3), 71–84.

MacInnis, D., & Nakamoto, K. (1990). *Cognitive associations and product category comparisons: The role of knowledge structure and context.* Unpublished manuscript, University of Arizona, Tucson.

MacKenzie, S. B., & Lutz, R. J. (1989). An empirical examination of the structural antecedents of attitude toward the ad in an advertising pretesting context. *Journal of Marketing, 53*(2), 48–65.

McDowell, W. S. (2006). Issues in marketing and branding. In A. Albarran, S. M. Chan-Olmsted, & M. Wirth (Eds.), *Media management and economics handbook* (pp. 229–250). Mahwah, NJ: Lawrence Erlbaum Associates.

McDowell, W. S., & Sutherland, J. (2000). Choice versus chance: Using brand equity theory to explore TV audience lead-in effects. *Journal of Media Economics, 13*(4), 233–249.

McGovern, G. (2001). Content builds brands on-line. *International Journal on Media Management, 3*(4), 198–201.

Mitchell, A. A., & Olsen, J. C. (1981). Are product attribute beliefs the only mediator of advertising effects on brand attitudes? *Journal of Marketing Research, 18*(3), 318–332.

Murphy, J. M. (1987). *Branding: A key marketing tool.* New York: McGraw-Hill.

Nykiel, R. A. (1997, October). Brand marketing paramount to success. *Hotel & Motel Management,* p. 22.

Owen, S. (1993). The Landor ImagePower survey: A global assessment of brand strength. In D. A. Aaker & A. L. Biel (Eds.), *Brand equity and advertising* (pp. 11–32). Hillsdale, NJ: Lawrence Erlbaum Associates.

Quelch, J. A., & Kenny, D. (1999). Extend profits, not product lines. In E. Joachimsthaler, D. Aaker, J. Quelch, D. Kenny, V. Vishwanath, & M. Jonathan (Eds.), *Harvard Business Review on brand management* (pp. 109–115). Boston: Harvard Business School Press.

Rangaswamy, A., Burke, R., & Oliva, T. A. (1993). Brand equity and the extensibility of brand names. *International Journal of Research in Marketing, 10*(1), 61–75.

Ries, A., & Trout, J. (1993). *Positioning: The battle for your mind.* New York: Warner Books.

Ries, A., & Trout, J. (1997). *Marketing warfare.* New York: McGraw-Hill.

Shocker, A. D., Srivastava, R. K., & Ruekert, R. W. (1994). Challenges and opportunities facing brand management: An introduction to the special issue. *Journal of Marketing Research, 31*(2), 149–158.

Sunde, L., & Brodie, R. J. (1993). Consumer evaluations of brand extensions: Further empirical results. *International Journal of Research in Marketing, 10*(1), 47–53.

Uncles, M. D. (1996). Reflections on brand management: An introduction to the special issue. *Marketing Intelligence & Planning, 14*(1), 4–9.

Wilkie, W. (1990). *Consumer behavior* (2nd ed.). New York: Wiley.

Chapter 5

Strategy and Competition in the New Broadcast Industries

The environmental changes that have occurred since the 1980s as a result of technological advances and shifting audience demands have impacted the broadcast media profoundly. As the pioneer of electronic media products, the conventional characteristics of radio as a local, over-the-air commercial medium have to be reexamined as commercial-free satellite radio subscription services have become popular nationally among many music lovers and as technologies have enabled the delivery of radio signal worldwide via the Internet and the arrival of customized music CDs and portable music players (e.g., iPod). Broadcast television, once a favorite of most American media consumers, now competes against multichannel programming services such as cable and DBS as well as streaming content on the Internet. The broadcasters now have to fight for shares in a fragmented audience market, invest heavily in digital technology, and rethink their strategic role in a consolidated media marketplace where most competitors are verticall integrated and operate businesses in many other media sectors.

It is evident that the general environment for broadcasters has changed dramatically. But how have these external forces shaped today's broadcast market? Adopting the strategic framework proposed in chapter 2, this chapter attempts to answer this question with a review of the economic, technological, political, and sociocultural changes that have influenced the state of broadcast industries and discusses the factors that have affected the competitive dynamics of both the broadcast radio and television markets.

CHANGES IN THE GENERAL ENVIRONMENT

Elements in the broader context of a society influence the operations of industries and the firms within them. Although firms have no control over these environmental changes, they can respond to them with appropriate strategies. Followings are some major trends that have impacted the broadcast media industries.

Economic Changes

Several economic developments have indirectly shaped the direction and nature of today's broadcast media. First, the growth of a global economy has positively contributed to the market potential of broadcasters. The fact that most television broadcast networks are integrated with production studios means that the development of a global programming market would lessen the programming financing burdens of television broadcasters as more overseas media outlets become potential revenue sources. The interconnectedness between different media systems also presents more coproduction cost-sharing/reduction opportunities. Second, the relatively low interest rates in various time periods between the 1980s and 2000s fostered a favorable environment for mergers and acquisitions, which gave birth to numerous media conglomerates and created many consolidated local broadcast markets. The development of larger media groups means a different strategic role for today's broadcasters when their corporate parents compete multilaterally (i.e., multipoint competition). Finally, because the U.S. economy grew more than 56% in gross domestic product (GDP) per capita from 1980 to 2000, we are faced with a more affluent media consumer who can afford new subscription or pay-per-event media services that compete with the traditionally free broadcast products. Note that the economic condition of the United States, a market economy, also directly impacts the core income source—advertising revenues—for broadcasters. By comparison, the broadcasters have had a mere 16% increase in total ad revenues since 1996, whereas their cable counterparts, which only partially rely on advertising income, had a 150% increase (Standard & Poor's, 2004). The attractiveness of the cable sector often means the development of more alliances and/or consolidations between broadcasters and cablecasters.

Technological Changes

The technological advances in computing and communication technologies in the last two decades have brought tremendous changes to the broadcast industries. There are continuous product innovations in computing devices that enable the widespread ownership of personal computers and network connections, which take shares from media consumers' investment in broadcast media products and leisure time. There are new digital communication technologies that facilitate the delivery of digital signals and make better audio-visual quality, more content options, and interactivity possible and even demanded. Most evidently, although the arrival of cable, satellite, and Internet/broadband distribution technologies has reduced the dominant position of broadcasters, advances in digitization and compression have also offered broadcasters new business opportunities. More recently, the introduction of personal digital recorders and on-demand content services is beginning to transform how audiences use the television medium, prompting the need to reevaluate the existing broadcast business model of a free over-the-air commercial system. In essence, the continued technological evolution has redefined the nature and boundaries of broadcast products as well as how and how much the consumers use broadcast products.

Political Changes

Beginning with the sweeping changes brought about by the Telecommunications Act of 1996, the regulatory environment of broadcast industries has been largely relaxed to encourage cross-media competition and the introduction of new media technologies. The adoption of more liberal ownership rules by the Federal Communications Commission (FCC) has made it easier for broadcasters to own a number of broadcast properties as well as develop cross-media ownership. These deregulatory moves effectively facilitate the application of cross-promotion strategies, sharing of resources, and negotiation power of broadcast group owners. In essence, the recent deregulatory development has changed the strategic options and priorities for many broadcasters, making corporate strategies a critical aspect of competition. There also have been global political changes toward privatization and commercialization of media systems. The opening of media borders and commercialization means the option of global diversification and increase of programming demands and thus revenue potential for the vertically integrated U.S. broadcasters.

Sociocultural and Demographic Changes

Sociocultural and demographic changes have profound impacts on the broadcast business because these external forces ultimately shape the audience type, size, preferences, and behavior. A number of developments in this area have influenced the market for broadcast products. First, the aging of the baby boomer audience segment has widened the desirable age bracket for broadcast advertisers, thus somewhat altering the programming approach (e.g., more health-related content) and competitive positions of different broadcasters. Second, the growing income disparity between different socioeconomic audience segments has pushed further the application of market segmentation strategy, a specialty for cablecasters rather than broadcasters. Third, more women in the workforce as well as increasing workplace diversity have significant implications in both programming content and scheduling strategies. In general, most television broadcasters' conventional day-parting scheduling and general-appeal programming strategies seem to be less responsive to such societal developments. Fourth, the attitudes toward quality of life and environment have influenced both broadcasters' promotional approaches and news focuses. For examples, the busy lifestyle of today's audiences has resulted in diminishing audience loyalty and leisure time, which prompted the increase of programming modularity (i.e., shorter plot lines) and cross-platform marketing. Finally, the fast growth of two demographic groups—the Hispanic and African American markets—has considerable connotations for the programming and diversification strategies of broadcasters. The lure of the increasing Hispanic population and its buying power has spawned a new array of Spanish radio formats and the acquisitions of Spanish programming sources (e.g., NBC's acquisition of Telemundo). The expansion of the African American demographic segment also has some notable programming and marketing implications for broadcasters because anecdotal evidence suggests that this segment comprises a large number of young people and spends more on cable services and entertainment than the general population.

CHANGES IN BROADCAST INDUSTRIES

As depicted previously in chapter 2, the external environment of an industry shapes the nature and state of competition between the firms operating in it. Accordingly, the aforementioned changes have impacted the relationships between broadcasters in the market and the strategies adopted by these firms. To examine these competitive dynamics and their implications, we adopt Porter's five-force competition assessment framework, reviewing the bargaining power of suppliers, bargaining power of buyers, threat of substitute products, threat of new market entrants, and rivalry among competing firms.

Bargaining Power of Supplier

In the context of broadcast markets, suppliers are the content producers/suppliers for broadcast networks and stations. Historically, the bargaining position of the television content suppliers was not particularly strong because broadcast television networks and stations held the control of the conduits to audiences. With the proliferation of electronic media outlets (i.e., the number of content buyers has increased), the content suppliers have garnered somewhat more bargaining power. Nevertheless, the active consolidations at both the network and station levels seem to have also solidified the countering negotiation power of the broadcast buyers. For example, the formation of large station groups has resulted in a significant increase of television broadcasters' bargaining power over syndicators. Table 5.1 shows the considerable numbers of stations and extensive reach controlled by the top network/station groups. It is virtually impossible to launch a new syndicated program without the support of these station groups. In addition, in recent years, television broadcasters have attempted to mitigate the power of content suppliers through vertical integration. As a result, all broadcast television networks are now affiliated by ownership with major studios (see Table 5.2).

TABLE 5.1
Top Broadcast Television Station Groups

Corporate Owner	Viacom				News Corp.	
	CBS Network (3)[a]		UPN Network (6)		Fox (1)	
DMA Size	Reach	Station #	Reach	Station #	Reach	Station #
1–5	19.8(19.8)[b]	6		2	17.6(14.7)	7 (of 3 are UPN affiliates)
6–10	6.1(5.2)	3	1.9(0.9)	4	10.0(8.9)	7 (of 1 are UPN affiliates)
11–25	6.3(6.3)	5	6.6(4.8)	6	12.2(9.6)	13 (of 5 are UPN affiliates)
26–50	0.7(0.7)	1	3.9(1.9)	6	4.2(4.2)	6
50+	0.9(0.7)	2		0	0.6(0.6)	2
Subtotal	33.8(32.7)	17	12.4(7.7)	18	44.6(37.9)	35 (of 9 are UPN affiliates)
Total	46.2(40.3)	35		35	44.6(37.9)	35

Corporate Owner	NBC-Universal				Disney		Tribune (2)			
	NBC (4)		Telemundo (7)		ABC (5)		WB Affiliates		Fox/ABC Affiliates	
DMA Size	Reach	Station #	Reach	Station #	Reach	Station #	Reach	#	Reach	#
1–5	19.9(19.9)	6	0	4	19.8(19.8)	5	17.6(16.2)	4	0	0
6–10	4.1(4.1)	2	2.2(1.1)	2	0	0	8.2(4.1)	4	0	0
11–25	2.8(2.8)	2	3.0(1.5)	3	1.7(1.7)	1	9.0(7.0)	7	1.2(0.6)	3
26–50	3.2(2.3)	4	2.2(1.4)	3	0.9(0.9)	1	2.5(1.2)	3	1.3(0.6)	4
50+	0	0	0.9(0.4)	2	1.3(1.1)	3	0.5(0.3)	1	0	0
Sub Total	30.1(29.1)	14	8.3(4.5)	14	23.7(23.5)	10	37.8(28.8)	19	2.4(1.2)	7
Total	38.3 (33.6)			28	23.7(23.5)	10	40.2 (30.0)			26

Note. Compiled from "Top 25 Station Groups" (2004).

[a]Ranking of the station group's reach in the United States. Note that Viacom will be the number one group when CBS and UPN stations are combined. (DMA = Designated Market Area)

[b]First number is the actual audience reach as a percentage of the nation's television households. Second number is the reach according to the FCC discounted definition for UHF stations.

TABLE 5.2

Broadcast Television Network and their Affiliate Production Properties

CBS & UPN (Viacom)	Fox (News Corporation)	NBC (NBC Universal)	ABC (Disney)	WB (Time Warner)
		Affiliate Production Properties		
CBS Productions	Fox Television Studios	Universal Studios	Walt Disney Television	Warner Bros. Television
CBS Television City	20th Century Fox	NBC Studios	Walt Disney Animation	Warner Bros. Studios
King World Productions	Television		Touchstone Films	Telepictures Productions
Spelling Television	Twentieth Television		Buena Vista Pictures	TBS Productions
Viacom Productions				
Big Ticket Television				
DNA Productions				

Note. Compiled from OneSource (2004).

81

For the radio market, its content suppliers, mainly the major record companies, had relatively strong bargaining power when most stations were independently owned. With the consolidation of local stations in recent years, radio station groups now control the lifeline of these music labels through the selection of their playlists. The recent controversy in the practice of "pay-for-play," whereby record companies pay independent promoters to get their singles on radio playlists, is an excellent example of such a power struggle. The "payola" laws prohibit radio stations from accepting payment in exchange for playing certain songs, but the addition of the middleman—the independent promoters—has enabled radio stations to sidestep the laws. It was estimated that the recording industry spent more than $150 million in 2004 on pay-for-play, with labels paying anywhere from $250,000 to $1 million to get and keep a single on the radio (Hoovers Online, 2004). Many independent record companies have complained about the tremendous negotiation power of large radio groups such as Clear Channel and Viacom (Infinity). In summary, although the suppliers in the broadcast industries have generally grown in importance, the trend toward vertical and horizontal integration has also elevated the position of the broadcast buyers and, at the same time, amplified the significance of effective corporate strategies.

Bargaining Power of Buyer

In the context of broadcast markets, there are two groups of buyers for broadcast products: audiences and advertisers. From the perspective of the audiences, the source of their power resides in the investing of their "time" in the programming offered by one of the broadcast outlets. Have broadcast audiences become more or less powerful amid the environmental changes discussed earlier? Broadcast audiences have historically possessed significant power over broadcasters because they are indirectly the only source of income for broadcasters. Such power has been strengthened further as the audiences are now presented with more alternative products from other media systems that they could switch to at little cost. In addition, the availability of abundant information about alternative products through a wide variety of sources including the Internet has shifted even more power to media consumers. Nevertheless, although losing ground in some less differentiated programming areas, television broadcasters still possess certain unsubstitutable products (e.g., the Super Bowl) that they can use to maintain some degree of negotiation power over audiences. It is important not to minimize the power of these superproducts because they might serve as the most effective marketing avenues to build other products to compete with the competitors' offerings. For example, television broadcasters have been very successful in developing and promoting reality-based programming (e.g., promotion of *Survivor* during

Super Bowl breaks), although the origin and acceptance of this programming genre can actually be traced to cable networks such as MTV with the *Real World* series.

From the perspective of advertisers, historically they have also been powerful because their purchases constitute the only major revenue source for broadcasters. Nevertheless, there is a balancing intricacy in this relationship because advertisers traditionally also have been largely dependent on broadcasters to promote their products. Although the essentiality of the broadcast media as the primary advertising conduit still holds true today, there has been a gradual shift in validating the effectiveness of other advertising alternatives and in questioning the value of the tremendous investment in the broadcast media as audiences migrate to other newer media. To counter such a potential tip of market power, broadcasters now have to contemplate ways of minimizing the effect of ad revenue loss through diversification of ownership into other media sectors or new broadcast business models that diversify their revenue sources.

Threat of Substitutes

By definition, substitutes are different products from outside of an industry that perform the same or similar functions as a product that the industry offers (Hitt, Ireland, & Hoskisson, 2001). In the context of broadcast markets, multichannel video programming distributors (MVPD) such as cable television and DBS services are logical substitutes for broadcast television products, and geographically unconfined audio services through new media conduits such as online streaming audio content and satellite radio services are likely substitutes for the traditional radio broadcast products. The key to gauging the degree of threat posed by substitute products is to assess two factors: how hard it is for audiences to switch to the substitute and how valuable is the differentiated quality of the substitute to the audiences. From the perspective of radio broadcasters, as the prices of portable, customizable music devices such as iPod and satellite radio services like XM and Sirius continue to decrease, the switching cost to migrate to these competing services is getting lower. The radio broadcasters, especially the music format stations that do not offer differentiated local, editorial added value, are facing an increasing threat from these substitutes. In addition, Internet radio, though still not self-sustaining financially in its current state, also offers a variety of content unmatched by local stations and is a strong substitute for certain listeners (Ren & Chan-Olmsted, 2004). From the perspective of television broadcasters, it would be fair to conclude that the switching cost to cable is minimal (perhaps a bit more for DBS in the initial investment of time and money, but the difference is disappearing as well). In addition, MVPDs have been relatively successful in differentiating and demonstrating the value of their programming products. As a result, ad-supported cable had acquired a prime-time audience share of 50.3% in 2003, versus a combined 44.8% for the four major broadcast networks (Standard & Poor's, 2004). To counter the threat posed by the MVPD substitutes, broadcasters have either diversified into the MVPD sector (e.g., NBC's investment in MSNBC and CNBC) or attempted to differentiate their products along the dimensions that the audiences might value (e.g., sports, celebrity sitcoms, reality-based shows, etc.). The presence of increasing competition, in essence, reveals the importance of branding for today's broadcasters.

Potential Entrants

Because of the substantial barriers against entry into broadcast industries, there is little continuous threat of potential entrants to the existing incumbents. With the addition of Fox and two other minor networks, the market of broadcast television networks seems to have reached its saturation point with declining audience market shares and the fact that most local stations have already aligned with a network. Furthermore, the entry barriers, namely, governmental policy (e.g., localism), economies of scale (e.g., ownership of many stations, especially in major markets), and access to distribution channels or programming (e.g., network affiliation or high-profile programs), are likely to persist in these markets. In other words, existing broadcasters can expect minimal threats posed by potential entrants to their markets to further divide up the shrinking market shares or dilute their bargaining power with suppliers or buyers. There is also very limited room for new entrants to the radio market as the radio syndication and network segment is already crowded with suppliers although there has been no increase in the number of local radio stations. The growth of large radio station groups also means a tremendous scale economy advantage possessed by these group owners.

Internal Rivalry Intensity

The nature of competition in broadcast industries has changed significantly since the 1980s with the injection of more broadcast networks, the growth of station groups, and the formation of media conglomerates with broadcast holdings. Specifically, in the television industry, there has been a slight increase in the number of competitors, which typically contributes to more rivalry intensity. Nevertheless, the existence of a still relatively small number of equivalent competitors (e.g., the big four networks or the major affiliates in a local market) points to oligopolistic, mutually dependent behavioral patterns (i.e., the don't-rock-the-boat syndrome). By comparison, radio markets are generally more crowded and thus more competitive, but the growth of radio station groups has also led to more strategic, selective competition (e.g., format saturation). In fact, faced with a stagnant industry with

little growth, many broadcasters have chosen the strategy of differentiation rather than direct pricing competition because differentiated
products typically induce loyalty, which lessens the need for the
rivalrous behavior that might lower a firm's profitability.

Although conventional wisdom tells us that with more competitors
and saturating consumer demands, there should be more rivalry in the
broadcast industries, the result is really best reflected by the strategic
stakes of broadcast properties as an investment for diversified media
corporations, considering the extent of media consolidations involving
broadcast outlets in recent years. As Hitt et al. (2001) put it, competitive
rivalry is more intense when achieving success in a particular industry
is crucial to most companies. In other words, broadcasters' competitive
rivalry is also determined by the importance of success in the broadcast
sector in influencing a media conglomerate's effectiveness in other markets. In this context, broadcasters are strategically significant in that
they offer the most extensive brand communications channels and efficient cross-promotional tools for their corporate owners. Broadcast stations also generate one of the highest profit margins compared to other
media sectors (Albarran, 2001). Thus, it is still crucial for media conglomerates to compete aggressively in broadcast markets. In essence,
the rivalry in broadcast markets today is more intense but different. The
concentration of ownership means a certain degree of mutual dependency with selective rivalry. Competitive behavior is more likely to be
based on corporate interests rather than responses to local or single-sec-
tor rivalry.

Several themes seem to permeate throughout our discussions thus
far of the changes impacting the broadcast media: (a) the development
of networks and ownership groups that make corporate and alliance
strategies more relevant nowadays, (b) the transforming role of broadcast networks that requires a more holistic, resource-based reexamination of the broadcast business, (c) the necessity of brand management
that goes beyond tactical applications but is also full of application challenges, and (d) the reformulation of business models that might allevi-
ate broadcasters' reliance on one single revenue source and perhaps
make them more competitive in the new digital marketplace. The following sections elaborate on each of these themes.

FORMATION OF STRATEGIC NETWORKS
AND CONSOLIDATED OWNERSHIP

Chapter 3 alluded to the benefits of corporate acquisition and alliance
strategies for gaining access to critical resources, reducing costs, generating scale/scope economies, improving competitive positions, and entering new markets. Evidence shows that broadcasters have adopted
these strategies in their attempt to align with the changing environment. The following section assesses the specific approaches they have
taken and examines the implications of these actions.

Strategic Alliances

Why do broadcasters choose to form alliances and how have they allied? Adopting an RBV approach of strategic network formations, we first investigate the drivers for alliances in this market. From an RBV perspective, strategic alliances are formed because firms seek partners that have resources complementary to their own or allow them to acquire new capabilities (Eisenhardt & Schoonhoven, 1996; Harrison, Hoskisson, & Ireland, 2001). Strategic alliances can take a variety of forms. Das and Teng (2000) categorized alliances in terms of dichotomy of alliance structure: equity alliances versus nonequity alliances, differentiated by the creation or absence of new entities, or ownership transfer of existing entities (Gulati, 1995). As described in chapter 3, Das and Teng further suggested that a firm will prefer an equity joint firm if it primarily contributes property-based resources, and its partner primarily contributes knowledge-based resources; a firm will prefer a minority equity alliance if it primarily contributes knowledge-based resources, and its partner primarily contributes property-based resources; a firm will prefer a bilateral contract-based alliance if both partner firms primarily contribute knowledge-based resources; and a firm will prefer a unilateral contract-based alliance if both partner firms primarily contribute property-based resources. Utilizing the Das and Teng alliance typology, Liu and Chan-Olmsted (2003) found that the broadcast television networks' preferences for alliance structure were indeed influenced by the resources they brought to the alliances. In cases of expansion into online businesses, broadcasters used their property-based resources as a basis to form alliances with Internet firms, and in return they acquired access to the Internet firms' knowledge-based resources that were essential to their Internet strategies. Liu and Chan-Olmsted also noticed that this group of broadcasters was most interested in developing flexible access to content (knowledge) resources (e.g., minority equity alliances with niche Web sites that are content-based firms). Specific alliance examples include NBC's partnership with iVillage, CBS's investments in the content sites MarketWatch and SportsLine, and News Corp./Fox's alignment with Yahoo!

It is also our observation that broadcasters have attempted to capitalize on the growth of new media services through strategic alliances with members of the Internet, computing, and other media markets in the following three categories: community/content building, access facilitating, and e-commerce enabling.

Community/Content-Building Alliances. Broadcasters have formed alliances aimed at building virtual communities of similar interests, topical or geographic. For example, CBS partnered with ThirdAge, a Web destination that offers news, expert advice, and self-assessment tools with interactive chat and forums to create an online community of baby boomers. NBC entered an agreement with TalkCity, which in turn provided chat room services for NBC.com. NBC also invested in iVillage.com and created a presence in a virtual community of women. Similar to the attempt to enrich the overall media experience of their audiences through virtual communities, broadcasters have also formed alliances to enhance their content competency, and they have even been contemplating the possibility of collaborating with local television stations to offer multichannel services using the new digital spectrum. For instance, NBC, Hearst-Argyle Television, and Gannett Broadcasting formed a syndication-programming development and distribution partnership to share their content resources and capabilities (McClellan, 2000). NBC also entered programming joint ventures with MGM and Court TV, and Tribune Broadcasting entered a programming joint venture with Universal Television Enterprises (McClellan, 2002a, 2002b). The community- and content-building effort is critical because it offers brand identity–building opportunities and brand image assessment avenues, as well as a way of interactively connecting with audiences, which would compensate the broadcast media for its characteristicly inadequate, one-way appeal to a general audience.

Access-Facilitating Alliances. Broadcasters have formed alliances to ensure that they are one of the players in the emerging, converging Internet-led broadband world of media. Specifically, they have tried to explore new ways of reaching audiences and distributing their contents on multiple platforms through partnerships. For example, Granite Broadcasting Corp. entered an alliance with WB Network to form a Fort Wayne, Indiana, cable television station ("Granite Broadcasting Alliance," 1999). NBC allied with Videoseeker, a video directory that offered streaming online content in entertainment, news, business, and shopping. Through an agreement with AOL, CBS is the exclusive broadcast news provider to AOL. CBS.SportsLine.com serves as the primary sports content provider for AOL, Netscape, and Excite. To position themselves for the potential convergence between online and television content, the network broadcasters sought partnerships with computer and network heavyweights such as Microsoft (with NBC), Oracle (with CBS), and Compaq (with ABC) (Elkin, 2000; "Walt Disney Internet," 2000). To facilitate their technological capability in the new digital marketplace, the broadcasters have also allied with firms that produce software for interactive television. For instance, NBC invested in DigitalConvergence.com to facilitate its plan to allow NBC viewers to watch NBC programming and advertising via their personal computers interactively (Mermigas, 2000). Such strategic networks are important in that they reduce the risk of equity diversification into a new emerging market that is critical for the future of broadcast products while speeding up the broadcasters' entrance into a new media market with their partners' knowledge (e.g., online marketing experience) and property (e.g., proprietary software) resources.

E-Commerce-Enabling Alliances. Broadcasters have also formed alliances to explore new business models via the Internet conduit. By allying with the e-commerce experts, broadcasters seek to develop additional revenue sources and experiment with the Internet's effectiveness in paid content delivery (e.g., selling fee-based or subscription content products) and online merchandising (e.g., selling program or station merchandise). Besides numerous partnerships between e-commerce developers/stores and local broadcasters, networks such as NBC entered partnerships with leading e-commerce sites like Auto-By-Tel, Golf.com, Polo.com, and Preview Travel (Kaufman, 2000). ABC was affiliated with Pets.com (now Petsmart.com) and MBNA.com, an online banking service, whereas CBS, through its parent company, Viacom, allied with e-commerce sites such as RX.com and MVP.com. The alliances with e-commerce partners, although not most critical to the future direction of broadcasters, are significant in that they give broadcasters the opportunity to develop online content distribution capabilities and experience in exploring nontraditional business models.

Mergers and Acquisitions

Under the justification that the nation is moving toward electronic abundance and that broadcasters increasingly face new electronic entrants and should be fully free to meet these new competitors, media ownership rules have been relaxed since the early 1980s. As a result of the deregulatory climate as well as other environmental changes discussed in chapter 1, broadcast markets have witnessed tremendous waves of mergers and acquisitions. Many significant transactions occurred in the 1990s. There were conglomerate mergers such as the Westinghouse-CBS, Disney-Capital Cities/ABC, and GE/NBC-Vivendi Universal deals; concentric mergers such as the Tribune Co.-Renaissance Communications Corp., Viacom-CBS, and News Corp.-New World Communications transactions; vertical mergers such as the acquisition of King World by CBS and Paramount by Viacom; and station group combinations such as those between Hearst-Argyle and Pulitzer Broadcasting, Chancellor Media and LIN Television, and Fox and Chris-Craft. In the other broadcast market, there were major combinations of radio groups such as the mergers of Westinghouse/CBS-Infinity, Liberty Broadcasting-SFX Broadcasting, Sinclair Broadcast Group-River City Broadcasting and Sullivan Broadcasting, and Clear Channel's acquisition of Paxson's station properties (Bodipo-Memba & Brannigan, 1997; Brown, 1998a, 1998b; "Disney to Acquire," 1995; Freeman, 1996a, 1996b; Gay, 2000; Heuton, 1995; Laureen, 1995; Miller & Jensen, 1996; Sherman, 2004; "Time Warner to Buy," 1995; Trigoboff, 2001; "Westinghouse Will Make," 1995). Today's radio station group owners such as Clear Channel have more than 1,000 local stations (see Table 5.3). These major mergers and acquisitions changed the competitive dynamics in broadcast industries by creating horizontally consolidated, vertically integrated markets and giving birth to more multimedia conglomerates.

THE NEW NETWORK BUSINESS

It is evident that the content packagers—broadcast networks—have encountered the most dramatic environmental changes among all broad-

TABLE 5.3

Top 25 Radio Station Groups

Rank by Revenue	Radio Station Group	Corporate Owner	#of Stations
1	Clear Channel	Clear Channel Communications	1,216
2	Infinity	Viacom	185
3	Cox Radio	Cox Enterprises	78
4	Entercom	Entercom Communications	104
5	ABC Radio	The Walt Disney Co.	74
6	Citadel	Citadel Broadcasting Corp.	216
7	Radio One	Radio One Inc.	66
8	Emmis	Emmis Communications Corp.	27
9	Cumulus	Cumulus Media Inc.	270
10	Univision	Univision Communications Inc.	57
11	Susquehanna	Susquehanna Pfaltzgraff Co.	33
12	Bonneville	Deseret Management Corp.	35
13	Greater Media	Greater Media Inc.	19
14	Spanish Broadcasting	SBS Broadcasting	27
15	Salem	Salem Communications Corp.	92
16	Jefferson-Pilot	Jefferson-Pilot Corp.	17
17	Beasley	Beasley Broadcast Group Inc.	41
18	Saga	Saga Communications Inc.	71
19	Entravision	Entravision Communications Corp.	58
20	Regent	Regent Communications Inc.	76
21	Journal Broadcast	Journal Communications Inc.	36
22	NextMedia	Next Media Group LLC.	60
23	Inner City	Inner City Broadcasting Corp.	19
24	Sandusky	Sandusky Radio Inc.	10
25	Lotus	Lotus Communications Corp.	24

Note. Data compiled from "Ad Sales Show" (2003).

casters in the last two decades, especially in the television industry. Amid the growth of the MVPD services, broadcast television networks are fighting for a much smaller audience share while at the same time trying to figure out their strategies in the new digital media market full of opportunities as well as risks. The decisions the networks make also have rippled effects on different parts of the industry. For instance, as the traditional scripted shows gave way to reality-based programming, there was a reduction of programming products in the syndication pipeline. Nevertheless, CBS became the highest-ranked network recently in overall demographics thanks to this programming approach (Standard & Poor's, 2004). The competitive picture today is very different from the time when the big three networks garnered almost all the primetime-viewing shares and held the upper-hand bargaining position with both the upstream producers and downstream stations.

Exactly how has the network business evolved in response to all the challenges? Using an RBV approach, we examine here how these broadcasters have adapted to the environment by investigating the evolution of network resources since the rise of MVPD services. Note that as a firm's environments become turbulent and uncertain, the relevance and flexibility of its resources become more significant to achieving success (Chatterjee & Wernerfelt, 1988). Similarly, the network broadcasters would have to acquire specific resources to achieve competitive advantage and profitability during this period.

Landers and Chan-Olmsted (2004) reviewed precisely the changing property and knowledge resources during four time periods of increasing uncertainty (i.e., 1985, 1990, 1995, and 2001). They noted that property-based resources of station ownership, market reach, and overall/top content properties seem to become more prominent as the network television market becomes more unstable or uncertain. Affiliate contracts and top content property appear to be critical property-based resources for the minor networks in their attempt to gain market shares. Network news, on the other hand, does not seem to be influenced by the fluidity in the market as a property resource. As for the knowledge-based resources, the "breadth" of human resources such as media employee pools and multipurposing expertise appears to grow in importance as the market becomes more volatile. International expertise, mostly in forms of cable programming expansion, is also becoming more vital. Generally, access to a diverse set of knowledge resources (in product and geography) seems to become more essential as the level of uncertainty in this media market increases. As for the resource attainment strategies, Landers and Chan-Olmsted also observed that whereas NBC was aggressive in acquiring certain property-based resources such as broadcast media and affiliate contracts properties, developing some knowledge-based resources like management and audience expertise, and employing a "focus" strategy of building electronic media outlets and content, CBS and Fox emphasized expanding property resources such as O&O stations and top content properties. Fox was especially successful in developing competitive content expertise that aided its segmentation strategies.

The analysis thus far reveals that channel/content access and expertise in expanding, marketing, or coordinating into other media domains are crucial resources in the changing broadcast television market. Viewing these resources now in the broader context of corporate resources (i.e., broadcast networks as a resource of media conglomerates), we can see that the broadcasters' contribution to their corporate owners is necessarily shifted. Table 5.4 shows the top U.S. media conglomerates' diverse holdings and the fact that half of them own at least one broadcast network. Historically, without the complicated affiliations with firms from other media sectors and the presence of multipoint competition, the network business was the source of television programming and what defined a television station. Today, networks play the multifaceted roles of a content developer (for multiple media outlets), channel manager (on behalf of the stations), lead cross-media promoter, and brand-marketing tone setter. After GE-NBC's acquisition of Universal from Vivendi, the media conglomerate is already actively pursuing a strategy of integrating Universal's studio assets with those of NBC and marketing its Universal movie properties via DVD and other MVPD networks with NBC's promotional arms. In conclusion, the network business has evolved from a one-dimensional programming distributor to a critical platform for executing corporate strategies.

BROADCAST BRAND MANAGEMENT

Marketing researchers have long advocated that managers need to start managing their brands more like assets—increasing their value over time (Keller, 1993). Management has to invest in understanding its brand today to make better brand decisions tomorrow. Such a notion holds true for the broadcast industries as well. As the theory of "brand life cycle" suggested, a brand, if well managed and perceived, may enter a stage of fortification with the utility of leveraging a brand's value by extending the brand to other related product categories (Liebermann, 1986). With the arrival of digital media technologies, broadcasters have the opportunity to explore new media services that may bring new revenues and/or develop competitive advantages. A successfully branded broadcaster has the foundation on which to begin such service expansions.

Among all broadcasters, radio stations are most experienced in branding related marketing techniques such as segmentation, differentiation, and positioning. Because of their narrowcasting nature, radio broadcasters have long embraced the idea of assessing the audience perceptions of their stations (i.e., brand images). On the other hand, with the product of traditionally mass-appeal content, television broadcasters have approached the branding concept quite differently.

The three major broadcast networks have historically branded themselves based on their news divisions and newscaster personalities.

TABLE 5.4
Top U.S. Media Conglomerates and Their Media Holdings

Rank	Company	Total Net U.S. Media (In mil., 2003)	Broadcast Networks/Station	MVPD	TV/Film Production/Distribution	Print	Other
1	Time Warner	$29,247	The WB Network	Time Warner Cable Bright House HBO TBS CNN Cartoon Network TNT Court TV Cinemax	Warner Bros. Pictures Warner Bros. Studios Warner Bros. Television Telepictures Production Castle Rock Entertainment Turner Ent. Network New Line Cinema Fine Line Features	Time Inc. Warner Books Little, Brown, & Co.	America Online Warner Bros. Records The Atlantic Recording
2	Comcast Corp.	$17,492		Comcast Cable Comcast SportsNet E! Entertainment Golf Network Outdoor Life Network Style QVC			
3	Viacom	$17,252	CBS Network UPN Network Viacom Stations Group CBS Radio Infinity Broadcasting Corp.	MTV BET Nickelodeon Nick at Nite CMT VH1 Spike TV Comedy Central Showtime The Movie Channel FLIX	Paramount Pictures Paramount Television CBS Productions CBS Television City King World Productions Spelling Television Viacom Productions Big Ticket Television DNA Productions	Simon & Schuster The Free Press	Blockbuster Viacom Outdoor Famous Music Publishing
4	News Corp./ DirecTV	$15,224[a]	Fox Network Fox Stations Group UPN Stations Group Fox Sports Radio Networks Chris-Craft Industries	DirecTV PanAm Sat Fox Sports Net Fox Movie Channel Fox News Channel FX National Geographic Ch. Speed Channel	20th Century Fox Film Fox Television Studios 20th Century Fox Television Twentieth Television	HarperCollins Publishing TV Guide New York Post	

	Company	Revenue	Broadcast / Radio Stations	Cable / Communications	Film & Television Studios	Newspapers / Publishing	Music / Other
5	Walt Disney Co.	$11,239	ABC Network, ABC Stations Group, ABC Radio, Radio Disney, ESPN Radio	ABC Family, The Disney Channel, ESPN, A&E, The History Channel, Lifetime, E! Entertainment	Walt Disney Pictures, Walt Disney Television, Walt Disney Animation, Touchstone Films, Buena Vista Pictures, Platinum Dunes Prod.	Disney Publishing	Buena Vista Music
6	NBC Universal	$8,177	NBC Network, NBC Stations Group, Telemundo Network, Telemundo Stations Group, PAX Network	CNBC, MSNBC, Bravo, USA, Sci-Fi, Trio	Universal Pictures, Universal Studios, Universal Television, NBC Studios		Universal Music
7	Cox Enterprises	$8,108	Cox TV Stations Group, Cox Radio Stations Group	Cox Communications		Cox Newspapers, Trader Publishing	
8	Gannett Co.	$6,330	Gannett Station Groups			*USA Today*, *The Detroit News*, *The Indianapolis Star*, *The Cincinnati Enquirer*, *The Tennessean*, *The Courier Journal*, *Asbury Park Press*, *The Desert Sun*	
9	Clear Channel	$6,138	Clear Channel Stations Group Clear Channel Radio Stations Katz Media Group	Operations with Time Warner			Clear Channel Outdoor
10	Advance Publications	$5,909				Conde Nast Publications, The Business Review, Herald Company, Fairchild Publications, Newhouse Newspapers, The Star Ledger, Oregonian Publishing	

Note. Data compiled from "100 Leading Media" (2004), "Who Owns What" (2004), and OneSource (2004).
ªTotal amount for both companies.

Branding via news programming seems to be widespread among local stations because local news often generates ratings, revenues, and visibility for these stations (Upshaw, 1995). The continuity and consistency of a news brand is especially important for an affiliated station as it tries to capitalize on the lead-in power of its network's news brand and the more established, identifiable overall network brand. A survey of local television station managers revealed that the local broadcasters had a very high awareness of the branding concept (Chan-Olmsted & Kim, 2001). Nevertheless, they often treated branding as "promotional" tasks. In addition, although the managers believed that branding plays an important long-term strategic role in the success of a station, they frequently associated branding with tactical operations such as graphical consistency, unique selling points for local news, and network affiliation image. Station promotions and news functions were more readily identified as related to branding rather than to strategic management, and most branding activities included news-oriented promotions, network brand association, and station logo designs. This is not surprising considering the fact that the broadcast networks, the ones that local TV stations often model themselves upon, have embraced the term of branding mostly with a frenzy of logo designs as well as tactical placement of these signatures and promotion of the accompanying slogans. The same study also found that the managers' commitment to brand research, not their industry experience, was linked to a more accurate understanding of branding. Also, the perceived long-term role of branding is negatively related to managers'(general managers') experience and current position in the industry. It seems that branding is a managerial function that is applied more readily by an industry newcomer than a seasoned veteran. The same study also showed that market sizes matter in a station's branding endeavor; the upper management in bigger markets tended to hold a more positive, long-term view of branding, thus offering a better environment of building station brand equity.

Branding and the Internet

Chan-Olmsted and Kim (2001) found that most local television stations perceived the Internet as a good branding tool, especially for news. According to the *Internet Age Broadcaster Report* released by the National Association of Broadcasters (NAB), two major strategic approaches have been adopted by broadcast networks: one used the Internet as a promotion tool for competing, and the other used the Internet to develop a better brand relationship with customers (Sonne, 1999). Lin and Jeffres (2001) also suggested that local TV stations use their online ventures to secure and enhance audience brand loyalty. Hashmi (2000) put forward that television networks generally perceived the Internet as a platform for repurposing, brand extension, and promotion. Along the same line of proposition, Chan-Olmsted and Ha (2002) concluded that broadcast television networks largely use the Internet to complement their core off-line business (i.e., on-air content) rather than delivering new online content or generating e-commerce or online ad revenues.

So how have the broadcasters incorporated the Internet in their branding efforts? The broadcasters have utilized the Internet to enrich their off-line products by distributing a certain online content that takes advantage of the new medium's capacity of interactivity and personalization. For example, ABC launched an Enhanced TV site that allows viewers to interact with its broadcasts of *Monday Night Football*. NBC created fresh online content for some of its series, such as *Homicide*, that allows users to get involved in solving crimes with a set of detectives not featured on the show. Fox started Sports Fantasy Network, one of the Web's active fantasy sports leagues, and TooHotForFox.com, a site containing original content that is more provocative and thus not available on the Fox network. These online sites certainly contribute to the building of network brand images. As broadcasters solidify their brand images both on-air and online, it is possible for them to use the Internet beyond marketing purposes. Working toward a market/product development strategy, a broadcaster can even attempt to sell content products online. The online distribution of content products, however, would be viable only when a broadcaster approaches the Internet with a brand identity that is based on solid, differentiated content.

NEW CHALLENGES AND OPPORTUNITIES: REFORMULATION OF BUSINESS MODELS

In response to the changing external environment, broadcasters have to revamp their traditional business models to diversify their revenue sources and position themselves for the opportunities offered by the new digital media marketplace. In exploring the applicability of different business approaches, this chapter now focuses on addressing three issues that have significant implications for broadcasters' creation of new strategies: the development of digital television, which revolutionized the capability of the television medium; the growth of satellite and Internet radio, which abolished the traditional geographic limitation of the radio medium; and the emerging broadcast-Internet business models, which could serve as a blueprint for broadcasters' expansion into new media businesses.

Digital Television: Opportunities and Challenges

Industry observers see the digital bandwidth, which enables high-definition television, interactive television, and related commerce functions, as the next big thing in the Internet–TV converged world (Ha & Chan-Olmsted, 2004). The FCC specifically stated in its report that digital television (DTV) could enhance the ability of broadcasters to compete in the video marketplace (FCC, 2002). Different television broadcasters have approached the arrival of digital spectrum with various degrees of enthusiasm. Whereas CBS and ABC are actively utilizing HDTV format during primetime, NBC and Fox are less aggressive in this endeavor. Compared to their U.S. counterparts, the Europeans have been much more successful with their consumers' adoption of DTV. Some suggested that DTV is less successful in the United States for reasons such as expensive reception equipment and poor business models. Others argued that the lack of a comprehensive copyright protection plan has slowed the transition to DTV (FCC, 2002). Furthermore, in spite of the fact that over 85% of TV households in the United States receive their TV signals via multichannel media systems such as cable or satellite TV, cable carriage of local digital broadcast signals is still a hotly contested issue. In a nutshell, DTV has the capacity to deliver clearer pictures, multicasting, better sound, and interactive functions for broadcasters. To speed up the DTV transition, the FCC has even imposed the mandate for TV set manufacturers to include digital tuners capable of receiving DTV signals over the air in all new TV sets larger than 13 inches by July 2007 (Harbert, 2002).

As important as DTV is to the future of television broadcasters, Chan-Olmsted and Chang (2004) found that there is a very low level of DTV awareness and knowledge among American consumers. The ownership of many entertainment and digital media was found to have an impact on how much consumers know about DTV. Consumer Internet usage and tenure were especially significant in increasing the knowledge of DTV. Interestingly, interactivity, the function that was touted as the critical driver for generating economic return for DTV, was considered by the consumers to be the least important DTV benefit. The findings here point to a few marketing implications. First, in the fluid, emerging DTV market, an established broadcast brand could serve as a base of consumer trust and for the possible transfer of equity to the new DTV product. In addition, the Internet and other newer media are valuable channels for communicating with potential DTV adopters. Second, as relevancy and fit are some of the keys to brand extension success, it is essential for broadcasters to contemplate these brand factors in their design of new products for the digital shelf space. There is a real danger of diluting their existing broadcast brands with inappropriate expansions into other product categories simply for the sake of diversifying revenue sources. Third, multicasting during non–HDTV times of the day presents an opportunity for broadcasters to develop differentiated brand identities to various audience segments, thus more effectively competing with MVPD services. Fourth, individual functions that consumers can easily relate to with their current television usage experience (e.g., time shifting, better picture quality, and more content choices), rather than new utilities such as interactivity, might be a more attractive differentiating identity or selling point at the initial DTV-marketing stage. Finally, with a total expected conversion cost of $16 billion (McConnell, 2004), broadcasters would need to not only explore new revenue sources and ways of developing competitive advantages from the new digital spectrum but also diligently pursue strategic networks in this process. For example, 12 station groups formed the Broadcasters' Digital Cooperative, a coalition of stations that dedicate part of their digital television space to distribute data by renting the spectrum to companies that want to distribute broadband data such as Internet content, digital audio files, or business-to-business information. Such an alliance approach is essential in an uncertain environment because it reduces the risk of introducing new products, shares partners' resources, and is able to test different business models much more quickly.

Satellite and Internet Radio: Redefining the Radio Medium

Satellite radio, a subscription-based service, offers about 60–100 channels of mostly commercial-free music, news, sports, and talk programming to subscribers that utilize a satellite antenna and receiver to receive the signal. The two major satellite radio providers, Sirius Satellite Radio Inc. and XM Satellite Radio Holdings Inc., offer a wide range of content that is unmatched by traditional radio services and are aggressively forming alliances with different outlets for the distribution of their services. For example, both companies have relationships with the major automakers, as well as car rental companies, which call for dozens of car models to come equipped with factory- or dealer-installed satellite radio receivers. Sirius Satellite Radio's digital broadcasts became available free of charge to some subscribers of DISH Networks ("Sirius Offered," 2004). Sirius is also exploring distribution agreements with cable operators. Through a partnership with Dell, XM is getting into the Internet music business by way of a subscription-based online radio service. In response to the rapid development of satellite radio in recent years, major radio station groups such as Clear Channel plan to begin limiting the number of commercials on more than 1,200 stations. Citing the desire to better compete with satellite radio, the radio industry leader, Clear Channel, also decided to improve the sound quality of its radio stations by aggressively converting 1,000 of its 1,200 stations to digital radio within 3 years at a cost of about $100,000 per station ("Radio Giant Moves," 2004). It is evident that as the switch cost for satellite TV becomes minimal, radio broadcasters, mostly through their corporate owners, are attempting to counter the differentiated value of satellite radio, namely, broadcast quality, commercial elimination, and variety. It is our assertion that although all these are important, localism would still be the key differentiating point for radio broadcasters. Thus, stations with brand images based on music variety, sound quality, or uninterrupted programming are likely to be more vulnerable as satellite radio continues to grow.

Internet radio, which includes terrestrial radio stations streaming online and Internet-based radio stations as defined in the context of this discussion, has grown tremendously since the late 1990s. According to Arbitron, American Internet users are not only flocking to the Internet for radio material, they are listening for up to 5 hours per week

(Arbitron, 2004). There are many inherent differences between the two groups of Internet radio stations. Most terrestrial radio stations webcast material that is similar to their on-air programs, whereas the majority of the Internet-based radio stations offer alternative, nonmainstream music. Terrestrial radio stations typically regard their online presence as a way of adding value to their off-line content, but Internet-only radio stations often need to find innovative, multiple revenue sources based solely on their online content (Palumbo, 2002).

Ren and Chan-Olmsted (2004) investigated the differences between these two groups of Internet radio stations based on their Web content and discovered that whereas both of them provided extensive informational content, Internet-based radio stations tended to be more conscious in collecting users' information and developing relations with users through more interactive Web functions. The study also found that although the two groups of radio stations operate under very different economic structures, they both relied mostly on advertising revenues. However, Internet-based stations also attempted to derive additional revenues from subscription, e-commerce, and affiliated programs. It is evident that Internet-based stations, although struggling to find a commercially viable means of operation, are able to differentiate themselves from the more established terrestrial webcasters by ways of unique content and personal relationships.

The impacts of Internet radio on traditional radio stations can be evaluated from two perspectives, its influence on audiences' radio usage and its impact on terrestrial radio stations' advertising revenues. Specifically, the development of Internet radio changes the competitive dynamics in the radio market in three ways: (a) It added a new group of competitors that appeal to certain niche audience segments with more variety and personal appeals; (b) it added another dimension of competition for traditional radio stations as online content became a tool for marketing and for adding value to off-line content; and (c) it added more choices for radio audiences in general. Note that most of these impacts do not directly take away local audience shares and thus advertising revenues from local radio stations; however, the influence on audiences' radio usage and expectations of online radio experience have important implications for how traditional radio stations should reformulate their marketing strategies. It is our assertion that Internet-based radio stations are unlikely to become major competitors of traditional radio stations because the value of their differentiated quality is somewhat limited (i.e., limited popular content). On the contrary, the growth of Internet radio, fueled by many Internet-based radio stations, has transformed traditional radio stations into a multifaceted medium with unprecedented potentials. In essence, the characteristics of unlimited geographical reach and the enhancement that furthers the personable nature of radio, now available through the Internet medium, present an attractive opportunity for the radio industry to boost its competitiveness in the increasingly crowded media marketplace.

Internet Business Models: A Work in Progress

Moving our focus again to television, television broadcasters have adopted a variety of Internet strategies, from outsourcing the Internet operations, utilizing the Web to create interactive advertising experiences, employing the Internet as a marketing tool for on-air content or station brands, and positioning Web sites as local portals, to producing content for enhanced television (Kerschbaumer, 2000). Specifically, various surveys of television stations revealed that the news and promotions departments were most frequently impacted by the Internet, most stations had focused on utilizing their Internet operations to generate advertising revenues rather than to develop e-commerce or content on demand, and different broadcast groups have internalized the Internet with various approaches. For example, whereas CBS stations explored ways to package existing sales forces, content, and promotion into profitable Internet businesses, Fox stations focused on online branding and developing local personalities and content with a national infrastructure and technical support. As NBC stations emphasized the building of local portals with their news products, station groups such as Tribune Broadcasting that also own newspaper properties integrated the print and broadcasting Internet operations to provide a more competitive local content. On the other hand, ABC stations worked toward a Web version of network–station programming relationships, whereas the Chris-Craft Industries stations developed niches that are database-driven (e.g., used cars and employment listings) and have immediate revenue potentials. Most station groups have also invested in the broadband and wireless sector, and some have supplied information content to their local broadband systems to ensure a presence in the growing broadband market (Greene, 2000; Nitschke, 1999). With the arrival of digital television, many television broadcasters are even contemplating the feasibility of Web-enhanced television applications such as on-screen links to advertisers' Web addresses, localized news services, late-breaking news, sports statistics, interactive polling, background to documentary material, online chat, and links to movie trailers and ticketing services (Nelson, 2001; Pavlik, 2001).

Because business models that evaluate ways in which firms may leverage the Internet to develop competitive advantage are still evolving, it is quite a challenge for firms to decide on the extent and approaches of involvement with this new medium. The development of an appropriate business model is especially critical as well as intricate for television broadcasters because the Internet offers an alternative distribution channel for its products and strengthens its position with the audiences while at the same time it competes with television for audience attention.

Chan-Olmsted and Ha (2003) put forward a framework for analyzing Internet business models of television broadcasters (see Fig. 5.1). They proposed that firm-specific, internal forces such as the types of core products, changes required to integrate the Internet operations, de-

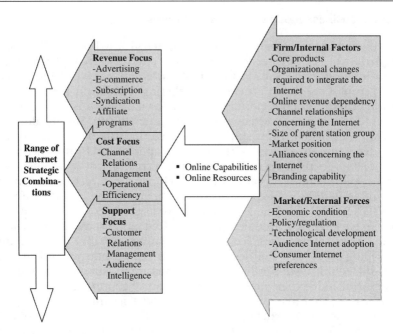

FIG. 5.1. A framework for analyzing broadcasters' Internet business models.

pendency of the online revenue, relationships with channel members regarding the Internet, size of the organization, market position, alliances relating to the Internet, and branding capability would affect a television broadcaster's Internet competency. Externally, market forces such as economic conditions, regulatory environment, technological development, and the audience's Internet adoption rate and patterns would impact a television broadcaster's Internet competency. Consequently, depending on its competency, a television broadcaster may choose to utilize the Internet to generate revenues from the sales of online advertising space or sponsorships, e-commerce (i.e., selling either merchandise or per-unit content online), content subscription (i.e., charging online users a monthly subscription fee for the right to access exclusive content online), content syndication (i.e., selling exclusive online content to other Web sites), and/or affiliate programs (i.e., receiving a percentage of all sales generated by customers traveling through a station's Web site to the online storefront of the partner). A broadcaster may use the Internet to reduce costs by managing its relationships with channel members like advertisers and programming syndicators more efficiently or by improving the overall operational efficiency within its station. The broadcaster may also utilize the Internet to support or complement its off-line operations by developing stronger customer (i.e., audience) relationships and collecting audience information through the Internet. It was suggested that most stations would have a combination of Internet operations that aim to accomplish multiple objectives (Chan-Olmsted & Ha, 2003).

Based on the proposed framework, Chan-Olmsted and Ha (2003) surveyed television stations nationally and found that a broadcaster's Internet competency is critically dependent on its manager's view of the relative revenue contribution of the Internet. These broadcasters have also focused their online activities on building audience relationships, rather than generating online ad sales. In other words, the Internet was used as a "support" to complement their off-line core products. Stations also felt inadequate about selling or syndicating content via the Internet. In fact, the revenue potential of "content" is minimal as perceived by the managers. Although continuing to view the strategy of customer/audience relations management as critical, the stations also began to value the importance of audience intelligence and the cost-cutting utility of the Internet in managing channel relations. The findings of this study point to a mix of business models that first utilize the Internet as a supplemental medium for developing a relationship with the audience of an off-line core product, and continue to increase the value of this relationship by building better audience intelligence, which then, in turn, improves the stations' ability to sell online ads and implement e-commerce, thus harvesting the value of its Internet operations (see Fig. 5.2). It is likely that not all broadcasters would go through this progression of Internet business models because they have different re-

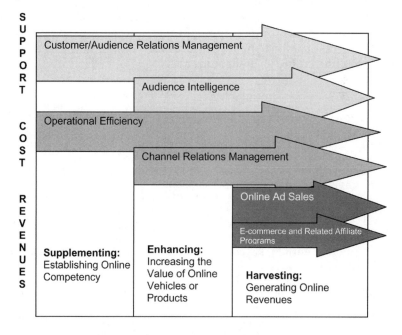

FIG. 5.2.   The Internet business models of television broadcasters.

sources and capabilities, set different goals for their Internet operation, and play different strategic roles in regard to their corporate holdings.

FINAL THOUGHTS

As the oldest incumbent in electronic media, broadcasters are facing the most threats from the emergence of new media services enabled by the tremendous technological advances in the last few decades. Although their primary revenue source, advertising, has not been significantly afftected, the fact that there have been a migration of audiences to the new media and a change of expections as well as consumption patterns indicates an urgent need for broadcasters to revamp their competitive strategies. This chapter identified several business and corporate strategies that seem to provide broadcasters with various ways to adapt to their changing environments. These strategies include: (a) consolidations/alliances that improve broadcasters' negotiation power and efficiency, (b) Internet and digital spectrum ventures that compensate broadcasters' one-way, mass-appeal shortcomings, (c) reexamination of networks' marketing utility for media conglomerates, (d) application of brand management tools, and (e) consumer-centered, brand-sensitive experiments of different business models utilizing the new digital shelf space and the Internet. It is our assertion that the broadcast media will continue to strive, not as the previously general-appeal electronic media dominator, but as an essential media property that develops the resouces (e.g., programming content, brand names, etc.) and marketing capability necessary for a media corporation to compete in today's uncertain, multifaced media environment.

REFERENCES

Ad sales show rebound in '02. (2003, September 29). *Broadcasting & Cable, 133*(39), 10.

Albarran, A. B. (2001). *Management of electronic media.* Belmont, CA: Wadsworth/Thompson Learning.

Arbitron. (2004). *Internet broadcast services.* Retrieved December 17, 2004, from http://www.arbitron.com/onlineradio/home.htm

Bodipo-Memba, A., & Brannigan, M. (1997, June 24). Clear channel to buy Paxson radio holdings. *The Wall Street Journal,* p. B14.

Brown, S. (1998a, June 1). Hearst-Argyle picks up Pulitzer. Broadcasting & Cable, 128(23), 12.

Brown, S. (1998b, April 8). Raycom adds stations from Malrite. *Broadcasting & Cable, 128*(15), 44.

Chan-Olmsted, S. M., & Chang, B. (2004). *Consumer awareness and adoption of digital television: Exploring the audience knowledge, perceptions, and factors affecting the adoption of terrestrial DTV.* Manuscript submitted for publication.

Chan-Olmsted, S. M., & Ha, L. (2002, August). *Internet business models for broadcasters: How television stations perceive and integrate the Internet.* Paper presented to the Communication Technology & Policy Division at the annual meeting of the Association for Education in Journalism & Mass Communication, Miami, FL.

Chan-Olmsted, S. M., & Ha, L. (2003). Internet business models for broadcasters: How television stations perceive and integrate the Internet. *Journal of Broadcasting & Electronic Media, 47*(4), 597–617.

Chan-Olmsted, S. M., & Kim, Y. (2001). Perception of branding among television station managers: An explanatory analysis. *Journal of Broadcasting and Electronic Media, 45*(1), 75–91.

Chatterjee, S., & Wernerfelt, B. (1988). Related or unrelated diversification: A resource-based approach. *Academy of Management Best Paper Proceedings*, pp. 7–11.

Das, T. K., & Teng, B. (2000). A resource-based theory of strategic alliances. *Journal of Management, 26*(1), 31–61.

Disney to acquire Capital Cities/ABC. (1995, August 7). *Corporate Growth Report Weekly* (855), p. 7975.

Eisenhardt, K. M., & Schoonhoven, C. B. (1996). Resource-based view of strategic alliance formation: Strategic and social effects of entrepreneurial firms. *Organization Science, 7*(2), 136–150.

Elkin, T. (2000, February 7). Nortel bets $10 mil. on global CNN deal. *Advertising Age*, p. 61.

Federal Communications Committee. (2002). *Ninth annual report on competition in video markets*. Washington, DC: Author.

Freeman, M. (1996a, July 22). On top of the world. *Mediaweek, 6*(30), 2.

Freeman, M. (1996b, April 22). Strength in numbers. *Mediaweek, 6*(17), 9.

Gay, V. (2000, January 24). World domination. *Mediaweek, 10*(4), 40.

Granite broadcasting alliance. (1999, October 6). *The Wall Street Journal*, p. 1.

Greene, T. (2000, August 14). Verizon takes NorthPoint to make national DSL move. *Network World, 17*(33), 10.

Gulati, R. (1995). Does familiarity breed trust? The implications of repeated ties for contractual choice in alliances. *Academy of Management Journal, 38*(1), 85–112.

Ha, L., & Chan-Olmsted, S. M. (2004, April). *Exploring the effects of cable television web sites on cable television network branding and viewership*. Paper presented at the annual meeting of the Management and Sales Division of the Broadcast Education Association, Las Vegas, NV.

Harbert, T. (2002). FCC plays chip makers' tune. *Electronic Business, 28*(10), 30.

Harrison, H. M., Hoskisson, R. E., & Ireland, R. D. (2001). Resource complementarity in business combinations: Extending the logic to organization alliances. *Journal of Management, 27*(6), 679–690.

Hashmi, Y. (2000). The impact of the internet. *World Broadcast Engineering, 23*(6), 26.

Heuton, C. (1995, December 4). The large get larger. *Mediaweek, 5*(46), 12.

Hitt, M. A., Ireland, R. D., & Hoskisson, R. E. (2001). *Strategic management: Competitiveness and globalization* (4th ed.). Cincinnati, OH: South-Western College.

Hoover's Online. (2004). Retrieved November 19, 2004, from http://premium.hoovers.com/

Kaufman, L. (2000, February 18). NBC helps Ralph Lauren fulfill a multimedia dream. *The New York Times*, p. C13.

Keller, K. L. (1993). Conceptualizing, measuring, and managing customer-based brand equity. *Journal of Marketing, 57*(1), 1–22.

Kerschbaumer, K. (2000, September 25). TV & the Internet: Old meets new. *Broadcasting & Cable, 130*(40), 55–58.

Landers, D., & Chan-Olmsted, S. M. (2004). Assessing the changing network television market: A resource-based analysis of broadcast television networks. *The Journal of Media Business Studies, 1*(1), 1–26.

Laureen, M. (1995, August 7). NBC picks up three stations. *Mediaweek, 5*(31), 4.

Liebermann, Y. (1986). The advertising-to-sales ratio along the brand life cycle: A critical review. *Managerial and Decision Economics, 7*(1), 43–48.

Lin, C. A., & Jeffres, L. W. (2001). Comparing distinctions and similarities across Web sites of newspapers, radio stations, and television stations. *Journalism and Mass Communication Quarterly, 78*(3), 555–574.

Liu, F., & Chan-Olmsted, S. M. (2003). Partnerships between the old and the new: Examining the strategic alliances between broadcast television networks and Internet firms in the context of convergence. *International Journal on Media Management, 5*(1), 47–56.

McClellan, S. (2000, December 11). Partners in programming. *Broadcasting & Cable, 130*(51), 6.

McClellan, S. (2002a, June 17). Getting together—on something. *Broadcasting & Cable, 132*(25), 33.

McClellan, S. (2002b, April 15). A new repurposing arena. *Broadcasting & Cable, 132*(16), 7.

McConnell, B. (2004, March 15). Millions could be without TV. *Broadcasting & Cable, 134*(11), 5.

Mermigas, D. (2000, June 5). NBC's fall lineup to spotlight new Web technology. *Advertising Age, 3*, 64.

Miller, J. P., & Jensen, E. (1996, July 2). Tribune to acquire TV broadcaster renaissance. *The Wall Street Journal*, p. A3.

Nelson, K. (2001, March 19). Cable show put new technology on front burner. *Electronic Media*, p. 13.

Nitschke, A. (1999). *Station Internet activities report*. Washington, DC: National Association of Broadcasters.

100 leading media companies. (2004, August 23). *Advertising Age*, p. S4.

OneSource. (2004). *OneSource Online Business Information*. Available from http://www.onesource.com/

Palumbo, P. (2002). *Streaming content sites favor advertising over subscription*. Retrieved August 16, 2002, from http://www.streamingmedia.com/article.asp?id=8240

Pavlik, J. (2001). *Journalism and new media*. New York: Columbia University Press.

Radio giant moves to limit commercials. (2004, July 19). [Electronic version]. *The New York Times*.

Ren, W., & Chan-Olmsted, S. M. (2004). Radio content on the World Wide Web: Comparing streaming radio stations in the United States. *Journal of Radio Studies, 11*(1), 6–25.

Sherman, J. (2004, May 17). NBC Universal looks forward. *Televisionweek, 23*(20), 3.

Sirius offered To DISH subscribers. (2004, May 21). *Satellite Today, 3*(98), 1.

Sonne, M. D. (1999). *Technologies & new business directions for broadcasters*. Retrieved July 10, 2001, from http://www.nab.org/Research/topic.asp

Standard & Poor's. (2004). Retrieved November 19, 2004, from http://www2.standardandpoors.com/servlet/Satellite?pagename=sp/Page/HomePg

Time Warner to buy Turner Broadcasting. (1995, September 11). *Corporate Growth Report Weekly* (860), p. 8035.

Top 25 station groups. (2004, April 19, 2004). *Broadcasting & Cable, 134*(16), 56.

Trigoboff, D. (2001, August 6). Chris-Craft, Fox move in. *Broadcasting & Cable, 131*(33), 14.

Upshaw, L. B. (1995). *Building brand equity.* New York: Wiley.

Walt Disney Internet, Compaq Computer set three-year pact. (2000, December 1). *The Wall Street Journal,* p. B2.

Westinghouse will make a $80 per share bid for CBS. (1995, July 31). *Corporate Growth Report Weekly* (854), p. 765.

Who owns what. (2004). Columbia University's Graduate School of Journalism, *Columbia Journalism Review.* Retrieved December 17, 2004, from http://www.cjr.org/tools/owners/

Chapter 6

Strategy and Competition in the Multichannel Media Industry

As a relatively newer challenger to traditional media incumbents such as print and broadcast media, multichannel media firms or multichannel video programming distribution (MVPD) services dramatically altered not only the competitive dynamics in the television industry but also audiences' viewing behavior since the 1980s. The MVPD market continues to evolve and remain a powerful contender as technological advances brought forth the Internet, digitization, broadband, and interactivity. Adopting the strategic framework proposed in chapter 2, this chapter first examines the economic, technological, political, and sociocultural changes that have influenced the MVPD industry and continue to discuss the factors that have affected the competitive dynamics of the MVPD market. Because cable television and DBS services comprise more than 96% of all MVPD subscriptions in the United States (Standard & Poor's, 2004), this chapter focuses on addressing these two multichannel video media.

CHANGES IN THE GENERAL ENVIRONMENT

As discussed in the previous chapter, elements in the broader context of a society influence the operations of industries and the firms within them. Although the general environmental trends are the same for all media industries, their impacts on individual markets are different. In this context, the major environmental developments and their implications to the MVPD sector are presented next.

Economic Changes

The growth of a global economy has substantially contributed to the market potential of MVPD services. The interconnectedness of different economies, including freer flow of products and the establishment of mechanisms enabling that flow, encourages multinational corporations to invest in communications infrastructures in various countries. The development of network capacities helped establish multichannel media services. The subsequent programming needs then fueled the international expansion of many MVPD firms. The relatively low interest rates during various time periods between the 1980s and 2000s also fostered a favorable environment for mergers and acquisitions. The M&A activities consolidated many smaller systems into large multiple system operators (MSOs), which significantly changed the competitive dynamics of the industry. The relatively robust growth of the U.S. economy from 1980 to 2000 also increased consumers' disposable income, making MVPD and many of its auxiliary services more affordable. In addition, the increase in consumer spending translated to advertising revenue growth for the cablecasters, which more than tripled over the last 10 years (Standard & Poor's, 2004).

Technological Changes

Technological advances in the last two decades have fundamentally shaped today's MVPD market. In fact, technologies underlie the very existence of DBS and cable television and drive the types of MVPD services that might be available in the future. From addressable converters that catapulted premium services like HBO and optical fibers and compression that stimulated the development of new channels to the more recent broadband and digital communication technologies that facilitate the arrival of better audiovisual quality, more content options, fast data transmissions, and interactivity, technological changes have constantly brought forth new business opportunities for MVPD firms. The essentiality of technology in this market also means that there is more strategic heterogeneity among MVPD services. That is, because of the product diversity enabled by technologies, there is more room for strategic competition and differentiation among the MVPD firms. In addition, many of the same technologies have also altered their broadcast counterpart's conventional capabilities, making the broadcasters more competitive (e.g., HDTV and multicasting).

Political Changes

The Telecommunications Act of 1996 and the recent, more relaxed regulatory environment has also impacted the MVPD market by fostering an environment for group ownership and technological development. Specifically, the deregulatory climate facilitated the formation of large MSOs, which are able to improve operational efficiency through clustering strategies; have better access to resources such as programming through their increasing corporate relationships with cable networks (i.e., vertical integration); and explore potential digital, interactive, and even telephone services via their improving broadband platform. Similar to the effect on broadcasters, the opening of media borders and commercialization made possible by the global political changes toward privatization and commercialization of media systems also led to the option of global diversification and the increase of programming demands and thus the expansion potential for MVPD firms such as cable networks.

Sociocultural and Demographic Changes

A number of developments in this area have influenced the MVPD market. The growing income disparity between different socioeconomic audience segments discussed earlier has elevated the competitiveness of MVPD firms, which are experienced in market segmentation strategies. More women in the workforce as well as increasing workplace diversity also point to the importance of programming content and scheduling flexibility, which are more feasible in a multichannel setting. The busy lifestyle of today's families makes more valuable the benefits of on-demand services provided by cable and DBS services. Finally, the fast growth of two demographic groups—the Hispanic and African American markets—has contributed to the value and development of Spanish-language and African American–focused programming channels. Besides the established specialty brands such as Univision and Black Entertainment Television (BET), mainstream networks like ESPN and HBO have extended their brands to include ESPN Deportes and the HBO Latino channel to target these specific audience segments.

CHANGES IN MULTICHANNEL MEDIA INDUSTRIES

To describe the nature and state of competition in the MVPD industry, we again follow the framework depicted in chapter 5 with a review of five factors that shape the competitive dynamics of a market: bargaining power of suppliers, bargaining power of buyers, threat of substitute products, threat of new market entrants, and rivalry among competing firms.

Bargaining Power of Supplier

In the context of the MVPD market, suppliers are the producers/suppliers that make available the MVPD contents like local origination and community access information, audio programming, electronic program guides, news, weather, sports, original programming, retransmitted broadcast signals, and syndicated, recycled programming. From this perspective, the main suppliers include information and audio services (e.g., *TV Guide* and XM), television syndicators (e.g., WB syndication), studio and independent producers (e.g., Universal Studio), cable networks and systems that produce original contents such as news, weather, public affairs, and sports (e.g., ESPN and CNN), and broadcast television stations. Because the audio and information components of MVPD services are typically not the primary attraction for an MVPD service (at least currently), our discussion of the bargaining power of suppliers focuses on the other four groups.

Because most MVPD services were originally developed as an alternative distribution system for retransmitting broadcast signals, historically studio producers and syndicators did not regard the MVPD market as a primary revenue source. Consequently, the exercise of supplier power has not been as evident as in the broadcast market. Also, because of the numerous sources of MVPD programming contents, diversity of MVPD buyers, and their specialized content preferences as a niche medium, there is less domination by a few content suppliers and thus less concentration of supplier power. In addition, the extent of vertical integration between MSOs, cable networks, and studio producers has somewhat neutralized the supplier–buyer power struggle in the market. For example, Time Warner, a major MSO, has ownership interests in movie producers New Line Cinema and Castle Rock Entertainment, news producer CNN, and even the sports teams Atlanta Braves and Atlanta Hawks. In fact, among the 339 cable networks at the end of 2003, about one third of them, with many producing their own original programming, are affiliated by ownership with an MSO (FCC, 2004). The pervasiveness of vertical integration between cable networks and MSOs actually characterizes the industry and very often changes the dynamics between many MVPD suppliers and buyers from competitive to cooperative.

As the multichannel industry continues to build its own identity, investing more than $11 billion in original programming (Cabletelevision Advertising Bureau, 2004), the linkage between content suppliers and MVPD firms is becoming more strategic. In fact, the success of a content product is no longer dependent simply on generating above-average revenues in a particular business sector but also on enhancing other relevant products under the same corporate umbrella. In other words, it is also strategically beneficial for MVPD firms to carry affiliated networks or buy programs from their sister studios. Table 6.1 shows that most cable networks that offer more original programming and/or dominate primetime cable viewing are, in fact, owned by media conglomerates. An examination of the most popular cable networks reveals that they are basically owned by two groups of media conglomerates: one group includes Time Warner and News. Corp., which have powerful MVPD properties along with production holdings, and the other group includes Disney and Viacom, which have powerful broadcast properties with production capabilities. It is clear that the competitive strategies nowadays are corporate and multilateral rather than segmented and vertical.

Another important negotiation power of suppliers that needs to be addressed is that of broadcasters because the carriage of broadcast signals is an essential part of MVPD services. This is indeed a contentious issue amid the expansion of the number of cable networks and the arrival of terrestrial digital television that also needs multichannel carriages. Historically, the broadcasters had more bargaining power over

TABLE 6.1

Top 10 MVPD Service Providers and Their Affiliate Programming Networks

Rank	Company	% of MVPD Subscribers	Affiliate National Networks (Ownership %)	Affiliate Regional Networks (Ownership %)
1	Comcast	22.69	Discovery HD Theatre (20) E! Entertainment (50) G4 Video Gaming Network (94) Golf Channel (99) iN Demand (50) Outdoor Life Network (100) QVC (57) Style (60)	CN8-The Comcast Network (100) Comcast SportsNet (78) Comcast SportsNet Mid Atlantic (100) Comcast Sports South East (72) Empire Sports Network (33) Fox Sports Net New England (50) New England Cable News (50) Tri-State Media News (100)
2	DirecTV	12.32	Fox Sports Net Fox Movie Channel Fox News Channel FX National Geographic Channel Speed Channel	Fox Sports Arizona Fox Sports Bay Area Fox Sports Chicago Fox Sports Detroit Fox Sports Intermountain West Fox Sports Midwest Fox Sports New England Fox Sports New York Fox Sports Northwest Fox Sports Ohio Fox Sports Pittsburgh Fox Sports RockyMountain Fox Sports South Fox Sports Southeast Fox Sports Southwest Fox Sports West Fox Sports West 2 Madison Square Garden Network Sunshine Network
3	Time Warner	11.62	Action Max (100) @Max (100) Cartoon Network (100) Cinemax (100) CNN (100) CNN En EspaZol (100) CNN Headline News (100) CNN International (100) CNNfn (100) Comedy Central (50) Court TV (50) 5 StarMax (100) HBO (100) HBO Latino (100) HBO 2 (100) HBO Zone (100) iN Demand (33) MoreMAX (100) OuterMax (100)	Bay News 9 (100) Central Florida News 13 (50) New York 1 News New York 1 Noticias News 8 Austin News 14 Carolina R News Rocheste Turner South (100)

			Ovation: The Arts Network (4.2)	
			TBS (100)	
			Thriller Max (100)	
			TNT (100)	
			Turner Classic Movies (100)	
			WMAX (100)	
4	EchoStar	9.35		
5	Charter	6.87		
6	Cox	6.67	Animal Planet (25)	Arizona News Channel (50)
			Discovery (25)	Cox Sports Television (100)
			Discovery En Español (25)	Local News on Cable (50)
			Discovery Health (25)	News Now 53 (50)
			Discovery HD Theater (25)	News on One (50)
			Discovery Home & Leisure (25)	News Watch 15 (50)
			Discovery Kids (25)	Rhode Island News Channel (50)
			Discovery Times (25)	Sunshine Network (6.3)
			Discovery Wings (25)	
			Health Network (25)	
			iN Demand (15)	
			Science Channel (25)	
			TLC (25)	
			Travel Channel (25)	
7	Adelphia	5.43		Empire Sports Network (67)
8	Cablevision	3.15	AMC (60)	Fox Sports Net Arizona (45)
			Fuse (60)	Fox Sports Net Bay Area (45)
			Fuse on Demand (60)	Fox Sports Net Chicago (45)
			Independent Film Channel (60)	Fox Sports Net Detroit (45)
			WE (60)	Fox Sports Net Florida (45)
				Fox Sports Net New England (45)
				Fox Sports Net New York (45)
				Fox Sports Net Ohio (45)
				Madison Square Garden Network (41.5)
				MSG Metro Guide (80)
				MSG Metro Learning Channel (80)
				Neighborhood News (75)
				News 12 Connecticut (75)
				News 12 Long Island (75)
				News 12 New Jersey (75)
				News 12 Bronx (75)
				News 12 Westchester (75)
9	Bright House[a]	2.19		
10	Mediacom	1.66		

Note: From Federal Communications Commission (2004) and "Who Owns What" (2004).

[a]Subsidiary of the Time Warner Cable Group.

cable systems when cable-only content was very limited. As cable continues to invest in its own original programming, the power of broadcasters is lessening. Nevertheless, the broadcasters will still have a certain degree of countering power as long as there are differentiated elements that cannot be satisfactorily substituted by MVPD programming (e.g., the Super Bowl). Finally, it is important to view the relationship between television-broadcasting suppliers and MVPD firms from a corporate perspective, given the fact that many broadcasters have corporate owners that are also heavily involved in the MVPD market (e.g., Disney and Viacom); the broadcasters' bargaining power may materialize as a means to advance other corporate interests.

A final note on the bargaining power of the suppliers is the potential of the pay-per-channel scenario (à la cart program pricing). Technological advances have made the offering of à la carte programming more feasible. That is, it is now possible for individual consumers to choose to pay for only the channels that they prefer to watch rather than paying by programming tiers. Industry practitioners argued that an à la carte pricing system would result in a restructuring of the cable-programming business that would harm consumers by reducing choice, eliminating programming diversity, and driving up prices (National Cable & Telecommunications Association, 2004). It is our assertion that such a fundamental change would place a substantial financial burden on the programmers. In other words, the entry barriers to the programming market would likely be raised because of the increased costs in product development and marketing. The need for additional resources (and greater bargaining power) might facilitate more mergers and acquisitions in this sector. The pay-per-channel system would also diminish the role of service providers and shift the "value" of the MVPD service to the programming packagers and other facilitators. As a result, competition might heat up between different MVPD service platforms because they would become less differentiated.

Bargaining Power of Buyer

In the context of the MVPD market, buyers include audiences and advertisers. From the perspective of the audience buyers, their bargaining power resides in the investment of their "time" in the programming offered by MVPD services and the subscription or per-unit fee that they pay to the service providers. It is our assertion that MVPD audiences do not in general possess strong bargaining power over MVPD service providers for the following reasons: (a) Though the audiences directly pay for MVPD services, the pricing structure of most MVPD services somewhat insulates consumers from pricing sensitivity through package marketing; (b) the switching cost is relatively high once MVPD subscriptions have been established; (c) most MVPD products are differentiated and branded; and finally, (d) there are no substitutes for MVPD products available in most local markets (note that both DBS and cable are considered MVPD products).

From the perspective of the advertising buyers, MVPD services have become viable commercial outlets over time. In fact, cable network viewership has grown steadily in recent years, largely at the expense of the major broadcast networks. Ad-supported cable had a prime-time audience share of 50.3% in 2003, versus a combined 44.8% for the four major broadcast networks. The growth in viewership has also translated to increased shares of ad dollars as cable services garnered over 33% of total ad spending in 2003 (Cabletelevision Advertising Bureau, 2004). MVPD services, namely cable networks, are now a necessary communications channel for brand marketers because of their ability to target specific audience groups. The essentiality of MVPD services in delivering defined market segments (e.g., Nickelodeon for children) and the fact that advertising revenue is not the only source of income for MVPD firms means that the bargaining power of advertisers is comparatively less significant than in the broadcast market.

Threat of Substitute

Substitute products are different goods or services from outside of the MVPD market that perform similar functions. In this context, broadcast content, video programming provided by local exchange carriers (LECs), Internet video, and home video sales and rental can be viewed as potential substitutes for MVPD services. In the case of broadcast signals, studies have shown that broadcast and cable television are highly substitutable (Waldfogel, 2002). Nevertheless, we believe that the substitutability is becoming moderate because many MVPD channels now offer highly differentiated, niche programming dissimilar to broadcasters' more mass-appeal content. As for competition from the telephone sector, most large incumbent LECs such as Ameritech (now SBC) and Qwest, despite various attempts to offer video distribution services via existing copper telephone lines using very high-speed digital subscriber lines (VDSL), have exited the video business, thus presenting limited substitution threats because of unavailability in most local markets (FCC, 2004). In terms of Internet video, notwithstanding the increasingly accessible real-time and downloadable online video, near broadcast-quality streaming video is still not widely available, making it a less direct competitor of MVPD services. Finally, the sale and rental of home video, including videocassettes, DVDs, and laser discs, do pose a certain degree of substitution threat for the premium and pay-per-view offerings of MVPD services. To counter such a threat, cable operators have aggressively invested in upgrading their infrastructure to allow for advanced video services such as digital video, video on demand (VOD), and even telephone services. In summary, MVPD services do face some degree of threats posed by a variety of substitutes; however, because of their continuous investments in original programming, differentiation, and technological development, MVPD firms have obtained some competitive advantages over their competitors from other sectors.

Potential Entrants

With the passage of the Telecommunications Act of 1996, the U.S. government attempted to create an environment that encourages competition from new entrants outside of the MVPD market. In this context, the potential entrants include LECs, broadband service providers (BSPs), electronic and gas utilities, and new DBS service providers (FCC, 2004). As mentioned previously, most LECs have decided to stay away from a pure video-programming business model or enter the market through comarketing with existing DBS providers. The LECs' choice to concentrate on expanding their broadband telecommunications services rather than video-programming products means limited potential addition of competitors from this sector. Another group of potential entrants, BSPs, on the other hand, have grown from simple local overbuilders to state-of-the-art services that offer bundled telecommunications services including video, voice, and high-speed Internet access. Nevertheless, there are significant entry barriers for this group of contestants (U.S. General Accounting Office, 2002b). First, BSPs' access to programming products has been difficult due to vertically integrated cable programmers and unaffiliated programmers that make exclusive agreements with cable operators. Second, BSPs often have problems accessing vital sports and regional news programming as a result of exemptions to the program access rules. Third, BSPs have difficulties obtaining franchises from local governments or gaining access to VOD equipment, public rights of way, and utility poles needed to expand their systems (FCC, 2002, 2004). As for potential entrants from the utilities sector, although some utility companies have engaged in the provision of video services through overbuilding incumbent cable systems, such services are not widespread. Though characteristics such as ownership of fiber-optic networks and access to public rights-of-way remove some of the entry barriers, in general, the entry by electric and gas utilities is limited mostly to rural areas where other telecommunications firms may not be willing or able to provide the full range of advanced services (FCC, 2004). Finally, the barriers to entry remain substantial for new DBS services. The economies of scale necessary to set up the satellite uplink and distribution system, required capital, access to programming, and even expected retaliation from the existing two established DBS services, DirecTV and DISH Network, translate to little incentive for a third DBS service.

Whereas there has been very modest threat of new entrants at the exhibition stage (e.g., distribution systems such as MSOs and DBS services), we have witnessed a tremendous growth in the number of MVPD programming networks in the last decade. Today's cable systems offer an average of 70 analog video channels and approximately 120 digital video channels, with additional bandwidth to provide high-definition television, VOD, and Internet access services. Through this expanding capacity, more MVPD programmers have entered the market, reaching a total number of more than 330 networks by the end of 2004 (by contrast, most local markets can sustain only one or at most two cable systems because of the extent of investment to wire a community). Nevertheless, it is quite a challenge for new programming networks to survive without the carriage by leading MSOs because the top four MSOs control as many as 56% of nation's cable subscriptions (FCC, 2004). The extent of vertical integration between MSOs and cable networks is therefore one of the most significant barriers to entry for stand-alone networks. In essence, the MVPD market is at a stage of development that represents a maturing industry with relatively high entry barriers, whereas the competitive dynamics materialize in the rivalry within the market.

Internal Rivalry Intensity

The MVPD marketplace in the United States has been through some transformations in the last few years because of technological advances, consolidations of services, and the growth of alternative satellite-based services. Only a decade ago, cable systems dominated this market with almost 100% of the nation's multichannel subscribers (National Cable & Telecommunications Association, 2003); the number now is close to 75% as DBS subscribership grew significantly, reaching 21.6% of all MVPD households. The remaining 3.5% of MVPD subscribers are shared by minor services such as satellite master antenna television (SMATV) (aka private cable), home satellite dishes (HSD), multichannel multipoint distribution services (MMDS) (aka wireless cable), BSPs, and open video systems (OVSs) (FCC, 2004). Because the majority of the MVPD services are offered by either cablecasters or DBS firms, we focus our following discussion on the rivalry between these two groups. Note that the focus here is on MVPD service providers rather than programming distributors such as HBO and CNN. The nature and state of the rivalry between these firms are addressed later in the chapter.

How do cable television and DBS compete, and will DBS continue to take shares away from cablecasters? There are different characteristics between DBS and cable that shape the competitive dynamics in this market. They can be discussed from the perspectives of programming access, service and pricing, and technology. In fact, barriers of access to programming were historically the major obstacles that hindered the early growth of satellite-related multichannel services. Two legislations, the Cable Television Consumer Protection and Competition Act of 1992 and the Satellite Home Viewer Improvement Act of 1999, successfully removed most of the barriers that prevented DBS operators from accessing vertically integrated programming on nondiscriminatory terms (the rules prohibit cable operators from forming exclusive deals with their affiliated cable networks in the sale and distribution of satellite-delivered programming and from distributing local broadcast signals) (FCC, 2004). It was actually found that DBS are able to compete with cable more effectively where they can offer local signals (FCC, 2004).

DBS became even more competitive when, at the end of 2003, News Corporation purchased 34% of Hughes Electronics, DirecTV's parent company, for $6.6 billion in cash and stock. Armed with the ownership of Fox, an important supplier of cable content, particularly news and sports channels such as the Fox Sports regional sports networks and the top-rated Fox News Channel, DirecTV now has access to an array of popular MVPD contents from its affiliated programming networks (Higgins, 2003). Furthermore, Liberty Media, the corporate owner of major MVPD networks such as the Discovery Channel and QVC, is the largest outside shareholder of News Corporation, owning 17% of its equity (Higgins, 2003; *Who Owns What*, 2003). The vertical integration provides DirecTV with an advantage long enjoyed by its cable MVPD counterpart.

The leveling of the playing field contributes to more internal rivalries in the MVPD industry, at least in markets where DBS is able to offer comparable local and national programming packages. In essence, programming access in the forms of extent, cost, and exclusivity significantly impacts the competitiveness of DBS as a newer entrant to the market versus the more established cable incumbents. The key strategies here for DBS are to strike a balance between the cost of adding local channels to more markets and raising subscriber numbers and to aggressively seek exclusivity of programming for which they have no ownership (e.g., DirecTV's NFL Sunday Ticket package) while controlling programming costs so they are able to offer comparable or lower package prices to consumers.

From the perspective of services, DBS was consistently ranked to have better consumer satisfaction and pricing than its cable counterpart (J.D. Power & Associates, 2003; Olgeirson, 2003; Schaeffler, 2003). As for technology issues, though the potential for broadband Internet access and other advanced video services such as VOD is promising, studies have found that the majority of the consumers did not find Internet access services to be a top concern when choosing between DBS and cable (U.S. General Accounting Office, 2002a). In other words, cable's aggressive deployment of cable modem is not, at least currently, considered a strong differentiating point between DBS and cable. In fact, channel variety and prices are the top considerations for choosing between the two MVPD platforms (U.S. General Accounting Office, 2003).

It is our assertion is that cable television will remain the dominant MVPD service for the following reasons. First, the MVPD industry growth rate has slowed down, which means that DBS would have to take customers from the incumbent cable systems to expand its customer base, most likely through pricing strategies. Such a competitive engagement reduces profitability and is sustainable on only a short-term basis. Second, there is a lack of major differentiation between cable and DBS programming offerings. Third, the switching cost from cable to DBS is relatively high considering the up-front expenses and the cost of equipment upkeep (though it is getting lower). In fact, industry reports have suggested that DBS has exploited its potential market and will focus on maintaining its modest market share (ZenithOptimedia, 2002). DBS, however, will continue to be a formidable competitor to cablecasters for the following reasons. First, there exist high fixed costs for distributing DBS signals, which means that DBS services are motivated to use pricing and packaging strategies to maximize their sales volume. Second, there are high exit barriers for DBS firms such as their specialized assets and strategic interrelationships with other media properties (e.g., DirecTV and News Corp.), which compel them to remain in the market and compete. Finally, a DBS service might carry high strategic stakes for its diversified corporate owner. For instance, DirecTV is critical for News Corp. because it is News Corp.'s only MVPD distribution arm when competing with a media conglomerate like Time Warner that multilaterally engages News Corp. in both the broadcast and MVPD markets.

Going from different platforms to individual competitors, the field of MVPD services is largely populated by major MSOs. The two DBS providers, DirecTV and DISH Network (i.e., EchoStar), were ranked the second- and fourth-largest MVPD service providers, serving close to 22% of the MVPD subscribers in 2003, slightly less than that of the top MSO, Comcast (FCC, 2004). Time Warner, with close to 12% of the MVPD market share, was number three on the list. The rest of the leading MSOs, including Charter, Cox, Adelphia, Cablevision, Bright House, and Mediacom, all garnered less than 7% share of the market.

How competitive are these MVPD services? One way of assessing competition is to examine the degree of concentration in a market because of structural effects on firm conduct, strategic options, and profitability as proposed by industrial economics' SCP notions. To this end, we can use concentration measures to benchmark industries by the market share (percentage of sales) held by the largest firms. Economic theory and empirical research suggest that highly concentrated industries (i.e., those in which most of the market is held by a few powerful firms) face little pressure to compete through services, pricing, or new technologies. There are two commonly used measures of industry concentration: the n-firm concentration ratio (CR), where n is the number of the largest firms included in the measure, and the Herfindahl–Hirschman Index (HHI). Whereas the n-firm CR is the sum of the percentage of market shares held by the number of largest firms, the HHI is defined as the sum of the squared percentage of market shares of all firms in the industry, which is generally a more comprehensive and revealing measure of industry concentration. According to Shepherd (1987), a CR4 between 40 and 60 identifies an industry with firm concentrations optimal for competitive behavior. Scherer and Ross (1990) identified the boundaries for the CR4 as 45 and 60. Scherer and Ross also reported finding that the optimal CR8 for a competitive industry is 70 (which roughly corresponds to a CR4 of 50 in the U.S. economy). The Federal Trade Commission (FTC) uses both the CR and the HHI to assess the extent to which a proposed merger will affect competition in that industry and is unlikely to challenge mergers when the HHI is below 1,000. According to the U.S. Department of Justice (DOJ), a market with an HHI of less than 1,000 is considered unconcentrated, between 1,000 and 1,800 moderately concentrated, and over 1,800 highly concentrated.

Nationally, the MVPD market had a CR4 of 56%, CR8 of 78, and HHI of 1,031 by the end of 2003 (FCC, 2004). The CR4 ratios have fluctuated over time from 47% in 1993 to 55% in 1998, and then dropped to 52% in 2001 and 50% in 2002, whereas the HHI moved from 880 in 1993 to 1096 in 1998, 905 in 2001, and 884 in 2002. Overall, today's national MVDP market is on the borderline of unconcentrated or competitive. Locally, however, most markets have only one cable system in addition to the two DBS options available to consumers. The significant local entry barrier due to cable's natural monopoly characteristic deters new entrants and protects the cable incumbent from other cable MVPD challengers, thus making most local markets oligopolistic with one dominant leading firm (i.e., cable franchise holder). The two-tier competitive scheme suggests that whereas we may observe more rivalries between MVPD service providers at the national level in regard to programming development and acquisitions, technology adoption, and audience marketing (especially from the DBS providers), there is relatively more limited competitive behavior between local MVPD units.

It is our assertion that the next stage of competitive strategy for MVPD providers will move from a focus on original programming development to advanced services marketing and advertising sales enhancement (for cablecasters). There is an increasing pressure to derive new revenues from new products (e.g., broadband, VOD, and personal video recorder [PVR]) as the demand for multichannel video is slowing and to improve the cable ad sales process because cable has successfully established itself as a differentiated, good target ad medium through its programming investment. In fact, technological advances at local cable systems have enhanced local cable advertising by making customized advertising possible. Advertisers now can reach more than 22 million households in the top 10 interconnects and more than 52 million in the top 100 interconnects, making cable a more competitive advertising medium (Cabletelevision Advertising Bureau, 2004).

Several themes seem to permeate throughout our discussions thus far of the changes impacting the MVPD market. They include the pervasive consolidations that reshaped the structure and competitive behavior of this industry, the increasing strategic diversity among different MVPD firms, and the essentiality of realigning resources to capitalize on the new broadband technologies and new media services for MVPD firms. The following sections elaborate on the alliance and M&A factor, apply a strategic management concept to evaluate the strategic multiplicity in this market, and reexamine the MVPD value chain considering the addition of new media services and the trend toward convergence.

FORMATION OF STRATEGIC NETWORKS AND CONSOLIDATION OF OWNERSHIP

As discussed earlier, consolidations in the MVPD industry have created large, clustered, and vertically integrated MSOs. We now examine how the MVPD firms have formulated strategic networks such as joint ventures and acquired more properties to enhance their competitive positions.

Strategic Alliances

To gain access to programming products and provide better coordinated marketing of MVPD services, to increase speed in product development or market entry, and to share knowledge and develop industry standards, MVPD firms have geared up the formation of strategic networks with programmers and producers, technology firms, and even telephone companies.

Alliances With Programmers. The integration of MVPD service providers and MVPD programming distributors has been increasingly accomplished not only by mergers and acquisitions but also by joint ventures and other marketing agreements. The partnerships are especially evident in the area of pay-per-view/VOD development and marketing. For example, Starz Encore Group has formed various marketing alliances with DBS MVPDs such as DirecTV and EchoStar Communications to increase the subscription of pay-per-view services ("Starz Inks Multi-Tactical," 2004). Comcast, the largest MSO, has entered a joint venture with Sony to develop new cable networks and utilize Sony's movie properties to enhance Comcast's video on demand service (Grant, 2004). In essence, the MVPD service providers, with a growing strategic network of content producers and distributors, are better positioned to quickly deploy attractive content products for a platform that is increasing in capacity and interactivity.

Alliances With Technology Firms. Another alliance strategy for the MVPD service providers seems to be developing a network of technology-driven services to explore new revenue opportunities. Parise and Henderson (2001) once suggested that technological advances tend to induce strategic alliances as firms strive to acquire technology complementarity, reduce innovation time span, lessen uncertainty in terms of emerging technologies, and position themselves when there is a convergence of several industry segments. News Corp. and TiVo Inc. agreed to work together on a PVR-digital satellite television venture in the

U.K. The companies even cobranded their PVR-based personal television services TiVo and Sky (Dickson & Kerschbaumer, 2000). Many MSOs eyeing broadband and new media expansions have also configured a strategic network of telecommunications technology firms. For example, AT&T Broadband (now part of Comcast) and Matsushita Electric Corp. of America formed a joint initiative to develop advanced digital set-top boxes to stimulate the introduction of new broadband video, voice, and data services via cable set-tops ("Panasonic Announces Alliance," 2000). Time Warner also has a strategic marketing and technology agreement with Samsung Electronics to collaborate on an AOLTV set-top box that would feature TiVo PVR functionality. To explore the potential of new interactive services, Time Warner and Royal Philips Electronic even formed a so-called global strategic alliance to develop new e-commerce platforms for cable television ("AOL Forms Tech Partnerships," 2001).

The expansion of broadband services via strategic networks is also important for the wireless MVPD service providers. EchoStar Communications joined force with PanAmSat in an alliance to distribute content through Excite@Home's broadband network. EchoStar also entered another agreement with Geocast Network Systems to deliver broadband services to personal computers (PCs) through EchoStar's DISH Network satellite TV service (Connell, 2000). On the other hand, DirecTV and Microsoft collaborated in their delivery of a branded UltimateTV that features PVR technology exclusively for DirecTV subscribers. The strategic networks of technology firms and broadband networks accelerate MVPD service providers' new media diversification efforts with less risk and more resources.

Alliances With Telcos. In the attempt to position themselves more competitively for broadband services, DBS MVPD providers have also chosen to partner with telephone companies in bundling and comarketing products. For instance, EchoStar Communications and SBC Communications entered a strategic alliance that combined DISH Network's digital satellite television offerings with SBC's broadband digital subscriber line Internet access service (Carter, 2002). The EchoStar–SBC plan offers five bundled services—local phone, long distance, cell phone, satellite TV, and broadband Internet access—and is branded as SBC DISH Network. DirecTV Broadband also entered an agreement with WorldCom to expand DirecTV DSL service across the western and midwestern United States via access to WorldCom's nationwide DSL services ("SBC Changes DSL," 2002). Qwest, on the other hand, formed comarketing partnerships with both DirecTV and EchoStar (Latour & Grant, 2003). Similar RBOC–DBS partnerships were formed between BellSouth and DirecTV and Verizon and DirecTV. The alliances with another wired network, telcos, present wireless MVPD providers with an experienced partner in broadband network deployment and marketing, thus elevating DBS's competitive position concerning new broadband-based MVPD services.

Mergers and Acquisitions

Mergers and acquisitions have characterized the cable industry for years (Chan-Olmsted, 1996). In fact, the pervasive ownership interests of MSOs in programming networks has been one of the most prominent features of the cable industry structure (Parsons & Frieden, 1998). As of 2003, one third of the satellite-delivered national MVPD programming networks were vertically integrated with at least one cable MSO. Table 6.1 shows that most top MVPD providers have extensive ownership interests in cable networks. Leading firms like Comcast, DirecTV, and Time Warner are vertically integrated with a substantial number of popular sports, news, and entertainment cable networks. Table 6.2 further demonstrates the importance of such ownership interests for MVPD service providers to stay competitive with the broadcasters because 9 of the 15 most highly rated MVPD programming networks are owned by conglomerates with top broadcast properties such as Viacom (CBS), NBC Universal (NBC), and Disney (ABC).

To assess the M&A strategies in the MVPD sector, we now examine the top MVPD service providers' activities involving the acquisitions of programming properties and the horizontal consolidations of MVPD services.

TABLE 6.2

**Top MVPD Programming Networks (Primetime Viewing)
and Their Corporate Owners**

Rank	MVPD Service	Corporate Ownership
1	TNT	Time Warner
2	Lifetime Television	Disney and Hearst
3	Disney Channel	Disney
4	Nickelodeon	Viacom
5	TBS	Time Warner
6	Cartoon Network	Time Warner
7	USA Network	NBC Universal
8	A&E	Disney, Hearst, & NBC Universal (GE)
9	Fox News Channel	News Corp.
10	Discovery Channel	Liberty Media
11	MTV	Viacom
12	TLC	Liberty Media
13	Spike TV	Viacom
14	ESPN	Disney and Hearst
15	Sci-Fi Channel	NBC Universal

Vertical Acquisitions for Programming Access.   As indicated earlier, many leading MVPD service providers are vertically affiliated with programming producers and distributors by ownership. Comcast, the number one MVPD firm, which reaches more than 22% of the multichannel media subscribers, however, is not the most active acquirer of MVPD programming properties as it has developed its programming mostly through joint ventures (e.g., with Sony for MGM and with Disney for E! Entertainment) and internal expansions (e.g., QVC, Comcast Sportsnet, and G4). Only recently has it started acquiring programming units to enhance its current programming holdings. For instance, Comcast purchased Home Team Sports and combined it with its SportsNet in 2001 to create a powerful regional sports MVPD network. It also acquired some specialty sports networks such as the Golf Channel and the Outdoor Life Network. Most recently, in 2004, Comcast merged its G4, a network dedicated to entertainment, news, and information about video games and the interactive entertainment industry, with TechTV, a network that showcases the development, business, and lifestyle of the technology world ("Comcast Acquires Tech TV," 2004). Besides focusing on horizontal M&A (discussed in the next section), the largest MVPD service provider seems to aim at establishing access to regional sports, specialty sports, and technology-oriented programming.

Time Warner, on the other hand, has amassed its programming properties mostly through its acquisition of Turner Broadcasting, which gave Time Warner a vast array of cable networks, production units, and extensive film libraries (Dizard, 1997). It is evident that the programming assets of Time Warner are most established in the areas of news and movies, continuing its highly valued news and film studio brands (e.g., Time Magazine and Warner Bros. Studio) outside of the MVPD industry. As for the other two major MVPD firms, whereas DirecTV has just been fitted with the tremendous content assets of Fox's programming properties through its merger with News Corp., Cox has developed access to programming mostly through its investment in Liberty Media's Discovery channels.

It is our assertion that the acquisition of DirecTV by News Corp. is one of the most significant M&A activities in this sector because it positions a major broadcaster to be also a strong contestant on the MVPD platform. In fact, broadcasters have been increasingly involved in this market through mergers and acquisition, but this has mostly occurred in the programming segment of the market. For example, Westinghouse spent some $1.55 billion in stock to purchase The Nashville Network and Country Music Television from Gaylord Entertainment Co. (Burgi, 1997). Viacom acquired BET, the largest cable network targeted at African Americans, for $2.9 billion (Hay & Saxe, 2000). Disney also acquired the Fox Family Channel for $5.3 billion and renamed it ABC Family whereas NBC added Bravo, the arts and entertainment network, to its cable holdings for $1.25 billion (Chunovic & Greppi, 2002). These acquisitions have extended the broadcast networks' reach into the MVPD programming arena; however, only News Corp., with its DirecTV unit, has an integrated access to major popular programming networks and media outlets in both the broadcasting and MVPD industries. The strategic significance of a strong presence in both the MVPD and broadcasting sectors can be further illustrated by Comcast's failed attempt to merge with Disney in 2004. Though Comcast subsequently withdrew its offer, citing dilution concerns and Disney's lack of interest, the proposed consolidation underscores the corporate strategy of dual presence in relevant markets and multilateral competition.

Horizontal Acquisitions for Market Expansions. Since the passage of the 1996 Telecommunications Act, there has been a tremendous amount of M&A activity involving horizontal expansions of MVPD service providers. It began with US West's acquisition of Continental Cablevision; then the United States' third-largest cable firm ("US West Acquisition," 1996), AT&T, also added Tele-Communications Inc. and later MediaOne to its networks (Higgins, 1999b). The wave of telco–cable mergers seemed to be a response to the potential of convergence and to the exploration of new services such as broadband Internet access and phone services over cable-system lines (Marcial, 1998). However, various divestitures of the cable properties following these high-profile cable–telco combinations demonstrate the difficulty of integrating a network-driven telephone business with a content-driven MVPD industry.

Many other MSOs such as Adelphia Communications Corp. also aggressively began expanding their cable properties with purchases of cable systems from Harron Communications Corp., Century Communications Corp., and FrontierVision Partners LP. Another major MSO, Cox Communications Inc., grew considerably in size with its acquisition of Gannett Corp.'s Multimedia Cable unit (Higgins, 1999a, 1999c), whereas Comcast became the number one MSO with its purchase of AT&T's cable assets for about $45.7 billion in stock, plus the assumption of nearly $25 billion in debt and liabilities, giving it nearly twice as many subscribers as the industry's next-biggest MSO, Time Warner (Dreazen, 2002; Higgins, 2001). Many of these mergers and acquisitions are about executing a regional strategy of "clustering," which creates economies of scale and scope, and thus enhances an MSO's ability to transform its cable systems into "advanced broadband platforms" (FCC, 2004). The FCC has reported that at the end of 2002, there were 109 clusters with approximately 51 million subscribers compared to 97 clusters with 20.1 million subscribers 8 years ago. In a sense, through mergers and acquisitions, the MSOs are attempting to develop a two-way infrastructure capable of providing advanced services such as broadband Internet and interactive television more efficiently, to create attractive regional programming, and to enhance their competitiveness in the regional advertising market.

Our examination of the formation of strategic networks and system consolidation between MVPD service providers highlighted the importance of certain corporate strategies at the exhibition stage of this market. We now review the competitive dynamics between MVPD programmers at the distribution stage of the MVPD market.

MULTICHANNEL STRATEGIC GROUP COMPETITION

Past economic discussions of the broadcast television industry have assumed that all programming distributors in the industry use the same funding mechanism and deliver products to a fairly homogeneous group of buyers. Such a presumption does not apply to MVPD programmers. For example, whereas CNN charges MVPD service providers relatively high license fees to carry its signals, many new start-up multichannel video programmers offer the providers incentives to induce carriage. Whereas USA Network carries commercials, the Independent Film Channel does not offer any local or national avails. Furthermore, most MVPD programmers have invested in branding and differentiating their content products, which are sold to service providers using various distribution platforms. The traditional emphasis on "industry" as a unit of analysis seems to be less appropriate for analysis of these heterogeneous programmers. In other words, MVPD programming networks operate under a more complex business system than their broadcast counterparts and are capable of more diverse strategic competition. The observation that strategic diversity within an industry has a significant bearing on market behavior is central to the theory of strategic groups and grounds our discussion here.

Porter defined a strategic group as a cluster of firms that follow similar strategies in terms of the key decision variables (Cool, 1985; Porter, 1985). Firms within a strategic group resemble one another closely, recognize their mutual dependence, and thus coordinate their behavior effectively. Furthermore, when one considers intergroup market dynamics, the existence of different strategic groups affects the overall level of rivalry in the industry. When firms are associated with different strategic groups, they have different preferences about pricing, research and development (R&D), advertising, optimal output, and other market conduct. As a consequence, operational differences complicate the process of cooperation (either explicitly or implicitly) between groups (McGee, 1985). Hence, it is more likely for groups with similar strategic approaches to cooperate than it is for groups that use diverse strategies. Moreover, cooperation is easier and more likely to happen within groups than between groups. Also, environmental changes do not have equal impact on different strategic groups due to their different strategic postures, assets, and skills. As for the performance differences among strategic group members, many strategic group scholars have argued that there are group-specific entry barriers (i.e., mobility barriers) that provide protection to group members (Olusoga, Mokwa, & Noble, 1995). Such structural forces impede firms from freely changing their competitive positions and explain intraindustry profit differentials in a cross section of industries (Caves & Ghemawat, 1992).

Incorporating the strategic groups concept, Chan-Olmsted (1997) proposed that the MVPD programmers would, by their heterogeneous nature, exhibit monopolistically competitive market behavior at the industry level. In other words, these firms attempt to build differential advantages (e.g., programming differentiation) and "selectively" interact with certain competitors' strategic actions. She also suggested that the industry-level analysis alone would not accurately reveal the competitive dynamics between these MVPD firms because they also compete in a group setting within the industry with oligopolistic market behavior (e.g., recognition of mutual dependency; Chan-Olmsted, 1997). Adopting this analytical framework, Chan-Olmsted and Li (2002) empirically examined the strategic patterns of the MVPD programming networks and the relationship between group membership and performance using the strategic dimensions (i.e., grouping variables) of size, vertical integration, operating efficiency, differentiation, and pricing.

It was found that the MVPD programmers, in pursuit of monopolistic space (i.e., areas of natural advantage), are highly differentiated not only in their programming approaches but also in many of the strategic dimensions tested. By occupying different strategic positions, most of the MVPD strategic groups were able to carve out more definite and clear boundaries to avoid territory encroachment (i.e., direct competition). There were groups of programmers that focus on providing programming guides and information, offer commercial-free movies, are vertically integrated with differentiated programming, are vertically integrated with general-appeal programming, are stand-alone networks with niche programming, and are differentiated cable networks owned by broadcasters. The group composition reveals some interesting strategic patterns. While the presence of broadcasters may be felt through their niche cable properties, some cable-based MVPDs have tried to compete with the broadcasters with their own mass-appeal networks.

Chan-Olmsted and Li (2002) also concluded that delivering branded content that is highly valued (as suggested by per-subscriber license fees) is the key to better financial performance for the programmer with respect to revenues, both overall and in rate of return. More ad avails and reliance on ad revenue do not necessarily yield better margin or revenue numbers, nor does a heavy reliance on license fee revenues. Horizontal relationships with other programmers and increased operating efficiency seem to somewhat contribute to the performance measures. Nevertheless, vertical integration, although enhancing carriages by the service providers and/or marketing efficiency, is not essential for superior performance for these firms. Finally, smaller programmers may still outperform bigger programmers in rate of return when they rely mainly on license fee revenues and invest in programming to improve the value of their products.

VALUE CHAIN OF AN EVOLVING MVPD MARKET

Whereas the notion of strategic groups presented thus far illustrates the diversity of strategic postures for MVPD programmers, it also underscores the significance of the changing environment upon the competitive dynamics of this market. Because of the complexity of strategic postures among the MVPD firms, an environmental shift such as technological advances in one area might greatly enhance a firm's market opportunity while limiting another's expansion plan. Also because MVPD firms are generally more differentiated and branded, changes in the environment that brought forth the opportunity of new-product development would mean a welcome chance to harvest brand equity through brand extension strategies for certain firms. The addition of product variety from the introduction of new MVPD services would again contribute to this industry's heterogeneity and enrich its differentiation possibilities.

The MVPD market is truly in a revolutionary stage with many new media services developing to enhance and add to its current offerings. The list includes digital video, VOD, subscription video-on-demand (SVOD), PVRs, high-definition television (HDTV), interactive/enhanced television (ITV/ETV), Internet protocol (IP) telephone over cable, and high-speed Internet access. It is our assertion that the growth of these new products inevitably contributes to an integration of the Internet, computing, cable television, and telephone industries and thus the emergence of a multimedia market with a value chain that is multilateral and interwoven with previously segmented sectors. Some scholars have even suggested that it is increasingly more appropriate to examine three vertical industries—media, telecommunication, and information technology—not by individual markets but by five horizontal value-adding segments of content, packaging, processing, transmission, and devices (Bane, Bradley, & Collis, 1997).

As one of the most technologically equipped media markets, the MVPD industry has ventured into many new media and broadband-based services such as digital video, high-speed Internet access, and cable telephony, which certainly point to the emergence of a different value chain with changing functions, relationships, and players. The next section applies the concept of value chain to examine the new, evolving MVPD market.

The notion of value chain is closely related to the discussion of business models as the former scrutinizes the value that is added to a product or service in each stage of its acquisition, transformation, management, marketing, sale, and distribution (Picard, 2000). Value chain analysis allows a firm to understand the cost–value relationship for every stage of their operation and thus facilitate the implementation of appropriate strategies. Hoskisson, Hitt, and Ireland (2004) and Porter (1985) detailed that a firm's value chain includes primary activities (i.e., activities that create, sell, distribute, and service the product) such as inbound logistics, operations, outbound logistics, marketing and sales, and service and support activities (i.e., activities that provide the support needed to implement the primary activities) such as firm infrastructure, human resource management, technological development, and procurement. As a value chain shows how value is added from the raw-material stage to the final output, the key is to identify where the value typically resides and the value-creating opportunities for a particular product.

Figure 6.1 depicts a generic value chain for MVPD programming networks (i.e., multichannel media programmer or packager) using the Porter value chain framework. For this group of firms, the activities associated with receiving, storing, and disseminating inputs to the product (i.e., inbound logistics) and collecting, storing, and distributing the product to buyers—MVPD service providers and advertisers—(i.e., outbound logistics) have more limited value-creating opportunities compared to other parts of the value chain. The key to create competitive advantage at these two stages would probably be activities that improve efficiency and result in better cost control. The primary activities associated with transforming inputs into the final product form (i.e., operations), on the other hand, are vital to adding value to the MVPD product, especially in areas of content selection and scheduling. Marketing and sales are another critical set of primary activities because the selection of the right distribution channels (e.g., leading MSOs), effective promotion and branding of the programming products, and productive sales forces (e.g., ad sales) produce tremendous value for MVPD programmers. Finally, service activities, although not as significant at this stage, may become more important in creating value through content and function enhancement as more interactive, broadband-based programming services are introduced.

We also believe that among all supporting activities, infrastructure-related activities such as effective strategic planning and highly developed information systems that enhance these firms' understanding of customers programming preferences are essential sources of competitive advantages. Note that because numerous MVPD programmers are part of a diversified media firm, their infrastructure activities are split between the business unit and corporate levels. In many cases, the relevant corporate activities contribute significantly to creating value for the business unit. Procurement is another major set of supporting activities, especially in gaining access to creative talents, agents, and contents to control costs and increase the quality of their products, thus adding value in the process. Finally, whereas developing incentives to encourage creativity might be a source of value for human resource management activities, investments in technologies that enable better differentiation and multiplatform presentations would gradually be-

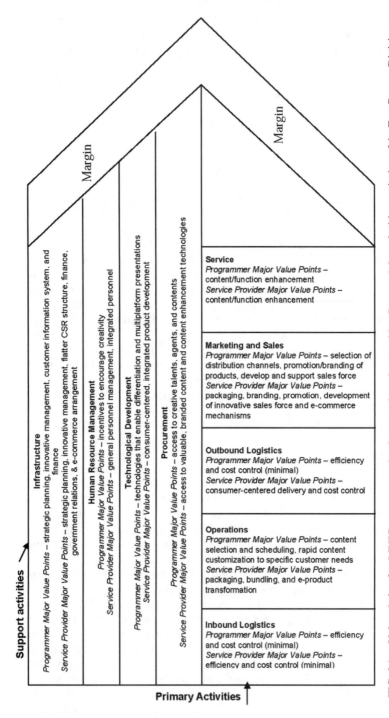

FIG. 6.1. Value chain of an MVPD programmer/packager and service provider. Source: Adapted with permission of the Free Press, a Division of Simon & Schuster Adult Publishing Group, from COMPETITIVE ADVANTAGE: Creating and Sustaining Superior Performance by Michael E. Porter. Copyright © 1985, 1988 by Michael E. Porter. All rights reserved.

come more essential for the success of MVPD programmers in the emerging digital media market.

Figure 6.1 also details the value chain for MVPD service providers. Although all the categories of primary activities are present and play a role in deriving competitive advantages, we believe that marketing and sales activities, especially those that enhance the packaging, branding, promotion campaigns, and innovative e-commerce and ad sales mechanisms, would add the most value to these firms. As more new media, broadband-based services become available, outbound logistics that improve the friendliness and efficiency of the service delivery (e.g., set-top box) and service activities that boost the perceived value of the products are likely to contribute to the building of competitive advantages for these MVPD firms.

There are many sources that a multichannel media service provider might look to for adding value through its supporting activities: a flatter customer service representative (CSR) structure that could respond more efficiently and effectively to subscribers who have bundled or a wide range of services (rather than a departmental, hierarchical CSR configuration); technological activities that focus on developing new consumer-centered rather than technology-centered media products; and procurement activities that emphasize access to valuable, branded content and the acquisition of content enhancement technologies.

A firm's value chain is also embedded in a larger stream of activities called the value system, where each channel member's output adds to the channel value of the overall system (Porter, 1985). Gaining competitive advantages would depend on understanding both a firm's value chain and how the firm fits into the total value system. Within the same industry-wide value creation notion, Wirtz (1999) proposed that there are five stages in a multimedia value chain. They are the content/service creators who provide program contents/services, the content/service aggregators who combine various contents/services to create multiple program bundles, the value-added service providers who develop and offer new services on existing platforms, the access/connecting facilitators who undertake the transmission of the contents and services to the customer, and the navigation/interfacing suppliers who provide customer navigation tools. In essence, the system of value chains here reinforces Porter's proposition of analyzing an industry by segmenting its market activities that add different values to the final product (Timmers, 1998).

Figure 6.2 depicts the total value system for the emerging MVPD industry, which takes into account the growing role of other new media, broadband-based services. The value system begins with the content creators' value chain. Whereas the core activity for this stage is content creation, the most critical competencies or resources that might generate significant value for the firms here are access to talents and capital for content development and the syndication rights for their creations (i.e., the right to maximize profit through the content-windowing

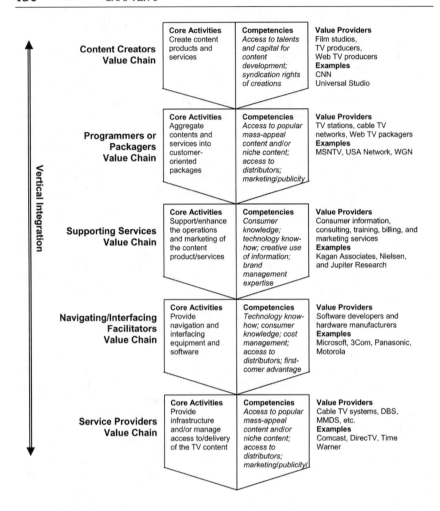

Vertical Integration

Content Creators Value Chain

Core Activities	Competencies	Value Providers
Create content products and services	*Access to talents and capital for content development; syndication rights of creations*	Film studios, TV producers, Web TV producers **Examples** CNN Universal Studio

Programmers or Packagers Value Chain

Core Activities	Competencies	Value Providers
Aggregate contents and services into customer-oriented packages	*Access to popular mass-appeal content and/or niche content; access to distributors; marketing/publicity*	TV stations, cable TV networks, Web TV packagers **Examples** MSNTV, USA Network, WGN

Supporting Services Value Chain

Core Activities	Competencies	Value Providers
Support/enhance the operations and marketing of the content product/services	*Consumer knowledge; technology know-how; creative use of information; brand management expertise*	Consumer information, consulting, training, billing, and marketing services **Examples** Kagan Associates, Nielsen, and Jupiter Research

Navigating/Interfacing Facilitators Value Chain

Core Activities	Competencies	Value Providers
Provide navigation and interfacing equipment and software	*Technology know-how; consumer knowledge; cost management; access to distributors; first-comer advantage*	Software developers and hardware manufacturers **Examples** Microsoft, 3Com, Panasonic, Motorola

Service Providers Value Chain

Core Activities	Competencies	Value Providers
Provide infrastructure and/or manage access to/delivery of the TV content	*Access to popular mass-appeal content and/or niche content; access to distributors; marketing/publicity*	Cable TV systems, DBS, MMDS, etc. **Examples** Comcast, DirecTV, Time Warner

FIG. 6.2.   Total value system of the new MVPD market.

strategy based on the notions of price discrimination and market segmentation) (Waterman, 2000). Some examples of the firms and business units involved at this level are film studios such as Universal and television producers such as CNN. The next stage of the value-adding process is packaging, which includes content aggregators (i.e., programmers), whose core activities are to assemble contents into packages that appeal to different segments of customers. The most critical core competencies or resources for these firms are access to popular mass-appeal content and/or niche content; access to distributors; capability of repackaging content for different user segments and/or distributions systems; and expertise in areas of marketing, brand management, and publicity. Examples of a programmer/packager would be MSNTV, USA Network, and broadcast stations like WGN. The next group on the value chain, though essential for the functioning of this market, is not as visible to MVPD consumers. The supporting services basically exist to enhance the operations and marketing of MVPD products, especially for the packagers and distributors. These services may include billing and marketing specialists, consumer information experts, and other consulting firms. Because of the complexity and importance of matching the right product with the right segment of audience in a market full of choices, the core competencies or resources for these firms are consumer knowledge, technology know-how, brand management expertise, and creative use of information. Examples here include companies like Kagan Media, Nielsen Media Research, and Jupiter Research. The next group, the interfacing/navigating facilitators, adds value to the overall system by providing navigation, interfacing equipment, and software programs that enable easy access to MVPD content, thus enhancing the value of the content. These firms' core competencies or resources for success are technology know-how, consumer knowledge, cost management, and access to distributors. The examples are software developers and hardware manufacturers such as Microsoft and Motorola as well as content management services like TiVo. Note that to be the first firm to introduce or market a navigating/interfacing technology will also increase the likelihood of success because of a first-comer's ability to set industry standards and influence consumer demands. The final group in the total value system is MVPD service providers, including cable system operators, DBS, and other minor multichannel media providers. The service providers offer an infrastructure for the delivery of multichannel video contents and manage the interactive access to these contents or additional services. The most significant competencies or resources are access to a mass consumer base for scale and scope economies; relationships with the navigating/interfacing facilitators; and the ability to provide a seamless, efficient network or infrastructure. Note that there are also critical linkages between different value chains and possible dynamic changes as a result of integrations between firms in various value chains through ownership (e.g., News Corp.'s acquisition of DirecTV).

Our discussions thus far of the value chains of the MVPD programmers and service providers and the value system of the overall market are based on the notion that by disaggregating a firm's activities into strategically relevant sets of actions, we might be able to identify the sources of competitive advantages. That is, we can identify components that an MVPD firm can work on to develop better cost structure, differentiation, technological applications, and other strategies that bring forth above-average returns. We believe that because of the multiplicity of this industry and the increasing service variety propelled by new technologies, such a value source analysis is becoming even more essential.

FINAL THOUGHTS

The MVPD market has grown tremendously in the last two decades with two major system contenders, DBS and cable television, and more than 330 programming networks. With limited threats of substitution and new entrants, as well as extensive clustered consolidations in the cable sector, the MVPD industry is well positioned to implement the next phase of new broadband and interactive video services. In fact, the growing multiplicity of product offerings, the existing diverse programming sources, and distribution platforms present an ideal mechanism for strategic competition and thus a fertile setting for media strategy studies. Vertical integration, international diversification, joint-venture alliances, brand extensions, innovation management, corporate entrepreneurship, and many more market behaviors are ripe for the empirical testing of strategic management and other economic theories in a media context. In fact, as technological advances transform the MVPD market, we are likely to see the addition of more broadband and telephone communications products available along with video programming offerings, making MVPD a contender also for advanced telecommunications services. This chapter has focused on the general issues of the MVPD industry. As it continues to evolve in response to technological developments, the interactive/enhanced television and broadband telecommunications aspects of the market will become more evident sources of competitive advantages. Thus, the next two chapters examine the MVPD as well as broadcast firms' activities in these two areas and their implications.

REFERENCES

AOL forms tech partnerships. (2001, July 23). *Cable World, 13*(30), 60.

Bane, P. W., Bradley, S. P., & Collis, D. (1997). Winners and losers: Industry structure in the converging world of telecommunications, computing, and entertainment. In D. B. Yoffie (Ed.), *Competing in the age of digital convergence* (pp. 227–246). Boston: Harvard Business School Press.

Burgi, M. (1997, February 17). TNN, CMT won't transplant Eye. *Mediaweek, 7*(7), 4.

Cabletelevision Advertising Bureau. (2004). *Cable TV facts.* New York: Author. Retrieved November 20, 2004, from http://www.onetvworld.org/?module=displaysection&section_id=139&format=html

Carter, R. (2002, April 18). SBC Communications enters alliance with EchoStar. *Journal Record,* p. 1.

Caves, R. E., & Ghemawat, P. (1992). Identifying mobility barriers. *Strategic Management Journal, 13*(1), 1–12.

Chan-Olmsted, S. M. (1996). Market competition for cable television: Reexamining its horizontal mergers and industry concentration. *Journal of Media Economics, 9*(2), 25–41.

Chan-Olmsted, S. M. (1997). Theorizing multichannel media economics: An exploration of group-industry strategic competition model. *Journal of Media Economics, 10*(1), 39–49.

Chan-Olmsted, S. M., & Li, C. C. (2002). Strategic competition in the multichannel video programming market: An intraindustry strategic group analysis. *Journal of Media Economics, 15*(3), 153–174.

Chunovic, L., & Greppi, M. (2002, November 11). NBC adds Bravo to its cable holdings. *Electronic Media, 21*(45), 1A.

Comcast Acquires Tech TV, Will Merge Network Into G4. [Electronic version] (2004, March 29). Retrieved October 15, 2003, from http://www.mediaweek.com

Connell, D. (2000, October 23). Alliances boost satellite B-band. *Cable World, 12*(43), 18.

Cool, K. O. (1985). *Strategic group formation and strategic group shifts: A longitudinal analysis of the U.S. pharmaceutical industry, 1963–1982.* Unpublished doctoral dissertation, Purdue University, West Lafayette, IN.

Dickson, G., & Kershbaumer, K. (2000, March 6). TiVo and BSkyB form alliance. *Broadcasting & Cable, 130*(10), 72.

Dizard, W., Jr. (1997). *Old media new media: Mass communication in the information age* (2nd ed.). New York: Longman.

Dreazen, Y. J. (2002, April 24). AT&T, Comcast assert benefits of cable union outweigh risks. *The Wall Street Journal*, p. D4.

Federal Communications Commission. (2002). *Ninth annual report on competition in video markets.* Washington, DC: Author.

Federal Communications Commission. (2004). *Tenth annual report on competition in video markets.* Washington, DC: Author.

Grant, P. (2004, September 14). Sony, Comcast strike content deals. *The Wall Street Journal*, p. A6.

Hay, C., & Saxe, F. (2000, November 18). BET, Viacom solidify merger. *Billboard, 112*(47), 5.

Higgins, J. M. (1999a, April 19). Adelphia buys Harron system. *Broadcasting & Cable, 129*(16), 88.

Higgins, J. M. (1999b, May 31). AT&T's incredible shrinking plan. *Broadcasting & Cable, 129*(23), 10.

Higgins, J. M. (1999c, August 2). Cox wins Gannett auction. *Broadcasting & Cable, 129*(32), 49.

Higgins, J. M. (2001, December 31). No holiday for consolidation. *Broadcasting & Cable, 131*(53), 6.

Higgins, J. M. (2003, April 14). Rupert's vertical reality. *Broadcasting & Cable, 133*(15), 1.

Hoskisson, R. E., Hitt, M. A., & Ireland, R. D. (2004). *Competing for advantage.* Mason, OH: Thomson/Southwestern Learning.

JD Power & Associates. (2003, August). *2003 residential cable/satellite TV customer satisfaction study.* Westlake Village, CA: Author.

Latour, A., & Grant, P. (2003, July 22). SBC, Qwest strike partnerships with providers of satellite TV; Alliances with EchoStar, DirecTV aim to fend off rivalry from cable firms. *The Wall Street Journal*, p. B11.

Marcial, G. G. (1998, December 14). AT&T brings new zing to TCI. *Businessweek*(3608), 128.

McGee, J. (1985). Strategic groups: A bridge between industry structure and strategic management? In H. Thomas & D. Gardner (Eds.), *Strategic marketing and management* (pp. 293–313). Chichester, England: Wiley.

National Cable & Telecommunications Association. (2003, September 11). *NCTA calls on FCC to declare the multichannel video marketplace "full competitive."* Retrieved October 15, 2003, from http://www.ncta.com/press/press.cfm?PRid=393&showArticles=ok

National Cable & Telecommunications Association. (2004). *Cable developments 2004.* Washington, DC: Author.

Olgeirson, I. (2003, June 9). Burned by churn. *Cable World,* p. 22.

Olusoga, S. A., Mokwa, M. P., & Noble, C. H. (1995). Strategic groups, mobility barriers, and competitive advantage: An empirical investigation. *Journal of Business Research, 33*(2), 153–164.

Panasonic announces alliance with AT&T broadband to drive advanced digital cable set-top boxes in retail marketplace. (2000, October). *Cableoptics Newsletter, 11*(10), 6.

Parise, S., & Henderson, J. C. (2001). Knowledge resource exchange in strategic alliance. *IBM Systems Journal, 40*(4), 908–925.

Parsons, P. R., & Frieden, R. M. (1998). *The cable and satellite television industry.* Needham Heights, MA: Allyn & Bacon.

Picard, G. R. (2000). Changing business models of online content services: Their implications for multimedia and other content producers. *International Journal on Media Management, 2*(2), 60–68.

Porter, M. (1985). *Competitive advantage: Creating and sustaining superior performance.* New York: The Free Press.

SBC changes DSL speeds, prices. (2002, August). *High-Speed Internet Access, 18*(8), 8.

Schaeffler, J. (2003, August 4). Robust DirecTV puts pressure on cable. *Satellite News, 26*(30), 1.

Scherer, F. M., & Ross, D. (1990). *Industrial market structure and economic performance* (3rd ed.). Boston: Houghton Mifflin.

Shepherd, W. G. (1987). Concentration rates. In J. Eatwell, M. Milgate, & P. Newman (Eds.), *The new palgrade: A dictionary of economics* (pp. 563–564). New York: Stockton Press.

Standard & Poor's. (2004). *Standard & Poor's.* Retrieved November 19, 2004, from http://www2.standardandpoors.com/servlet/Satellitepagename=sp/Page/HomePg

Starz inks multi-tactical marketing campaigns. (2004, April 27, 2004). *Satellite Today, 3*(80), 1.

Timmers, P. (1998). Business models for electronic markets. *Electronic Markets, 8*(2), 3–8.

U.S. General Accounting Office. (2002a). *Critical infrastructure protection: Commercial satellite security should be more fully secured* [Electronic version]. Washington, DC: Author.

U.S. General Accounting Office. (2002b). *Telecommunications: Issues in providing cable and satellite television services* [Electronic version]. Washington, DC: Author.

U.S. General Accounting Office. (2003). *Satellite communications: Strategic approach needed for DOD's procurement of commercial satellite bandwidth* [Electronic version]. Washington, DC: Author.

US West acquisition of Continental clears FCC with condition. (1996, October 21). *The Wall Street Journal,* p. B6.

Waldfogel, J. (2002). *Consumer substitution among media.* Washington, DC: Federal Communications Commission.

Waterman, D. (2000, December). *Economic models for Internet TV content providers.* Paper presented at the TV over the Internet Conference, Düsseldorf, Germany.

Who owns what: Liberty Media Corporation. (2003). *Columbia Journalism Review,* Columbia University, New York. Retrieved November 9, 2003, from http://www.cjr.org/tools/owners/libertymedia.asp

Wirtz, B. W. (1999). Convergence processes, value constellations and integration strategies in the multimedia business. *International Journal on Media Management, 1*(1), 14–22.

ZenithOptimedia. (2002). *Television in the Americas.* London: ZenithOptimedia.

Chapter 7

Strategy and Competition in the Enhanced Television Market

Enhanced television (ETV) or interactive television (ITV) has been touted as the key to transform the television industry since the 1980s. Though the actual product offerings and consumer demand have fallen short of expectations over time and the introduction of ETV (ETV represents all relevant terms hereafter) turned out to be a slow evolution rather than a dramatic revolution, technological advances in distribution systems and computing in recent years have again put these services on the forefront of the industry road map. Much has been written about the nature of consumer demand for ETV (Gunter, 2003; Ha & Chan-Olmsted, 2002; Vorderer, Knobloch, & Schramm, 2001), the arrays of ETV ventures (Kerschbaumer, 2004), and the technical aspects of these services (Martin, 2002; Ranger, 2004); however, few scholars have tackled the strategic and competitive implications of these market activities for media firms. This chapter first discusses the historical development of ETV from the perspectives of strategy and competition. It then reviews the major ETV applications in recent years, discusses the strategic implications of these ventures, assesses leading media firms' strategic portfolios concerning ETV, and finally proposes a value chain framework that depicts the value creation process, sources of competitive advantages, and major players in the evolving ETV market.

The term enhanced television is often used to describe many software-enhanced television services from streaming online to PCs and shopping via television to video games on all platforms. The fact that the enhancement of a traditionally passive television-viewing behavior encompasses many perspectives of interactivity actually creates confusing definitions. Whereas some view ETV as any experience that gives viewers more programming selection, customization, and control, others insist on certain degree of real-time interactivity in both text and video format. There is so far no clear consensus on what ETV means or what it should include. In fact, some cable operators have indicated that they shied away from the unproven ETV services because they wanted to pursue the more profitable VOD service, which is an ETV activity by some definitions. In the context of this study, ETV is defined as services that enhance an audience's television experience by giving people more entertainment, information, and control through a mechanism capable of interaction between the audience and television (and between audiences) and customizing and delivering content in real time. PC-based broadband video and high-speed Internet access services, though also important for this market, is discussed mainly in next chapter.

THE DEVELOPMENT OF ENHANCED TELEVISION

The trials of ETV began in the 1970s, not by market force or consumer demand, but by a desire to improve education and community services through the newly established cable television systems from governmental agencies ("Symposium on Experiments," 1978). With the introduction of a then new, multichannel distribution system, public institutions such as the U.S. Department of Health, Education, and Welfare initiated ETV tests in an attempt to realize the potential of providing health care information and worker training via this media platform. During this introductory stage (see Table 7.1), the most publicized ETV venture was QUBE, an interactive cable service offered by the then Warner Communications in Columbus, Ohio. QUBE subscribers were able to use set-top decoder boxes to participate in game shows and surveys, call plays in a college football game, take part in electronic town meetings, and simulate a vote for the Academy Awards (Constantakis-Valdez, 2004). In a sense, services like QUBE and other trials were driven by either a public-service mandate or technological advancement in the distribution system. Nevertheless, these early services were very expensive to maintain with little added value to the existing television experience. Furthermore, the content provided was of low quality with limited repurposing utilities.

As the expensive QUBE system failed to survive, the ETV ventures in the 1980s regressed back to simplified text services on television. The videotext-like services continued to have difficulties with the expensive equipment and costly service maintenance. In addition, given the unaffordability of set-top boxes, the use of ETV services at this stage was strategically more for gaining franchising advantages than actual new-product development. Beginning in the late 1980s and into the 1990s, cable operators and telcos, in an effort to define the market of ETV, began a complex strategy of competition and cooperation (Constantakis-Valdez, 2004). AT&T and Bell Atlantic conducted interactive television services trials and reported strong interest in games and

TABLE 7.1
Developmental Stages of ETV/ITV

	Major Drivers	Technical Aspect	Distribution/Service Aspect	Content Aspect
Introductory Stage	Political: Public service Technological: Arrival of cable distribution system Strategic: Experimental	Expensive set-top decoders Unreliable equipment Upstream data path problems	Early cable television system Equipment subsidization	Public services such as health info Textual, participatory content Low-quality interactive original program
Videotex Stage	Strategic: franchising advantage for cable, Very limited market exposure	Less high-end but still expensive equipment Costly content service maintenance	Cable television systems Videotex, teletext-like services	Home banking, shopping, information/education services (text and graphics only)
Cooperative Exploration Stage	Strategic: market definition, Competitive cooperation	Expensive two-way service and set-top boxes Network upgrade	Telephone networks Cable television systems	Limited original content Movies-on-demand (trials) Educational programming (trials)
Revolutionary Trial Stage	Technological: Digitization, computing, and arrival of the Internet Strategic: Competitively explore all ITV services	Expensive terminals/set-top boxes and infrastructure	Telephone networks Cable television systems	Full service (Time Warner) Limited original content
Evolutionary Strategic Focus Stage	Technological: Broadband networks/high-speed Internet Strategic: Brand value enhancement, New revenue sources	More affordable set-top boxes More bandwidth Better infrastructure Gradual upgrade when financially feasible	DBS and cable television systems Broadband telecoms	VOD DVR

educational programs for children. TCI, AT&T, and US West introduced a movies-on-demand service. TCI and Viacom even formed an alliance to lay fiber-optic lines linking cable systems to serve as a basis for interactive services. In a sense, this stage is marked by the introduction of competitive behavior regarding ETV and market efforts (e.g., trials and alliances) to define ETV services.

As television entered the mid-1990s, in addition to the two interactive television full services, Interactive Network and Videoway, which were in place in different regions of the country offering somewhat different services, many trials were conducted by cable television systems such as Time Warner, computer firms such as IBM, and telcos such as BellSouth and US West. The focus was to explore the most desirable service packages. Nevertheless, nearly all trials were either scaled back or canceled because of cost concerns over equipment and content development. Amid the arrival of compression, digitization, and early online technologies in the late 1990s, the approach at this stage was revolutionary in nature with various players aiming to be the first comer to find the holy grail of ETV that would transform traditional television services.

Cautioned by the dismissal of previous trials because of laggard consumer demand and high costs, both telcos and cable television systems decided to switch to an evolutionary approach to ETV ventures. Under this strategy, the wannabe ETV players such as cable MSOs and telcos began to focus on developing simpler services with less costly technology, waiting for consumer demand to pick up, and investing in the necessary infrastructure only when the upgrade made financial sense considering these firms' other offerings (Carey, 1997). In summary, the business of ETV today is in a stage characterized by careful cost–benefit analyses and step-by-step rollout of services in a much more matured network environment with less expensive set-top devices. Strategically, ETV is no longer a pure revenue-generating potential but also a tool to enhance the brand value of a conglomerate ETV provider.

ETV DRIVERS, VENTURES, AND THEIR STRATEGIC IMPLICATIONS

While ETV ventures offer a potential for additional revenues from new consumer services and interactive advertising, research has also shown that viewers who interact with ETV programs spent more time watching the programs, paid more attention to and had better brand recall of the commercials, and in general reported having a better viewing experience than with traditional passive viewing (McClellan, 2003). Such a positive effect on consumer attitude, perception, and behavior has significant strategic implications in an already competitive media marketplace. Though most media firms would consider the goal of generating more revenues and/or creating intangible competitive advantages through ETV ventures worthy of investment considerations, not all would engage in the adoption of these new media services. For those choosing to appropriate their resources in this type of new-product development, not all would invest with the same intensity. Treating the implementation of ETV ventures as firm adoptions of new media technologies, we now review the factors that play a role in impacting the adoption and timing of such strategies.

Factors Influencing ETV Ventures

Figure 7.1 depicts the factors that we proposed to affect the ETV venture decisions of media firms. There are core, supporting, and environmental features with various degrees of influence on a firm's decision whether, when, and how much to invest in an ETV venture.

The first set of factors includes the collective qualities of an organization. Similar to personality trait factors that influence individual predispositions toward innovativeness, novelty, venturesomeness, and risk,

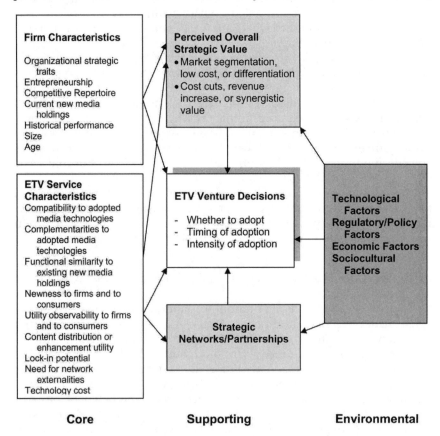

| Core | Supporting | Environmental |

FIG. 7.1. Factors that affect media firms' ETV venture decisions.

we believe that two sets of media firm characteristics—organizational strategic traits (which describe a firm's strategic tendency toward a new-media product/market) and degree of entrepreneurship (which depicts a firm's attitude toward opportunities and risks)—play a role in the decision to implement ETV ventures. We can evaluate a firm's strategic predisposition using a strategy profile taxonomy such as Miles and Snow's (1978) typology of firms: (a) prospectors that continuously seek and exploit new products and market opportunities and are often the first to market with a new product or service; (b) defenders that focus on occupying a market segment to develop a stable set of products and customers; (c) analyzers that have an intermediate position between prospectors and defenders by cautiously observing and following the prospectors, while at the same time monitoring and protecting a stable set of products and customers; and (d) reactors that do not have a consistent product–market orientation but act or respond to competition with a more short-term focus (Zahra & Pearce, 1990). Such an organizational strategic taxonomy can be applied effectively to assess how firms with different strategic predispositions approach ETV ventures. Another firm predisposition, degree of entrepreneurship, including a firm's proactiveness, autonomy, innovativeness, risk-taking propensity, and competitive aggressiveness, is also likely to affect propensity to invest in new media services such as ETV ventures.

It is our assertion that a media firm's past competitive market decisions (i.e., competitive repertoires) and current new-media holdings would also serve as indicators of the firm's predisposition to implement an ETV venture because the it might acquire experience that helps its future adoption decision-making process. As for the factor of historical performance, past output records are indicative of the resources a firm has available for commercializing a new ETV technology. They also point to possible directions or areas that a firm needs to enhance. Finally, the firm characteristics of size and age present the fundamental attributes of a firm in terms of its available resources and experience for implementing ETV ventures.

Besides firm characteristics, the nature of a new ETV service is likely to play an instrumental role in determining a media firm's decision regarding such a venture. Factors like the ETV service's technological compatibility, complementarities, and functional similarity to current media products that the firm offers; newness; utility observability; efficiency; content distribution or enhancement utility; lock-in potential; the need for network externalities; and technology cost are likely to shape if and how a venture will be implemented.

Specifically, the value of a new ETV service can be first assessed by the degree of disruptiveness of its integration into the existing organization. A good gauge here would be the degree of its compatibility to currently adopted media technologies. Taking a step further, complementarities refer to situations where a bundle of goods together provides more value than consuming the goods separately (Brandenburger & Nalebuff,

1996). In other words, the degree of complementarity provides insight on how a new product might add value to an organization. The last concept, functional similarity (i.e., how a new media service is perceived by consumers as being able to satisfy needs similar to those currently being fulfilled by an existing service), indicates the new product's degree of substitutability as perceived by consumers. Logically, a media firm's assessment of this substitutability will affect its new ETV plans. A new ETV service can also be examined by analyzing its degree of newness to the firm, newness to the market, or a combination thereof (Kotabe & Swan, 1995). Logically, the newer the related technology, the greater the uncertainty and the more hesitant a firm will be to invest in the technology. Furthermore, a media firm's ETV decisions are also likely to be affected by the apparent utility displayed by the anticipated service and the potential for the new service to in some way improve the delivery of a content product or enhance the appeal of a content product.

Lock-in refers to the ability of a service to create strong incentives for repeat transactions, thus preventing the migration of customers to competitors (Amit & Zott, 2001). A new ETV service that requires more upfront equipment investment by a consumer is likely to achieve a higher probability of lock-in and is typically regarded as more valuable. Another service characteristic, network externality, is a change in the benefit or consumer surplus that consumers derive from a product when more consumers purchase the product. Network externality might be a significant factor for many interactive services such as gaming and polling. Finally, the technology cost factor certainly affects a media firm's desire to adopt a new ETV service. In fact, because of the uncertainty of returns for new media services, even firms with sufficient resources might choose not to adopt a particular ETV venture if it is too costly.

Besides the two core characteristics, two supporting sets of factors also impact how a media firm might consider an ETV venture. The availability of strategic networks are important because they can provide a firm with access to information, resources, markets, technologies, credibility, and legitimacy (Cooper, 2002; Gulati, Nohria, & Zaheer, 2000). This is especially important for many ETV ventures, which often demand more resources and carry higher risks. For established media corporations, the benefit might be access to technologies and learning and sharing of information. Alliances or strategic networks are especially important for smaller innovative firms because such partnerships offer access to financial and marketing resources and economies of scale and scope. The value of a new ETV service can also be assessed by examining its perceived contribution to a firm's overall strategic posture. Porter (1980) suggested that there are three major strategic approaches: market segmentation, low cost, and differentiation. Depending on a media firm's strategic goal at the time of consideration, certain ventures might provide more utility in accomplishing one objective over others. Thus, the value of a new ETV service might be evaluated by analyzing how it helps a media firm reduce costs, increase revenue, and/or create synergistic advantage. Finally, environmental conditions such as technological, economic, sociocultural, and regulatory factors all affect a firm's ETV venture decisions.

It is important to note that the decision to offer an ETV service or enter an ETV venture involves multiple levels of decisions. Although the first level of a decision would be whether to adopt a new ETV service, there are also questions of timing and intensity. Timing of a business decision toward a new technology is often a strategic game of waiting for more information. In fact, the value of the wait might be proportional to the fixed adoption costs, potential reversal expenses, and the likelihood that the new technology will be unprofitable (Dong & Saha, 1998). The choice of timing is further complicated by the decision of intensity. As indicated earlier in the discussion of ETV development, many cable MSOs have chosen to approach ETV ventures with a lower, but more focused intensity after previous failed trials.

ETV Ventures and Their Strategic Implications

Many business ventures have been proposed and/or implemented to enhance consumers' television experience. From the perspective of their strategic contributions to a firm, they can be either revenue or brand value oriented. With a goal to generate additional revenues, ETV ventures may include on-demand programming, enhanced advertising, and television commerce (t-commerce). On the other hand, with a goal to enhance a consumer's television experience, thus adding value to a brand through increased audience loyalty, ETV ventures may include an electronic programming guide (EPG), a communication mechanism, and digital video recorders (DVRs). Some news, information, sports, and gaming ETV applications might even offer both benefits, depending on the degree of consumer demand and the nature of product offerings. In fact, the growth in broadband networks and decline in ETV equipment cost have accelerated the implementation of ETV infrastructures. It was estimated that ETV would be in 55 million households by 2006. The revenue potential was said to be up to $3.9 billion in t-commerce, $2.6 billion in interactive advertising, and $5 billion in ETV subscription by 2005 (Macklin, 2002). The following section reviews the ETV applications adopted by media firms in recent years and scrutinizes their strategic value for the firms.

Electronic Program Guide (EPG) or Interactive Program Guide (IPG).
A most basic form of ETV, EPG or IPG is an application used with digital set-top boxes and newer television sets to list current and scheduled programs that are or will be available on each channel and a short summary or commentary for each program. Assessed by a remote control device, a typical EPG or IPG includes options to set parental controls, or-

der pay-per-view programming, search for programs based on theme or category, and set up a video cassette or digital video recorder (VCR/DVR) to record programs. It is typically an important aspect of DTV service and is now built into a variety of consumer electronics devices, including digital TV sets and personal/digital video recorders (PVR/DVR). The EPG/IPG market is expected to grow at a compound annual growth rate of about 37% to a projected revenue of nearly $1 billion by 2008, with Gemstar-TV Guide, Microsoft, and Tribune Media Services dominating the market (Kerner, 2004).

While technology has been the main driving force for the early introduction of EPG, the smooth incorporation of this function into many existing television platforms made it the most widely used ETV feature. Because of the textual, informational nature of EPG content, the resources and degree of strategic entrepreneurship required from a firm to implement it is minimal. Though EPG does not really directly generate revenues, it has the potential to deliver brand awareness and serves as a tool for building brand images (see Table 7.2).

Television Commerce (T-Commerce)

Although definitions of t-commerce have sometimes included orders received via toll-free phone numbers for television offers, in the context of this chapter, we are concerned with the more advanced types of t-commerce: (a) transactions conducted by "clicking through" with the TV remote control or (b) offers presented on television and completed with an actual transaction on a PC Web page. T-commerce is basically e-commerce in a television environment. Ideally, t-commerce has the advantages of being placed in a comfortable home setting, garnering consumer attention through more involved content presentations, and building relationships while cutting costs. However, t-commerce is still expensive and might siphon away sales from existing sales channels, thereby adding to the cost of operations without increasing total revenues.

An industry study found that 46% of consumers are interested in t-commerce, but interest levels vary greatly among different applications. For instance, whereas 53% of consumers are interested in printing product information or coupons from their TV set, only 33% are interested in ordering restaurant meals for immediate delivery. The study also found that the most likely users for t-commerce services include premium cable and DBS subscribers, active online shoppers, and frequent customers of home shopping channels (Pastore, 2000). A Gallup-led survey found that household goods, appliances, and furniture were the most popular types of items that people wanted to purchase via t-commerce, followed by cosmetics and toiletries; clothes, movie, theater, or concert tickets; and CDs and videos. Age also plays a role in the t-commerce purchase pattern. Forty-two percent of respondents over age 50 expressed an interest in purchasing items via ETV, whereas

TABLE 7.2
Analysis of ETV Ventures

	Major Environmental Driver and Competency	Resource Requirement	Degree of Strategic Entrepreneurship	Brand Equity–Building Potential	Revenue Potential
EPG/IPG	• Technological • Operations	Low	Low	High	Low
T-commerce	• Economic • Operations • Strategic network	Medium	High	Low	High
VOD/SVOD	• Consumer preferences • Marketing • Strategic network	Medium	Medium	Medium	High
DVR/PVR	• Consumer preferences • Operations	Low	Low	High	Medium
Interactive Programming	• Consumer preferences • Strategic network • R&D • Operations	High	High	High	Low
Betting & Gaming	• Political/regulatory • Strategic network	High (Lower with alliances)	High	Medium	High
Communication	• Consumer preferences • Operations	Medium	Low	High	Low
Banking & More	• Strategic network	High (Low with alliances)	High	Low	Low
Enhanced Advertising	• Economic • Consumer preferences • R&D (Creativity)	High	High	High	High

only 25% of those between ages 18 and 34 expressed an interest in this service (Pastore, 2001). More consumer studies found that the majority of people prefer to have t-commerce transactions billed to their monthly MVPD statements, and consumers who use the Internet on PC and TV simultaneously have different levels of interest and price sensitivity for most t-commerce applications than consumers who engage in both activities separately (ClickZ Network, 2001).

The main drivers and competencies required for t-commerce include economy, efficient operations, and a strategic network with merchandise suppliers and/or fulfillment firms. Because of the new set of skills and knowledge necessary to carry out such ventures, it also requires a higher degree of entrepreneurship and resources. T-commerce could bring strong revenue potential. Nevertheless, its success is dependent on its ability to differentiate from the more established PC-based e-commerce by the type of products offered and target groups (e.g. the aforementioned likely users) as well as customer service (e.g., billing) implementations.

On-Demand Programming. On-demand programming generally involves either VOD or subscription video on demand (SVOD). VOD is a service that enables viewers to order and watch content on demand and to pause, rewind, and fast-forward the content. It is different from pay-per-view in that it allows "anytime" flexibility, whereas PPV is consumed at preset times. Thus, the audience has total control over the timing of the viewing and is able to pay on a per-event basis. An SVOD service offers a library of events typically from premium channel providers and is accessed from either a channel-based menu or the program guide. SVOD services also do not price on a per-title basis. With a subscription, viewers pay a flat fee to download all the on-demand content they want, as many times as they wish, rather than having to pay for each viewing. Industry studies have shown that consumers tend to prefer flat or stable pricing and MVPD programmers can readily repackage content and bundle on-demand services with basic or premium cable offerings, providing a tangible incentive for TV consumers and lucrative revenue potentials for MVPD firms. In fact, VOD and PVRs have been identified as the most appealing of all ETV features (Pastore, 2001). The benefits of consumer control and convenience seem to be the key drivers of adoption. On-demand programming is especially popular among younger demographics. An industry survey found "order movies on demand" to be the most popular ETV activity, preferred by over 33% of those between ages 18 and 34 (Pastore, 2001).

VOD/SVOD is comparatively the ETV service that offers the most potential with the most conservative entrepreneur quality and resource requirement. Its key to success is in understanding consumer preferences, forming alliances with content providers, and instituting effective marketing programs to promote on-demand programs. It is worth noting that while VOD/SVOD provides a concrete new revenue source, it can also be packaged and marketed in a way to enhance a desirable brand image.

Digital Video Recorder (DVR) or Personal Digital Recorder (PVR).
DVR or PVR is a device that records TV programs to a hard disk in digital format that also allows for "trick modes" such as pausing live TV, instant replay of interesting scenes, and skipping commercials. The most popular stand-alone DVRs on the market are TiVo and ReplayTV. Newer entrants into the market include products such as Digeo's Moxi and Microsoft's UltimateTV. Many satellite and cable companies also incorporate PVR functions into their set-top boxes. The Yankee Group estimated that by 2007, nearly one fifth of all U.S. homes will have access to DVR (Greenspan, 2003). The optimistic growth rates might be attributed to cable operators bundling of DVR software into their set-top boxes and the falling prices of stand-alone DVRs.

An industry study found that DVR users actively delayed watching a TV show so that they can either skip ads or save time. In essence, DVRs are used to enhance audiences' viewing experience and to accommodate their busy schedules. In fact, DVR owners reported higher television satisfaction rates and even more viewing time (Greenspan, 2004). From an advertiser's perspective, DVRs have posed a significant a challenge because of the audience's tendency to skip ads. To counter this problem, some advertisers have resorted to certain marketing tactics such as brand integration (i.e., product placement) and entertaining short films with commercial messages. For example, Best Buy sponsored a short film on TiVo to reinforce its entertainment brand image (Morrissey, 2003).

It is our assertion that the consumer's lifestyle strongly drives the development of DVR. This type of ETV venture, while offering a good potential for building brand equity and generating some revenues, does not call for a high commitment of resources or entrepreneurship, thus presenting another attractive ETV business opportunity, especially for MVPD service providers.

Interactive Programming. Interactive programming here is referred to as a television program that enables broadcasters, cablecasters, and other content providers to engage viewers actively by enhancing the content on multiple levels so that it creates a more engaging, personalized experience for viewers. The services can include providing more information about the content a viewer is watching, allowing him or her to voice opinions through online voting, letting him or her choose how a content is presented, and enabling him or her to play games relevant to the content, thus providing consumers a richer, more involved viewing experience.

In reality, such an interactive programming is mostly accomplished either by the single-screen (push channel) approach, which lets a viewer interact directly with television through a digital cable or satellite set-top box that drives interactive Internet content as an overlay on part of the TV screen, or by the two-screen (pull channel) approach, which basically combines the passive experience of TV while adding interactivity through the online medium on a PC with synchronized material. For example, ABC sports fans use their set-top boxes to scroll through real-time stats, participate in polling, access the scores of other games, and obtain more information about different teams in a Bowl Championship Series in 2003 (Rodgers, 2003). World Wrestling Entertainment (WWE) has incorporated synchronized TV–Web content to increase its pay-per-view viewer involvement. It was suggested that when a more engaging entertainment element such as extra humorous footage or games is added, the new viewing experience is likely to change the fundamentals of brand consideration and likeability measures (Grimshaw, 2004). Many industry analysts have concluded that sports programming seems to provide the best avenue for interactivity (Rodgers, 2003). In fact, according to many ETV users, multiple camera angles for sports events is one of the most attractive interactive applications, along with additional programming information (Whitney, 2004).

It is our assertion that interactive programming provides a limited revenue potential because of the passive nature of television viewing. Although some interactive contents (e.g., sports) are attractive to many viewers, only a limited number of people will be willing to use and pay for the enhancement. It is more likely for a firm to use interactive features to increase audience involvement and enrich a viewer's television experience, thus solidifying the value of its brand. However, because of the needs to develop strategic networks with content providers and hardware/software facilitators and to invest in researching consumer preferences, there is a higher degree of required resources and entrepreneur mindset.

Betting and Gaming.   Online gaming has become more popular as the deployment of broadband networks expanded. As ETV continues to explore the so-called "killer app" in generating revenues to sustain ETV ventures, betting or gaming through television, the center of entertainment in the home, is also getting noticed. In an ETV gaming environment, a viewer may play along with a game show, participate in contests linked to a popular show that he or she regularly watches (the viewers might be charged a small fee to participate with the incentive of winning prizes), or place bets during a sports event. It was suggested that ETV will overtake the PC as the platform of choice for casual gaming and it will be imperative that games industry firms focus their strategy on this sector of the market (Pastore, 2001). An industry report has predicted that ETV gaming in Europe and the United States will generate revenues of almost $2.7 billion by 2006 (Pastore, 2001).

Whereas online and ETV gaming is generally more popular in Europe, the Game Show Network (GSN), a U.S. industry leader in interactivity, features 84 hours per week of interactive programming that allows viewers a chance to win prizes by playing along with GSN's televised games via GSN.com. GSN is jointly owned by Sony Pictures Entertainment and Liberty Media Corporation and distributed via MVPD services. Another potential major ETV gaming player is DirecTV because its new owner, News Corp., has extensive experience with BSkyB in the U.K., whose most popular ETV feature is gambling on sporting events.

Betting and gaming ETV ventures would be heavily driven by the strategic networks ETV services and gaming content providers are able to form because of the resources needed and traditional television firms' lack of experience in this area. While some form of gaming would be able to enhance the degree of audience involvement with certain programs, betting and gaming ventures on the television platform might be able to generate significant revenues. Nevertheless, it is also limited by state gaming regulations.

Communications, Banking, Financial Services, and Other Auxiliary Services.   The communication function is another important ETV application that is often integrated with other ETV services. For example, to create a sense of community, there are often interactive chat opportunities for viewers of an ETV program (e.g., especially for sports programming). Services like AOLTV and MSNTV with set-top boxes also allow viewers to surf the Internet and use their e-mail on TV. Nevertheless, the e-mail and chat functions have not been cited as top ETV features consistently by most ETV industry surveys. The same situation holds true for other less TV-relevant ETV services such as banking and financial services. Whereas online banking has grown tremendously in recent years, financial management via television has seen limited interest in the United States, with most people unwilling to pay to access accounts, transfer funds, and pay bills with their TV remote controls.

E-mail and chatting ETV features are likely to enhance the brand value of a firm because of the opportunity to build relationships and user communities. Though it does not offer good revenue potential, it also does not require a tremendous amount of resource commitment. Note that the ETV communication feature is influenced greatly by consumer preferences for PC versus TV e-mail/chatting platforms. Currently, because of the established PC-based electronic communication pattern, e-mail or chatting via television is less likely to be widely used or to become an attractive selling point for ETV. As for banking and auxiliary services, it is our assertion that there are limited utilities for these types of ETV functions in building brand equity or generating revenues, and the resource and entrepreneurial requirements, as well as the need for forming strategic networks, are relatively high, thus making it a less popular ETV venture focus.

Enhanced Advertising.   The promise of interactivity has also meant the opportunity to revamp advertising and create greater accountability. Some have even claimed that the desire to make television and television ads interactive was a way of reaching into the direct marketing budget, which is usually much bigger than advertising (Rodgers, 2003). The interactivity offered by ETV has spurred the introduction of many enhanced advertising formats on TV, including targeted advertising that enables advertisers to personalize ads with messages that are relevant to the specific group of consumers, direct-response/addressable advertising, sponsorship of ETV content, product placement in ETV programming, ads that are integrated into the program, ad-sponsored VOD, which is similar to the PBS model with a sponsorship message and commercials appearing at the beginning and the end of the program, and long-form commercials. For example, whereas Chase, Remax, and Pfizer tried the ad-sponsored VOD method, Ford Motor Co. carried a sole sponsorship of the entire interactive portion of ABC's Bowl Championship Series in 2003 as part of a multiplatform ad campaign to drive brand retention by getting people to interact with the content (McClellan, 2003). Most have cited that the biggest obstacle to advertising in an ETV environment is its lack of consistent measurement, the challenge of format variance, and support from the creative community (Grimshaw, 2004). Nevertheless, Jupiter Research estimates that ETV advertising will reach $2.3 billion by 2007, representing a 39 times per-household jump from 2003 (Grimshaws, 2004).

Enhanced advertising, though challenging to implement, holds tremendous potential for generating more revenues for ETV service providers and adding value to advertised brands. When interactive material simply provides information or entertainment, it is likely that the experience facilitates a viewer's involvement with the brand message, but when the ETV advertising feature also collects user information, it enhances the overall branding program. To utilize the new interactive platform successfully for advertising, however, means a commitment of resources and necessary entrepreneur mindset.

MAJOR MEDIA CORPORATIONS' ENHANCED TV VENTURES

Beginning with Time Warner in the early days of ETV, most major media corporations have tested the interactive water with various trials. Whereas cablecasters have concentrated on marketing VOD/SVOD and DVR, the recent acquisition of DirecTV by News Corp. may change the dynamics of ETV competition because News Corp. has acquired tremendous knowledge-based resources from its experience marketing the successful BSkyB DBS service in the U.K. To assess the recent trends of leading media firms' ETV adoption strategies, the following section examines the ETV ventures of major media corporations that have top broadcasting and/or MVPD holdings.

Time Warner

As the number one media conglomerate in the world, Time Warner has been actively searching for the right ETV mix for 30 years. AOLTV has been Time Warner's answer for Web-based ETV applications, whereas its cable system is the base for TV-platform ETV services such as VOD and SVOD. Because of its leading position in both the online and MVPD sector, Time Warner seems to have adopted a strategy of developing ETV services for both cable TV and broadband systems. To ensure access to content, it also has partnered with Universal Studios, Sony Pictures, MGM, and Paramount Pictures to create an on-demand movie service. To accelerate the introduction of digital entertainment at home, Time Warner also allied with the home network manufacturer D-Link to develop and deliver products and services that will allow broadband consumers to access secure high-quality VOD anywhere at home. Comcast and Time Warner, the two leading MSOs, in an attempt to enable applications to be portable and interoperable across all cable networks, formed a joint venture to create an OpenCable Applications Platform (OCAP) middleware implementation. Time Warner also utilizes its ETV venture to cross-promote its broadcast brands; for example, AOLTV offers previews of popular WB network programming. Overall, the focus of Time Warner's ETV investment has been on DVR and VOD via the cable platform and AOLTV via the broadband platform.

News Corp.

News Corp. has become a formidable player in the ETV arena with its acquisition of DirecTV, aggressive use of vertically integrated properties, and alliances with technology firms. For example, through its subsidiary, NDS, News Corp. has allied with Microsoft to develop ETV software for MVPD network operators. The relationship between Microsoft and News Corp. extends to another alliance for DirecTV to promote UltimateTV. News Corp. also strategically utilizes its vertically integrated assets as it decided to drop a popular set-top box middleware from OpenTV and adopted one that uses the technologies developed by its subsidiary, NDS (Kerschbaumer, 2004). To secure a position in content delivery, News Corp. and Disney even established a joint broadband entertainment service called Movies.com to provide movies and other entertainment content on demand to consumers in the United States. News Corp. has also enhanced its *NFL Sunday Ticket* programming with advanced interactive features like the ability to watch one game and see real-time scores, yet be alerted when teams playing in other games are in scoring positions. Another new feature is "Highlights on Demand," allowing subscribers with a DirecTV DVR or HD (high-definition) DVR receiver to view highlights of all *NFL Sunday Ticket* games delivered automatically to their DirecTV DVR.

Comcast

Comcast has also been active in the ETV arena through acquisitions of technologies and content development. It invested in SeaChange International Inc. to develop streaming media and interactive television and launched G4, a 24-hour television network dedicated to electronic games with original programming. Its recent acquisition of TechTV Inc., a network that showcases highly interactive factual and late-night programming (to be merged with G4), demonstrates its focus on gaming ETV ventures. To secure its position in providing on-demand programming, Comcast and Starz Encore Group, the largest provider of premium movie services in the United States, partnered to launch Starz On Demand on Comcast's cable systems. To expand its VOD market, Comcast added content from selected Viacom networks such as MTV, BET, Nickelodeon, Noggin, and The N to its ON DEMAND service at no extra charge for Comcast Digital Cable customers. Comcast also partnered with Disney in creating the Comcast Kids Channel, an interactive environment designed for broadband users with premier content from Disney Online, and with Gemstar-TV Guide International for a joint venture to develop EPG for its cable systems. Overall, Comcast is combining its existing ON DEMAND service with the heavily marketed DVR to deliver convenience and value for its Digital Cable, whereas it uses alliances and acquisitions to expand into other ETV services.

Disney

Utilizing its popular sports and game show programming such as college football and *Who Wants to Be a Millionaire*, Disney's ABC has marketed its ETV with both one- and two-screen systems. Disney collaborated with Microsoft to improve the quality and security of digital content, from movie clips to full-length feature films, which can be delivered to homes over the Internet. Because of the lack of a broadband distribution property, Disney has largely been exploring partnerships that could result in a deal to include the service in set-top boxes, computers, or other devices. Overall, ABC has been one of the most aggressive broadcasters to explore ETV applications (Whitney, 2004).

NBC Universal

By comparison, NBC Universal has been a less active ETV player. Besides Universal Studio's alliance with Time Warner for an on-demand movie service, NBC Universal relies on partnered business units like MSNBC.com for ETV ventures. MSNBC.com offers free exclusive news programming from NBC News on MSN Video and helped develop the new service with MSN. Users can view breaking news and top-story videos on demand with the ability to build playlists free of charge. MSNBC.com produces nearly 60 video clips per day including programming from *NBC Nightly News* and the *Today Show* as well as video from CNBC and MSNBC TV. Again, without a distribution system property, NBC Universal has focused on developing ETV content via strategic networks.

Cox Enterprises

One of the top MSOs, Cox Communications has ventured into the realm of ad-supported VOD called FreeZone for digital cable subscribers. The advertising platform also includes permission-based follow-up interaction between viewers and advertisers. Actively pursuing DVR and VOD services, Cox has also entered agreements with various tech firms such as Liberate Technologies, a leading provider of software for digital cable systems, and Harmonic Inc., a digital video and optical network firm, to enhance its Entertainment on Demand branded VOD service. These deployments reflect its emphasis on delivering user-controlled on-demand services, along with a strategy of exploring interactive advertising potentials.

EchoStar

EchoStar, the owner of DISH Network, also sought strategic networks with technology firms as it formed a joint venture with OpenTV, a provider of ETV software, to offer interactive set-top boxes. To beef up its VOD investment, it entered an agreement with Telecommunication Products Inc., a provider of VOD services, and BBC America for its content products. DISH Network also introduced "DISH Home," which includes four ETV services: movie reviews from Zap2it Entertainment Features, games from Playin'TV, Horoscope, and DISH Network Customer Support. To further expand into the gaming arena, EchoStar partnered with Buzztime Entertainment Inc. to launch an interactive trivia multiplayer game service on its DISH Network and later with Silverstar Holdings for its Fantasy Cup Auto Racing content. In an attempt to be present in both wired and wireless broadband networks, EchoStar allied with SBC Communications, the nation's second-largest phone company, to create a television set-top box that allows consumers to download movies over SBC's high-speed Internet network.

Charter Communications

Charter Communications is one of the most active MSO ETV providers. It actually deployed the first multiple interactive services by integrating Wink's Enhanced Broadcasting product with DIVA's VOD technology, which brings Charter's Digital Cable customers access to product information, on-demand news, coupons, and shopping on more than 20 digital channels. Charter also partnered with Starz Encore Group for SVOD on Charter Digital. Continuing to focus on more than DVR and VOD, Charter allied with Digeo, "The Interactive TV Company," in launching an ETV service that gives customers quick access to six virtual "i-channels" of news, weather, sports, entertainment, money, and shopping information. Charter and Digeo also introduced an interactive television channel dedicated exclusively to games. Called i-Games, the new channel features games that viewers play simply by using their remotes. Finally, Charter joined with QVC in a partnership for an ETV shopping application, the first real-time two-way ETV shopping option on a television channel in the United States.

Cablevision

Cablevision Systems Corp. and American Express Publishing formed an editorial, marketing, and advertising alliance to jointly develop and market VOD content. It also partnered with FOX Entertainment Group to provide Cablevision's iO: Interactive Optimum digital VOD access to certain Fox programming. Cablevision's ETV services include traffic, weather, games, varying camera angles for sports, and an interactive portal as well as the industry's first interactive subscription games package and play-for-fun casino games. With a special focus on gaming, Cablevision continued to partner with Zodiac Gaming, a leading developer of advanced interactive games for digital set-top boxes, doubling the number of interactive games available to all iO customers.

A STRATEGIC ARCHITECTURE OF THE ENHANCED TELEVISION MARKET

The aforementioned ETV ventures and their strategic implications clearly depict a complex value system of various stages and firms. To provide a framework that illustrates the value adding process and the dynamic relationships between firms at different stages, we propose a strategic architecture of the ETV market. The term *strategic architecture* is typically described by organizational or information systems management scholars as a notion of creating an infrastructure that provides the functional foundation of an enterprise or information system (King, 1995; Nadler & Gerstein, 1992; Nadler & Tushman, 1999). In this chapter, strategic architecture is used as a metaphor that likens the design of social systems such as an industry to the design of physical artifacts such as a building. Just as architecture is the infrastructure that shapes physical space to meet human needs, the strategic architecture of ETV is the basic structure that shapes a firm's behavior space in carrying out their strategic objectives in this market.

Figure 7.2 depicts the proposed strategic architecture, which is composed of two different infrastructures, the telephone (wire-line or wireless) and multichannel system (wire-line or wireless). We treat these two distribution systems separately because of our belief that converging activities such as telcos' investment in the cable sector and cable's offering of cable telephony are means of enhancement rather than replacement of their current core products (i.e., we subscribe to a confluence rather than convergence view). Note that the distinction between the telephone and MVPD platforms will not be a source of product differentiation in the ETV market because rarely is the distribution method of signals a major concern of consumers, assuming that there are no significant technical differences (e.g., speed, capacity, and security) between the two infrastructures in the long run.

As shown, there are three groups of content creators that produce ETV products with various degrees of interactivity components. The

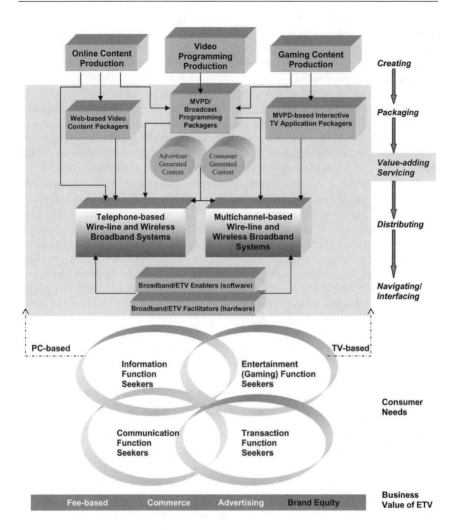

FIG. 7.2.   Strategic architecture of an enhanced television market.

online-content producers are most likely to provide textual and graphic informational content or shorter versions of entertainment video products, whereas the video-programming producers might offer longer-form content such as movies and traditional television programming. The gaming content creators such as Zodiac Gaming, on the other hand, present stand-alone or programming-linked interactive games. There are also three types of packagers: (a) Web-based video content packagers that offer mostly PC-based online television like MSNTV and AOLTV, (b) MVPD/broadcast programming packagers that assemble digital television programming services such as CNN, HBO, and ABC, and (c) MVPD-based ETV application packagers that put together ETV services such as Starz On-Demand. Because of the nature of ETV services, which often involve participant communication, polling, or gaming, ETV subscribers also generate part of the content, in addition to another type of content from interactive advertisers. The next group of market participants, the value-adding services, performs supporting functions to all players in the market. Value-adding services might include interactive advertising agencies, audience research services, and firms that carry out branding or t-commerce support functions.

The most visible firms in the ETV market are the distributors such as the MSOs, DBSs, and telcos. These companies hold the key to introducing, marketing, and managing ETV services to fulfill the different consumer needs for information, transaction, entertainment, and/or communication. The final group of ETV firms, the hardware facilitators like Scientific-Atlanta and Pioneer and software enablers like OpenTV and Microsoft, play an indirect but crucial role in the consumer adoption of ETV services through their design of navigating/interfacing software and equipment. A distributor's success in this market is strongly influenced by its relationships with these facilitators, especially in areas of cost management, negotiation, and sharing of consumer knowledge. The role of these facilitators, we believe, would become even more critical when most ETV functionality migrates to digital television sets or more sophisticated set-top boxes. In this scenario, the packagers' strategic role might diminish, whereas the interfacing/navigating facilitators' role becomes more significant as consumers bypass the packagers and are directly connected with content providers because of these facilitators' products and services. It is evident that there are more and more alliances formed between MVPD service providers and ETV software firms in recent years. Finally, the end business value created by the ETV market system includes a combination of brand equity and revenues from sales of fee-based content, commerce/transactions, and/or advertising.

FINAL THOUGHTS

The MVPD service providers have approached ETV with various degrees of enthusiasm. Because of numerous failed trials since the early days of ETV technology, most have chosen to introduce ETV services gradually with a current focus on DVR and VOD, ventures that are likely to create revenue or at least branding potentials with relatively less commitment of resources and entrepreneur mindset. Nevertheless, DBS service providers and some leading MSOs such as Charter and Cablevision have recently picked up the speed of ETV implementation amid various aggressive alliances with ETV software/hardware firms. The pressure to invest might be due to competition brought about by News Corp.'s entry into the U.S. ETV market and technological advances that make interactivity more practical and simple. The ETV market is still very fluid considering the continuous evolution of interactive technologies and changing consumer preferences. It is likely that many ETV firms will revise their business models and explore new ways of adding value to the system. For example, as TiVo faces more competition from big media companies like Comcast and EchoStar, which are incorporating nearly identical software in their cable and satellite set-top boxes and giving it to customers for free, it has to reinvent itself to identify sources of competitive advantages other than the manipulation of programming from traditional television broadcasts. To do so, TiVo has recently negotiated an agreement with Netflix, a mail-based DVD rental service, for TiVo subscribers to download Netflix DVDs over the Internet directly into the TiVo boxes in their homes, instead of receiving them in the mail. It is our assertion that the evolution of ETV is likely to continue with a much faster speed than in its earlier days because of the more mature broadband delivery systems, the trend toward resource/risk-sharing strategic networks, the financially sound roll-out plan, and attention paid to the nature of consumer demand.

REFERENCES

Amit, R., & Zott, C. (2001). Value creation in e-business. *Strategic Management Journal, 22*(6/7), 493–520.

Brandenburger, A. M., & Nalebuff, B. J. (1996). *Co-operation.* New York: Doubleday.

Carey, J. (1997). Interactive television trials and marketplace experiences. *Multimedia Tools and Applications, 5*(2), 207–216.

ClickZ Network. (2001). Digital TV grabs 20 million subscribers in 2000. Retrieved October 10, 2004, from http://www.clickz.com/stats/sectors/hardware/article.php/700971

Constantakis-Valdez, P. (2004). Computers in television. Retrieved December 17, 2004, from http://www.museum.tv/archives/etv/C/htmlC/computersin/computersin.htm

Cooper, A. C. (2002). Network alliances, and entrepreneurship. In M. A. Hitt, R. D. Ireland, S. M. Camp, & D. L. Sexton (Eds.), *Strategic entrepreneurship: Creating a new mindset* (pp. 203–222). Oxford, England: Blackwell.

Dong, D., & Saha, A. (1998). He came, he saw, and he waited: An empirical analysis of inertia in technology adoption. *Applied Economics, 30*(7), 893–905.

Greenspan, R. (2003). *Remote power: Can PVRs kill TV spots?* Retrieved October 12, 2004, from http://www.internetnews.com/stats/article.php/3080851

Greenspan, R. (2004). *Marketing, features drive DVR growth.* Retrieved October 12, 2004, from http://www.clickz.com/stats/sectors/retailin/article.php/3324151

Grimshaw, C. (2004, September 15). Interactive TV eyes mainstream. *Marketing,* p. 19.

Gunter, B. (2003). Digital information provision via interactive television: Understanding the digital consumers. *Aslib Proceeding: New Information Perspectives, 55*(½), 43–51.

Gulati, R., Nohria, N., & Zaheer, A. (2000). Strategic networks. *Strategic Management Journal, 21*(3), 203–215.

Ha, L., & Chan-Olmsted, S. M. (2002). Consumers' use of enhanced TV features and interest in e-commerce on cable network web sites. *Electronic Markets: The International Journal of Electronic Commerce & Business Media, 12*(4), 422–440.

Kerner, S. M. (2004). *TV 2.0: HDTV, program guide and DVR outlook.* Retrieved October 10, 2004, from http://www.clickz.com/stats/sectors/hardware/print.php/3421201

Kerschbaumer, K. (2004, May 3). Ready for iTV's closeup. *Broadcasting & Cable, 134*(18), 86.

King, W. R. (1995). Creating a strategic capabilities architecture. *Information Systems Management, 12*(1), 67–69.

Kotabe, M., & Swan, K. S. (1995). The role of strategic alliances in high-technology new product development. *Strategic Management Journal, 16*(8), 621–636.

Macklin, B. (2002). *What every marketer needs to know about iTV.* eMarketer.Retrieved September 28, 2004, from http://banners.noticiasdot.com/termometro/boletines/docs/consultoras/emarketer/2002/emarketer_itv.pdf

Martin, C. (2002, August). Interactive television is here. *Broadcast Engineering, 44*(8), 66.

McClellan, S. (2003, September 15). Report: No more baby steps for interactive TV. *Broadcasting & Cable, 133*(37), 23.

Miles, R. E., & Snow, C. C. (1978). *Organizational strategy, structure, and process.* New York: McGraw-Hill.

Morrissey, B. (2003). *Best Buy sponsors film on TiVo.* Retrieved November 3, 2004, from http://www.clickz.com/news/article.php/1563681

Nadler, D. A., & Gerstein, M. S. (1992). What is organizational architecture? *Harvard Business Review, 70*(5), 120–121.

Nadler, D. A., & Tushman, M. L. (1999). The organization of future: Strategic imperatives and core competencies for the 21st century. *Organizational Dynamics, 28*(1), 45–60.

Pastore, M. (2000). Interactive TV market remains complex. Retrieved November 4, 2004, from http://www.clickz.com/stats/sectors/hardware/article.php/489511

Pastore, M. (2001). *Internet becoming preferred information source.* CyberAtlas. Retrieved November 3, 2004, from http://cyberatlas.internet.com/big_picture/demographics/article/0,1323,5901_762881,00.html

Porter, M. (1980). *Competitive strategy.* New York: The Free Press.

Ranger, P. (2004, September). Interactive TV. *Broadcast Engineering, 46*(9), 38.

Rodgers, Z. (2003). iTV and the converged broadcast. Retrieved November 3, 2004, from http://www.clickz.com/features/case_studies/article.php/3314121

Symposium on experiments in interactive cable TV. (1978). *Journal of Communication, 28*(2).

Vorderer, P., Knobloch, S., Schramm, H. (2001). Does entertainment suffer from interactivity? The impact of watching an interactive TV movie on viewers' experience of entertainment. *Media Psychology, 3*(4), 343–364.

Whitney, D. (2004, April 5). Interactive boom predicted for 2004. *Televisionweek, 23*(14), 24.

Zahra, S. A., & Pearce, J. (1990). Research evidence on the Miles–Snow typology. *Journal of Management, 16*(4), 751–768.

Chapter 8

Strategy and Competition in the Broadband Communications Market

It is evident from our previous discussions about ETV that many telephone companies have had an interwoven relationship with multichannel media firms because of the increasingly blurry market boundaries between different communications networks. No longer regarded as a medium that carries merely user-generated voice content, the telco-based broadband system is now considered one of the essential building blocks of future digital entertainment because its platform enables the delivery of digital videos with the personalization and on-demand nature of the Internet via telecommunications networks (Bratches & Rooney, 2001). In fact, as the two leading broadband service providers (BSPs), DSL from the telephone sector and cable modem from the MVPD market, continue to expand, we are witnessing a new phase of development for the television medium. Just as the introduction of MVPD television added the multichannel, narrowcasting capability to broadcast television, the arrival of the Internet and the broadband infrastructure brought more enhanced functions such as interactivity and personalization to MVPD television. Such an expansion of television functions and content varieties means more opportunities for product differentiation in the marketplace and thus more strategic options for the market participants, now including the telecommunications firms (e.g., telcos) with broadband products. Considering the significant role telcos play in today's digital media environment, in this chapter, we tackle the broadband communications aspect of the telephone industry and compare the strategic differences between these firms and their MVPD counterparts in the emerging broadband multimedia industry.

THE DEVELOPMENT OF AND COMPETITION
IN THE BROADBAND MARKET

Broadband communications are the convergence of television, telephone, and computer networks that enables the interactive communication of voice, data, and video (Sawyer, Allen, & Lee, 2003). Because the increasing demand for higher-bandwidth networks is largely due to the growth in Internet traffic, broadband is typically discussed in the context of high-speed Internet connections. Accordingly, we begin this chapter by reviewing the market development of DSL and cable modem broadband access services. Note that the focus here is not on the growth of enhanced multimedia contents such as VOD, gaming, and interactive advertising, which have been covered in the previous chapter, but on the different strategic approaches and competition between providers of broadband networks.

The modern deployment of broadband communications can be traced back to the unsuccessful introduction of the integrated services digital network (ISDN) in the 1980s. Although various network companies such as GTE and Time Warner attempted to launch high-speed, interactive connections to homes in the early 1990s, most have faltered. The well-publicized broadband service Excite@Home floundered regardless of the backing by leading MSOs. It was not until the widespread popularity of the Internet that the utility of broadband communications was highlighted. In fact, most asymmetric digital subscriber line (ADSL) trials from telcos such as GTE and Pacific Bell (now SBC) were not introduced until 1996. SBC was one of the most active telcos in deploying ADSL, with an aggressive pricing strategy, serving up to 8 million residential customers by 1999 ("SBC Tries to Knock," 1999). The rollout of broadband was even cited by SBC's proposed buyout of Ameritech as a main reason of the merger, noting that the combination would enhance the efficient introduction of broadband technology to homes and neighborhoods (Rohde, 1999).

As the United States entered the 2000s, the deployment of cable modem led the race among high-speed data services due, in large part, to the fact that cable operators rapidly upgraded their passive one-way networks to two-way hybrid fiber/coax (HFC) networks and the 1996 Telecommunications Act, which opened up the telephone market to competition. Comparatively, the telcos' DSL service was distance sensitive and not available to many phone customers too far from the central office at that time. In addition, many telcos, although experienced in providing Internet access through their traditional dial-up services, were initially reluctant to push DSL in fear of cannibalizing their older, higher-priced services such as T-1 data lines. As a result, cable system operators have had a head start in attracting broadband consumers, signing up almost four times as many subscribers at the initial stage of broadband development (FCC, 2004).

Nevertheless, telcos began to forge ahead with their DSL services by improving operational efficiencies, marketing, pricing, and service area coverage, gradually surpassing the speed and service satisfaction offered by cable (Greenspan, 2002). The waves of mergers between RBOCs also enhanced the resources and access to potential customers for leading telcos. For example, Verizon, after combing the assets of Bell Atlantic and GTE, and Qwest, after its acquisition of US West, were able to significantly boost their broadband offerings with aggressive pricing strategies (Greene, 2000; "Qwest Communications Offers," 2001; "Qwest Offers New Broadband," 2000). By 2004, DSL acquired a collective market share of 39% whereas cable reached 61% of the market (wire-line only) (see Table 8.1). In fact, more than half of the at-home Internet connections were broadband by year 2004, largely fueled by the growth of DSL services (Greenspan, 2004; Horrigan, 2004a). Overall, 34% of all adult Americans had access to high-speed Internet connections either at home or at work by the spring of 2004, a 60% increase from the year before (Horrigan, 2004a). With a 58% broadband penetration rate in the spring of 2005, it was estimated that broadband connection for home users would break 80% by the fall of 2006 ("May 2005 Bandwidth Report," 2005). Most analysts believe that cable will continue to lead the U.S. residential broadband market with DSL remaining a formidable competitor (Greenspan, 2002; Leichtman Research Groups, 2004).

Table 8.1 depicts the state of competition between the top MSOs and telcos in terms of their perspective market shares in the broadband market in 2004. Whereas the top four cable firms commanded almost 45% of the market, their telephone counterpart had about 33% of the market. The top MSO, Comcast, and the top telco, SBC, were the most significant broadband market leaders, together controlling one third of all broadband subscriptions. Time Warner and Verizon are the other two noteworthy broadband players with a combined share of almost 22%. Overall, the top broadband services listed in Table 8.1 reached 95% of all subscribers. The CR4 in 2004 for this market is 55.7 and CR8 is 77.5. According to Shepherd (1987), a CR4 between 40 and 60 identifies an industry with firm concentrations optimal for competitive behavior. Scherer and Ross (1990) also reported findings that the optimal CR8 for a competitive industry is 70 (which roughly corresponds to a CR4 of 50 in the U.S. economy). According to these rules of thumb, the broadband communications market is relatively competitive with leading firms from both the cable and telephone sectors.

We believe that the race between cable and DSL is likely to stay competitive and become even more strategic while the growth rate tapers off. As an emerging industry, the broadband market exhibits the characteristics of technological uncertainty; high initial costs; entry barriers such as access to distribution channels, and input, and materials; and cost advantages due to experience (Hitt, Ireland, & Hoskisson, 2001; Porter, 1980). Consequently, market activities such as strategic alliances are becoming more critical as the broadband firms attempt to minimize

TABLE 8.1
Top Broadband Service Providers and Their Market Shares in 2004

Broadband Service Provider	No. of Subscribers	% of Market
Cable Firms		
Comcast[a]	6,005,000	19.9
Time Warner	3,548,000	11.8
Cox[a]	2,246,109	7.5
Charter	1,711,400	5.7
Cablevision	1,179,040	3.9
Adelphia[b]	1,167,802	3.9
Bright House Networks[c]	675,000	2.2
Mediacom	327,000	1.1
Insight	273,900	0.9
RCN[c]	210,000	0.7
Cable One	152,300	0.5
Total Top Cable	17,495,551	58% (61% of top firms)
Telcos		
SBC	4,277,000	14.2
Verizon	2,944,000	9.8
Bell South	1,738,000	5.8
Qwest	853,000	2.8
Covad	514,345	1.7
Sprint	383,000	1.3
ALLTEL	194,534	0.6
Cincinnati Bell	117,000	0.4
Century Tel	108,820	0.4
Total Top DSL	11,129,699	36.9% (38.9% of top firms)
Total Broadband for Top Firms	28,625,250	

Note. Data adopted from The Companies and Leichtman Research Group, Inc. Top cable and DSL providers represent approximately 95% of all subscribers. The percentages are based on the total subscriber number, not just the top broadband firms, as reported in the spring of 2004. Company subscriber counts may not represent solely residential households. Based on FCC data, about 6% of DSL subscribers and 0.2% of cable subscribers are classified as nonresidential or small business.

[a]Comcast and Cox totals are adjusted from last quarter of 2003 reflecting the closing of some minor transactions.

[b]Adelphia subscriber counts do not include properties owned by the Rigas family.

[c]Bright House Networks and RCN subscriber counts are estimates.

uncertainty, share resources, and obtain access. In this next section, we discuss how the broadband firms have formed strategic networks to gain competitive advantages.

STRATEGIC NETWORKS IN THE BROADBAND MARKET

Careful observations of the partnerships in the past few years involving BSPs reveal certain alliance tendencies. They include the formations of strategic networks with technology firms, retailers, content developers, and branded Internet firms.

Strategic Alliances With Technology Firms and Electronic Retailers

BSPs have sought alliances with software and hardware tech firms to enhance the value of their residential network services and reach potential customers through Internet access hardware (i.e., PC). For example, Comcast and Intel partnered to develop home networking products for Comcast broadband services. Comcast and Charter also formed alliances with PC manufacturers such as HP, Compaq, and Gateway, offering PC users easy signup for their broadband access services. In the telephone sector, SBC and Dell Computer partnered to equip Dell Dimension desktop PCs with ADSL modems and services ("Dell Computer Strikes," 1998). There was even a loose broadband consortium, the Universal Asymmetric Digital Subscriber Line Working Group (UAWG), formed by tech companies like Compaq, Intel, and Microsoft with the then five RBOCs (i.e., Ameritech, Bell Atlantic, BellSouth, SBC, and US West), as well as GTE, Sprint, and MCI ("Consortium to Push ADSL, 1998b). Most recently, SBC signed a 10-year, $400 million agreement with Microsoft to provide next-generation television services using Microsoft's TV Internet protocol television software platform. The high-profile move aims to counter cable's television advantage by enabling viewers to channel surf in a small window on their TV screens while watching another program. Subscribers also could get alerts for their upcoming favorite shows, caller ID, instant messaging, VOD, DVR, and program guides (Gonsalves, 2004).

BSPs have also attempted to form strategic networks with electronic retailers that have the most direct contact with potential broadband users to augment their marketing efforts. For example, Comcast partnered with Best Buy, RadioShack, and even Office Depot, working together to develop a point-of-sale presence at many of these retailers' stores nationwide.

Strategic Alliances With Content Developers/Providers

There are also alliances to enrich the variety of contents for broadband delivery and to comarket broadband access with branded content providers, thus increasing the attractiveness of the overall broadband service. For example, Comcast allied with RealNetworks, which offers its Rhapsody, an Internet jukebox service, via a cobranded Web site accessible on Comcast's broadband customer destination home page at Comcast.net. Working with Disney, Comcast launched Comcast Kids Channel, an interactive environment designed for the broadband family with content from Disney Online. Disney also formed a joint venture with the RBOCs BellSouth, SBC, and Ameritech to develop, market, and deliver video programming to consumers. Three other Bells (before the consolidation)—Bell Atlantic, Nynex, and Pacific Telesis—initiated a programming partnership aided by Hollywood agent Michael Ovitz, whereas the seventh Bell, US West, teamed up with Time Warner to explore video-programming opportunities (Leslie, 1995). Time Warner and Intellicast.com continued to ally to offer Broadband Weather, an online service that delivers weather information especially suited for high-speed Internet access.

Strategic Alliances With Branded Internet Firms

As the provider of connections to the Internet conduit, BSPs have also partnered with established Internet brands to take advantage of the existing brand equity of leading online brands in comarketing efforts. For example, SBC and Yahoo! formed a so-called "landmark alliance" to provide cobranded high-speed Internet DSL service to residential consumers in SBC's networks nationwide ("Yahoo, SBC Sign, 2001b). Microsoft jointly sold and marketed high-speed Internet services with Verizon Communications (Buckman, 2002). Verizon also partnered with Excite@Home to be the provider of directory services for all of Excite@Home's Web properties, whereas Charter and the MSN network allied to make MSN content and services available to customers of Charter high-speed Internet service.

TELEPHONE COMPANIES' VIDEO STRATEGIES

The promise of broadband Internet goes beyond the high-speed surfing of the Internet and VoIP (Voice over Internet Protocol) services. The capability of delivering ETV features is another exciting new area of revenues enticing many telcos that are faced with a decline in traditional landline telephone services. Chapter 7 has already examined the ETV ventures from the MVPD perspective. We now scrutinize the video ventures initiated by the telcos to assess their strategic emphases in this area.

Acquisition of Resources to Facilitate Video Services

Lacking the video services and marketing experience, telcos were at a competitive disadvantage initially compared to cablecasters who have acquired years of video programming expertise. To move from acting as a common carrier to a programming supplier, many telcos not only began to hire programming veterans like Sandy Grushow, former president of Fox Broadcast Group, and Howard Stringer, former president of CBS, from the broadcast and cable television industries (Sharkey, 1995), but also formed alliances with technology firms to facilitate their delivery of video services over phone lines. For example, Microsoft joined Southwestern Bell to provide software for the telco's interactive video service in the early 1990s (Cauley, 1994). To better their video offerings, telcos such as BellSouth and SBC also formed joint ventures with content firms like Disney and CinemaNow.com (Leslie, 1995).

From Video Dial-Tone (VDT) to Video on Demand (VOD)

Beginning with VDT ventures in the early 1990s, many telcos had tackled the complicated, expensive undertaking of delivering video services via telephone lines with mostly disappointing results ("FCC Approves BellSouth," 1995; Kapadia, 1995). For example, Bell Atlantic, the most aggressive telco in testing various VDT trials, failed to sustain its ambitious so-called "Stargazer" service, which offered shopping via television and more than 700 educational and entertainment program choices (Kapadia, 1995). Another high-profiled VDT service, Tele-TV, put forth by a consortium of three RBOCs—Bell Atlantic, Pacific Telesis, and Nynex—was formed to deliver programming content and link interactive elements to the video systems of the Baby Bells (Sharkey, 1995). The venture eventually folded after the 1996 Telecommunications Act, which distracted the RBOCs with the possibility of a more lucrative revenue stream, long-distance service. Citing the regulatory uncertainty and difficult application process for VDT ventures, telcos like Ameritech also decided to abandon their VDT services and instead use the cable TV model to build digital video networks with cable TV franchises offering both analog and digital video channels (Kapadia, 1995; McCarthy, 1995). In essence, the original VDT ventures by the telcos failed to materialize because of regulatory complications, problems of inefficiency in integrating a wide range of interactive options into a usable product not yet demanded by consumers, costly equipment, other business opportunities opened up by the 1996 Telecom Act, and the fact that interactive television was losing much of its luster as public interest began to shift to the Internet.

The new broadband VOD model seems to hold better prospects for the telcos. After waves of mergers, the remaining telcos are able to invest in broadband services with pooled resources and develop VOD as an application to enhance one of their core businesses, broadband services. To ensure a smooth transition to the VOD platform and the availability of attractive content products, telcos have formed alliances with technology and content firms. For example, SBC and Microsoft partnered to test an IP-based switched television service that enables features like standard and high-definition programming, customizable channel lineups, VOD, DVR, multimedia interactive program guides, and event notifications (OneSource, 2004). BellSouth entered an agreement with Movielink, an online movie rental service supported by the major studios that allows broadband users to download and watch hundreds of films on their PCs (Mahoney, 2003).

Strategic Alliances for DBS–Broadband Bundling Services

In recent years, we are also witnessing a new wave of strategic networks containing telcos and cable's wireless counterpart, DBS service providers. The move seems to be designed to blunt MSOs' marketing of bundled broadband and video services. For example, SBC formed a marketing and distribution agreement with DirecTV, making SBC's subsidiary Southwestern Bell a one-stop communications supplier for the apartment complex market ("SBC, DIRECTV Enter,", 1998). SBC continued to partner with the number two DBS firm, EchoStar, with both companies selling each other's services and offering discounts to customers who sign up for both video programming and high-speed Internet service. BellSouth has also allied with both DirecTV and EchoStar to bundle the DBS providers' TV services with BellSouth's voice and data services. Another telco, Qwest, took a more limited approach by signing strategic marketing agreements with both EchoStar and DirecTV to make satellite TV services available to customers in single-family homes in Qwest's residential phone market ("DBS Turns to Bells," 2003).

STRATEGIC DIFFERENCES BETWEEN TELEPHONE AND CABLE BROADBAND FIRMS

It is evident that the telephone and cable broadband firms have different core competencies and thus different strategic preferences in conducting their broadband businesses. In this section, we examine the different strategies adopted by telephone versus cable firms in the context of a broadband, ETV industry value chain. Because of the essential role of strategic networks and M&As in this market, we review how the two groups of competitors differ in alliance strategies and discuss the implications of this strategic divergence.

Using "industry" as the unit of analysis, Chan-Olmsted and Kang (2003) examined the alliance activities of the cable and telephone firms occurring during the period of 1996 to 2001 based on the ETV strategic architecture proposed in the previous chapter. In this empirical investigation, a series of criteria was established to identify the relevant structural (M&A) alliances occurring in the broadband television industry from a total of 63,452 domestic mergers and acquisitions recorded during the 5-year period. To be included in the dataset, the target or acquiring firm in a merger or acquisition has to: (a) belong to a primary SIC (i.e., Standard Industrial Classification) code that is one of the identified broadband SIC codes (e.g., Telephone service's SIC is 4813, whereas cable's is 4841), and (b) contain at least one of the broadband television key words in the officially filed description or synopsis of the transaction. All alliances were then classified into either structural alliances (i.e., mergers and acquisitions) or nonstructural alliances (i.e., joint ventures and non-M&A agreements) and as either related or unrelated based on the SIC codes of the participants (e.g., an alliance is classified as related when at least two of the participants' primary SICs are of the same first two digits).

The study analyzed more than 1,700 cases of mergers and acquisitions and 1,300 nonstructural alliances involving cable and telephone companies during this period. Whereas there were more M&A activities throughout the years, other alliances such as joint ventures were practiced modestly and remained fairly stable (see Table 8.2). The trends between M&A and non-M&A alliances were similar and increased gradually during the first 3 years (1996–1999) when non-M&A alliances were adopted somewhat more frequently than M&As (see Fig. 8.1). The number of activities increased substantially during the 4th year, especially for M&As. Whereas the number dropped sharply the following year, M&As continued to outperform non-M&A alliances by more than 110 cases. In sum, the levels of alliances have increased over the years as M&A moved from a slightly less favored model to the dominant method of structural alliances by the end of 1999.

Differences in Strategic Alliance Patterns Between Cable and Telephone Firms

In regard to M&A activities, cable has been a target of acquisition much more frequently than telcos during the 5-year period (16.2% vs. 4.7% of all M&As) (see Fig. 8.2). The difference, however, became much narrower in 2000–2001. Cable continued to be more aggressive than the telcos as an acquirer in M&As, though the range of difference was

TABLE 8.2
Broadband M&A and Alliances in the United States 1996–2001

Year	Total M&A (%)	Total Alliances/Joint Ventures (%)
2000–2001	448 (26.2)	237/14 (18.2/1.0)
1999–2000	674 (39.4)	409/52 (31.4/4.0)
1998–1999	261 (15.3)	303/36 (23.3/2.8)
1997–1998	187 (10.9)	170/29 (13.1/2.2)
1996–1997	140 (8.2)	182/33 (14.0/2.5)
Total	1710 (100)	1301/164 (100/12.6)

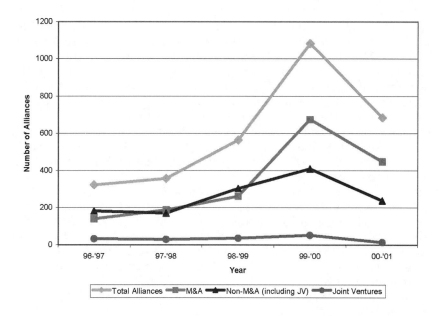

FIG. 8.1.   Total broadband-based enhanced television strategic alliances in the United States 1996–2001.

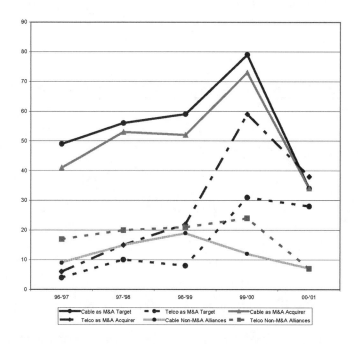

FIG. 8.2.   Broadband-based enhanced television strategic alliances by cable television and telephone firms 1996–2001.

somewhat smaller than it was for cable as a target of acquisition (14.8% vs. 8.2% of all M&As). The situation changed during 2000–2001 as telcos slightly passed cable as an M&A acquirer. In general, cable television firms were more likely to be the target than the acquirer, whereas telcos were more likely to be the acquirer than the target during this period. As for non-M&A alliances, telcos appeared to be more active than cable, though the difference is marginal and became minimal in the last year of comparison (see Table 8.3). Overall, cable's non-M&A alliances followed its trend of M&A activities except for the year 1999–2000 when cable was aggressively involved in M&A activities as the number of its non-M&A alliances dropped. In contrast, telcos preferred non-M&A alliances over M&A (as an acquirer or target) for the first 3 years until 1999–2000 when it changed its alliance strategy, actively acquiring firms through M&A in the broadband television industry. Its M&As continued to surpass non-M&A activities in the 5th year, even with a substantial reduction of alliance numbers. In general, cable firms were most interested in acquiring firms from their own industry (SIC 4841) (81.8%), followed by television broadcast stations (SIC 4833) (5.5%) and information services (SIC 7375) (4.7%) (see Table 8.4). On the other hand, telcos were most interested in acquiring firms from the information services sector (SIC 7375) (41.4%), followed by their own industry (SIC 4813) (24.3%) and the cable industry (SIC 4841) (16.4%) in broadband TV–related M&A activities. Finally, cable was more likely to form joint ventures than were the telcos (30.2% vs. 15.1% of all non-M&A alliances).

TABLE 8.3

Broadband Non-M&A Alliances by Comparable Industry Sectors 1996–2001

Year						By SIC Code						
	3651	3661	3663	3669	4813	4833	4841	7372	7375	7379	7812	7822
2000–2001		5	5	1	**7**	9	**7**	73	111	4	7	1
1999–2000	1	7	5	2	**24**	10	**12**	112	188	11	7	2
1998–1999		5	7	3	**21**	16	**19**	72	115	6	16	1
1997–1998	2	4	9	3	**20**	12	**15**	54	25		16	
1996–1997	1	11	4	5	**17**	14	**9**	69	32	3	15	1
Total: 1301 (100%)	4 (.3)	32 (2.5)	30 (2.3)	14 (1.0)	**89 (6.8)**	61 (4.7)	**62 (4.8)**	380 (29.2)	471 (36.2)	24 (1.8)	61 (4.7)	5 (.4)

Notes. The SIC codes for the non-M&A alliances here were from the participants of the alliances, not the newly formed alliances because the two are not always identical. Note that only the primary SIC codes were used.

TABLE 8.4

Broadband M&A Activities in the Cable Television (SIC: 4841) and Telephone (SIC: 4813) Sectors 1996–2001

Year	Acquiring Firm		Target Firm									
	Cable-4841	3651	3663	3669	4813	4833	4841	7372	7375	7812	7822	
2000–2001	34 (13.4%)		1	1		3	26		2		1	
1999–2000	73 (28.9)		2		5	4	57		5			
1998–1999	52 (20.6)						47	2	2	1		
1997–1998	53 (20.9)	1	1		1	3	43		2	2		
1996–1997	41 (16.2)		1		1	4	34		1			
Total	253	1	5	1	7	14	207	2	12	3	1	
	(100)	(.6)	(2.0)	(.6)	(2.8)	(5.5)	(81.8)	(.8)	(4.7)	(1.2)	(.6)	

Year	Acquiring Firm		Target Firm									
	Telephone-4813	3651	3661	3663	4813	4833	4841	7372	7375	7379	7812	
2000–2001	38 (27.1%)	1		1	14	2	2	5	14	1		
1999–2000	59 (42.1)				15		7	7	27	1		
1998–1999	22 (15.7)		2		2		5		11		2	
1997–1998	15 (10.7)				3		5	1	4	1	1	
1996–1997	6 (4.3)						4		2			
Total	140	1	2	1	34	2	23	13	58	3	3	
	(100)	(.7)	(1.4)	(.7)	(24.3)	(1.4)	(16.4)	(9.3)	(41.4)	(2.1)	(2.1)	

Alliances for Relatedness Versus Complementary Resources

It was found that cable firms were overwhelmingly more likely to acquire related communications firms (90.1% for SIC 48). The partner preference seems to go beyond relatedness as more than 81.8% of the cable
acquirers chose firms within their industry (see Table 8.4). In contrast,
telcos were more likely to branch out of their industry as only 42.1% of its
M&A targets were in the related industries. Telcos were aggressively tar-
geting the business services sector (52.8% for SIC 73), especially aiming at
the information services market (41.4% for SIC 7375). The telcos considered firms from their own industry as an M&A target only about a quarter of the time. It's interesting that whereas cable rarely pursued telcos
for M&As (2.7%), telcos were much more likely to approach cable as an
M&A target (16.4%). As for non–M&A alliances, both cable and telcos
were much more likely to form such partnerships with firms from related industries (see Table 8.5). Cable television was slightly more active in
forming related non–M&A alliances than the telcos (81.3% vs. 73%). Cable
was also more likely to ally with firms from the same industry than the
telcos (61.5% vs. 43.7 %). As in the case of M&As for the telcos, the information services sector was most likely (more than the telcos) to be involved with nonstructural alliances in the telephone sector, whereas cable

TABLE 8.5

**Industries Involved in the Formed Non-M&A Alliances by the Cable Television
and Telephone Firms 1996–2001**

SIC	Formed Alliances (%)	
	4813	4841
3661	9 (7.1%)	0
3663	1 (.8)	5 (5.2)
4813	27 (21.4)	6 (6.3)
4833	3 (2.4)	15 (15.6)
4841	4 (3.2)	45 (46.9)
7372	16 (12.7)	4 (4.2)
7375	64 (50.8)	16 (16.7)
7379	2 (1.6)	1 (1.0)
3651	0	3 (3.1)
7812	0	1 (1.0)
Total	126 (100)	96 (100)

Note. The SIC codes for the alliances were for the formed non-M&A alliances, not the
participants of the alliances because the two were not always identical.

companies continued to be the major players for such alliances in the cable market. In sum, relatedness seemed to be the main partnering strategy for the cable television firms, whereas the telcos were more likely to look for partners that complement their resources, except in the case of non-M&A alliances in which the telcos might ally with related but not necessarily similar communications firms.

In summary, M&As have played an important strategic role for these broadband firms in their quest for competitive advantages in the emerging broadband market. It is clear that the cable firms have in general been more active in forming alliances than the telcos. Specifically, cable television was a more attractive target as well as more active acquirer for M&As than the telcos. Nevertheless, telcos have changed their alliance strategy, moving away from non-M&A alliances and becoming a more aggressive acquirer in recent years. This change in alliance strategy suggests a learning curve as the telcos increasingly regard many components of the television industry as relevant and valuable while they reposition themselves beyond the traditional common carrier role and extend to the content/integrated telecommunications services sector. "Relatedness" appeared to be a more important M&A strategy for the cable firms than the telcos because the latter have aggressively pursued firms outside of their market in the information services and software sectors (i.e., the ETV enablers and facilitators), practicing a complementary resource alliance strategy (see Fig. 8.3). The different alliance strategies between the telcos and cable firms affirm the notion

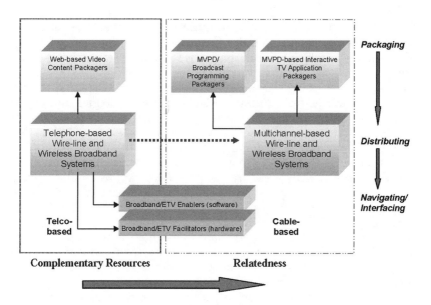

FIG. 8.3.   Patterns of alliances and the broadband-based enhanced television strategic architecture.

of "path dependency" in this industry as cable played to its historical strengths through the M&As with related television firms while the telcos attempted to counter their resource weaknesses in this emerging industry by extending into complementary sectors via M&As. Note that when it comes to non-M&A alliances, both cable and telcos were more comfortable allying with firms from related sectors; it seems that flexible access to specific, related resources is an important alliance strategy for both the telcos and cable firms.

The differences in alliance strategies between telcos and cable illustrate the two groups' different emphases in the development of their core competencies for the broadband-based ETV market (see Fig. 8.3). It seems that the telcos have focused on expanding their ability to offer a seamless, top-down, integrated broadband television service by securing access to Web-based content packagers and better navigating/interfacing tools. In contrast, the cable firms have emphasized developing their ability to offer attractive, enhanced cable programming by allying with the traditional as well as new television-programming packagers. However, it is plausible that television applications of broadband may yet become the top priority in telcos' broadband strategies at this stage because the telcos have chosen to focus on their existing core competencies in areas of communication networks and informational services, rather than on consumer television content services.

FINAL THOUGHTS

The analysis of the broadband communications market thus far depicts the current competitive dynamics and points to the prevalence of certain strategies. Although the overall market is still emerging and remains relatively competitive, dominant industry leaders have emerged from each sector, namely, Comcast from cable and SBC from telephone market. Both firms have actively pursued M&A/alliance strategies and experimented with different broadband trials. Both firms have also acquired their leading status from a series of aggressive M&As, which enabled them to explore new broadband business opportunities with more resources. In fact, M&A and strategic network strategies that facilitate the sharing of risks as well as resources appeared to be central to the development of broadband services. Specifically, alliances seem essential in acquiring access to technology firms' expertise, content firms' attractive products, electronic retailers' consumer contacts and knowledge, and Internet firms' established brand images. One interesting recent phenomenon is the partnership forged between cablecasters' two prime competitors, DBS and the telcos. The strategic networks between these two parties allow both to remain truthful to their core competency while compensating for the telcos' lack of video expertise and DBS's inability to provide reliable broadband access. It might prove to be the best transitional strategy in competing with cable's current bundling advantage.

It is important to note that many past ETV services have failed because of the lack of interest from consumers. Thus, it is fruitful to also review the characteristics of today's broadband subscribers in anticipating the effectiveness of potential broadband deployment strategies. It is said that the current broadband subscribers tend to be well educated, younger, and of higher socioeconomic status and choose broadband subscription mainly due to impatience with the dial-up speed than dissatisfaction with service pricing. Broadband users are also big spenders online as they account for almost a third of online spending although representing only 19% of online adults in the United States (they spend about 50% more than narrowband users) (Kerner, 2004). In terms of content preferences, broadband users are very active information gatherers, multimedia users/downloaders, group/forum participants, and content creators/managers. Furthermore, broadband users engage in multiple online activities on a daily basis. They not only search more for information about products and services, but also generate content about their thoughts and share them in online forums (Horrigan & Rainie, 2003). Interestingly, most broadband users would be willing to download a branded interactive video channel to their computers and accept content from a trusted marketer on that channel (Newcomb, 2004). What are the strategic implications for these consumer traits? First, it is obvious that broadband holds tremendous marketing utilities. It offers an attractive target market and great opportunities for marketing communications with the group (e.g., short-form video communication delivered directly to the consumer). It also highlights the importance of information, communication, brand equity, and multiplatform marketing.

This chapter has not discussed extensively another nonvideo broadband service, VoIP, which is becoming a more viable product option as broadband continues to expand. Although about 27% of Internet users in the United States have heard of the service, it still has a relatively low consumer adoption rate. While many have a favorable impression of VoIP, they are mostly early adopters and small in number (Horrigan, 2004b). Both telcos such as AT&T, SBC, and Verizon and cable companies like Cablevision, Cox, Charter, Time Warner, and Comcast have entered the residential VoIP market with various trials. Note that whereas telcos are more experienced in providing such voice services, many cable companies, including the five largest MSOs, are certified local exchange carriers in more than 15 states across the country, serving approximately 2.7 million residential subscribers of circuit-switched cable telephony across the country (National Cable & Telecommunications Association [NCTA], 2004). We believe that VoIP service, although it will not become the core application of broadband for cable firms, would add to the multiplicity, versatility, and thus value of cable-based broadband services. Especially, it might serve as an effective tool for reducing churn rates for cablecasters in a bundling marketing strategy. In fact, a triple-play, multi-point competition of cable TV, broadband, and telephone services is becoming a corporate strategy that drives many leading MSOs' recent market activities. On the other hand, VoIP is the new force that continues to reshape the competitive landscape of the core business of the telcos. From RBOCs' competition with long-distance companies like AT&T, MCI, and Sprint, to the rapid growth of cell phones, to the deployment of VoIP, the voice market is evolving to include more crossover competition, different technologies, smaller service providers like Vonage, VoicePulse, and Pocket8 from the VoIP segment, and thus more complex business strategies, amid regulatory uncertainties toward VoIP provision. In light of the triple play strategy of the MSOs, VOIP is also becoming an important engagement point that the telcos cannot ignore.

In essence, considering the multitasking tendency of broadband users and the multiplicity of broadband functions, the future of broadband may not rest on what many considered to be the deployment of one or two killer broadband applications, but rather on the integration of various applications that offer the most efficient interactive broadband access with the best user experience and content variety. In other words, the key to success for these broadband firms might be the implementation of strategies that develop a multiplicity of services, ensure the smooth integration of these services, and focus on communicating the versatility and value of these services to the consumers. Currently, with its television expertise and the lead in broadband service deployment, cable television seems to be better positioned in the broadband communications market. For telcos to remain competitive and even develop a strategic advantage, they have to not only offer comparable product bundles through alliances but also leapfrog cable by employing technologies that smoothly integrate a variety of services and provide the friendliest consumer interface compared to their cable counterparts.

REFERENCES

Bratches, S., & Rooney, J. (2001, October 29). Seizing the broadband opportunities [Electronic version]. *Multichannel News.*

Buckman, R. (2002, June 21). Microsoft to offer broadband through accord with Verizon. *The Wall Street Journal*, p. B5.

Cauley, L. (1994, September 26). Microsoft, Baby Bell form video alliance. *The Wall Street Journal*, p. B9.

Chan-Olmsted, S. M., & Kang, J. (2003). The emerging broadband television market in the United States: Assessing the strategic differences between cable television and telephone firms. *Journal of Interactive Advertising, 4.* Retrieved December 17, 2004, from http://jiad.org

Consortium to push ADSL to mass market deployment. (1998, February 3). *Broadband Networking News, 8*(3), 1.

DBS turns to Bells for edge. (2003, July 28). *Satellite News, 26*(29), 1.

Dell computer strikes marketing agreements with telecom giants. (1998, September 29). *Broadband Networking News, 8*(20), 1.

Federal Communications Commission. (2004). *High-speed connections to the Internet increased 20% during the second half of 2003 for a total of 28 million lines in service.* Washington, DC: Author.

Gonsalves, A. (2004). *SBC signs digital-TV software deal with Microsoft.* Retrieved December 17, 2004, from http://www.techweb.com/wire/networking/53700328

Greene, T. (2000, August 14). Verizon takes NorthPoint to make national DSL move. *Network World, 17*(33), 10.

Greenspan, R. (2002). *Slow but steady speed subscribers.* Retrieved October 15, 2004, from http://cyberatlas.internet.com/markets/broadband/article/0,,10099_1016281,00html

Greenspan, R. (2004). *High-speed hits 28.6M subscribers.* Retrieved December 17, 2004, from http://www.clickz.com/stats/markets/broadband/article.php/3396871

Hitt, M. A., Ireland, R. D., & Hoskisson, R. E. (2001). *Strategic management: Competitiveness and globalization* (4th ed.). Cincinnati, OH: South-Western College.

Horrigan, J. B. (2004a). *55% of adult Internet users have broadband at home or work.* Washington, DC: Pew Internet & American Life Project.

Horrigan, J. B. (2004b). *27% of online Americans have heard of VOIP telephone service: 4 million are considering getting it at home.* Washington, DC: Pew Internet & American Life Project.

Horrigan, J. B., & Rainie, L. (2003). *The broadband difference: How online America's behavior changes with high-speed Internet connections at home.* Washington, DC: Pew Internet & American Life Project.

Kapadia, R. (1995, November 27). Carriers wade slowly into video waters. *Telephony, 229*(22), 58.

Kerner, S. M. (2004). *More document usage means more online spending.* Retrieved December 17, 2004, from http://www.clickz.com/stats/markets/broadband/print.php/3419281

Leichtman Research Group. (2004). *Research notes: Actionable research on the adoption and impact of broadband media.* Durham, NH: Author.

Leslie, C. (1995, April 18). Baby Bells plan video venture with Disney. *The Wall Street Journal,* p. B6.

Mahoney, R. (2003, August 15). BellSouth adds films-on-demand to DSL services. *Birmingham Business Journal, 20*(33), 11.

May 2005 Bandwidth Report. (2005, May). Retrieved May 19, 2005, from http://www.websiteoptimization.com/bw/0505/

McCarthy, S. (1995, May 8). Regulations imperil video dial tone. *Telephony, 228*(19), 7.

National Cable and Telecommunications Association. (2004). Voice over Internet Protocol. Retrieved November 10, 2004, from http://www.NCTA.com

Newcomb, K. (2004). *Survey finds consumer Internet in branded video.* Retrieved November 10, 2004, from http://www.clickz.com/news/print.php/3419921

OneSource. (2004). *OneSource Online Business Information.* Retrieved November 10, 2004, from http://www.onesource.com/

Porter, M. (1980). *Competitive strategy.* New York: The Free Press.

Qwest Communications offers new bundle of broadband services. (2001, October). *High - Speed Internet Access, 17*(10), 17.

Qwest offers new broadband bundle. (2001, September 28). *Communications Today, 7*(184), 1.

Rohde, D. (1999, October 4). SBC merger support: Grass-roots with a twist. *Network World, 16*(40), 14.

Sawyer, S., Allen, J. P., & Lee, H. (2003). Broadband and mobile opportunities: A socio-technical perspective. *Journal of Information Technology, 18*(2), 121–136.

SBC, DIRECTV enter multi-year pact. (1998, March 3). *Journal Record*, p. 1.

SBC tries to knock cable broadband off its perch. (1999, January 13). *Communications Today*, p. 16.

Scherer, F. M., & Ross, D. (1990). *Industrial market structure and economic performance* (3rd ed.). Boston: Houghton Mifflin.

Sharkey, B. (1995, October 23). Programming a paradigm. *Mediaweek, 5*(40), 20.

Shepherd, W. G. (1987). Concentration rates. In J. Eatwell, M. Milgate, & P. Newman (Eds.), *The new palgrade: A dictionary of economics* (pp. 563–564). New York: Stockton Press.

FCC approves BellSouth, Nynex video-service plans. (1995, February 8). *The Wall Street Journal*, p. B6.

Yahoo, SBC sign broadband pact. (2001, November 15). *Communications Today, 7*(215), 1.

Chapter 9

Strategy and Competition of Global Media Conglomerates

Just as in the oil and automotive industries earlier this century, the media industry has gone through a profound transformation, progressing from a primarily national to a global commercial-media market, and in the process created a group of media conglomerates with worldwide reach (McChesney, 1999). The move toward an international business of media products corresponds to the shift away from nationalistic economic policies toward the internationally free-market economy of post–World War II facilitated by the establishment of international agencies like the World Bank and the International Monetary Fund (Gershon, 1997). Some have asserted that the internationalization of media is intractable and irreversible as managers increasingly view the expansion of media in a global context and not necessarily with an aim to fulfill the cultural needs of specific audiences (Smith, 1991). In fact, the trend toward media conglomeration has generated heated debates among communication scholars, policymakers, and industry practitioners (Croteau & Hoynes, 2001; C. Davis & Craft, 2000; S. Davis, 1999; Demers, 1999; Teinowitz, 2001). Drawing from a social/public-sphere theory, opponents have called such an acceleration of consolidation the homogenization of media and a threat to democracy (Parker, 2000; Smith, 1991; Wellstone, 2000). Proponents of the development, coming mostly from an economic/market perspective, have argued that the advent of technologies and proliferation of media outlets would minimize the threat of monopoly power and that economies of scale/scope are necessary when a firm competes in a global marketplace (Mandel-Campbell, 1998; Shearer, 2000).

Considering the significant role media corporations play in the production of culture and the delivery of important news and information and the fact that corporate structure, strategy, management, and behavior ultimately impact the nature and supply of "content" (Hollifield,

179

2001), a better understanding of the competitive patterns, international business strategies of media firms, and determinants of these strategies would contribute to the body of knowledge about the potential effects of media globalization and transnational/global media management.

This chapter contains two general sections: (a) a review of the world media landscape from the perspectives of the degree of media multiplicity, diffusion, openness, and new-media potential along with an investigation of how various environmental factors—including economic, cultural, social, political, technological, and other supporting industrial characteristics—influence the media markets in these countries and (b) an examination of the diversification patterns of the leading global media conglomerates along with discussions of the factors that affect media firms' strategic choices regarding international business in this sector and the relationship between diversification and performance. Whereas the macrolevel, general overview of the world's media systems provides an assessment of today's market environment, the microlevel, firm-specific analysis of diversification strategies offers insight into how global media conglomerates have responded to the market forces and the consequences of their strategic actions.

INTERNATIONAL BUSINESS AND GLOBAL MEDIA CONGLOMERATES

Before we dive into the discussions of a global media marketplace and global media conglomerates (i.e., media firms that have overseas operations in multiple countries), it is essential for us first to be familiar with various relevant terms used in the international business (IB) discipline. Though transnational corporations (TNCs), multinational corporations (MNCs), and multinational enterprises (MNEs) are used interchangeably in many literatures, they are sometimes referred to as companies of different operational philosophies concerning overseas operations. For instance, MNC and MNE are often used to describe either a company that takes a global approach to foreign markets and production, integrates operations that are located in different countries, and develops capabilities with an eye toward diffusing them throughout the company's home countries or a multidomestic company that allows each of its foreign-country operations to act relatively independently. TNC, on the other hand, is frequently used to describe a company that leverages the capabilities of both home and foreign countries where it operates and might have a geographically dispersed power structure (Daniels & Radebaugh, 1998). Although these distinctions are important in denoting the degree of international control and strategic emphasis for a media firm, in the context of this study, the terms global, multinational, transnational, and multidomestic are used interchangeably because it is not the objective of this chapter to investigate the comparative merit of different international corporate structures but to assess generally the patterns of operations of media firms with overseas operations. Thus, global media conglomerates are defined here as media firms that operate in multiple media sectors and multiple countries concurrently. Accordingly, a study of global media conglomerates involves the examination of IB practices of diversified media firms in a global marketplace.

Why do companies engage in IB? Four operating objectives are said to influence such strategy: to expand sales, to acquire resources, to diversify sources of sales and supplies, and to minimize competitive risk (Daniels & Radebaugh, 2003). In reality, there is an evolution of strategy in this international expansion process. Rarely is a media company conceived to be a global media giant. It is more likely that different firms evolve over time with different levels of international ambition and capabilities, which influence the most advantageous strategic alternatives available to the firms. CNN was launched in 1980 as a U.S.-based 24-hour cable news network, but it is now available in many countries around the globe and a part of the world's biggest media conglomerate, Time Warner. On the other hand, Knight-Ridder, established in 1974, remains largely a newspaper firm that focuses on domestic print and online operations. Figure 9.1 illustrates the typical patterns of international expansion with varying degrees of IB ag-

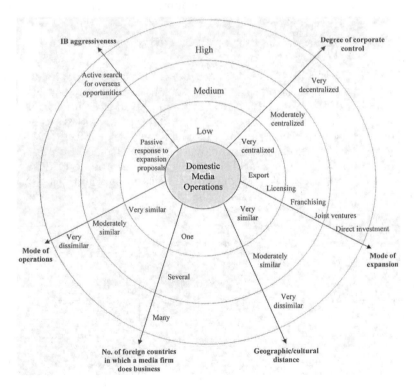

FIG. 9.1. Patterns of global expansion for media firms. Source: Daniels, John D. & Radebaugh, Lee H., *International Business Environments and Operations*, 8th ed. © 1998. Adapted by permission of Pearson Education, Inc., Upper Saddle River, NJ.

gressiveness and corporate control, different modes of operation and expansion, and various extents of geographic diversification. Note that not all media firms follow the order of progression in the figure. Whereas global media conglomerates like Time Warner and News Corp. have diversified extensively utilizing all modes of expansion, Viacom is comparatively much more conservative in both corporate control and international expansion. A number of factors seem to play a role in affecting these strategic differences. Figure 9.2 details the external and internal forces that might influence a media firm's choice of expansion modes from exporting to foreign direct investment (FDI), functional operations from marketing to human resources management, and other strategic decisions such as market selection and control mechanisms (Daniels & Radebaugh, 2003). The external factors include forces specific to a country such as economic and regulatory conditions of a target country and the competitive environment, which dictates the potential competitive advantages available to the firm for expansion. Internal factors such as corporate objectives, core competencies, and a firm's strategic networks also play a significant role in shaping the IB strategy of a media firm. The following section reviews some of these country-based media environments and their determinants.

THE WORLD MEDIA LANDSCAPE

It was suggested that most MNCs are formed because of (a) the uneven geographical distribution of national assets, (b) the exploitation of these assets by transferring them across national boundaries, and, more recently, (c) the acquisition, development, and integration of strategically important assets in other countries (Gooderham & Nordhaug, 2003). In 2003, more than 60,000 MNCs had over 800,000 affiliates abroad, generating about half of the world's industrial output and accounting for two thirds of world trade (Gooderham & Nordhaug, 2003). The media sector is no exception. There is a global disparity in supplies and access

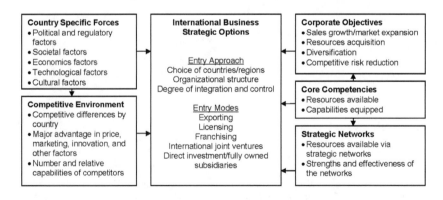

FIG. 9.2. Factors impacting the IB strategies of media firms.

to information and media due to different country environments. For example, one fifth of the world's people who live in countries with the highest income generated 86% of the world's GDP, 82% of the world's export markets, 68% of the foreign direct investments, and 74% of the world's telephone lines, whereas the bottom fifth, in the poorest countries, possessed about 1% in each sector (United Nations Development Programme, 1999).

Environmental Factors That Shape a Country's Media Systems

In the process of examining mass media either as a social component or as an industry, researchers have identified a number of factors that might play a role in shaping media systems at the country level. They may be summarized as economic, IB, political, social/consumer, cultural, technological, and other supporting determinants. These factors, individually and collectively, capture the multifaceted experiences that countries have with mass media. The following review discusses how the country-specific characteristics affect the development of media markets.

Economic Factors. Studies have found that economic wealth affects a country's adoption of new technologies (Rogers, 1995). For example, residents of industrial countries are 25 times more likely to have access to a daily newspaper than those in African countries, as measured by newspaper circulation. The difference between the reach of radio and the reach of other media is much greater in developing than in industrial countries (World Bank, 2002). It was also found that general economic strength does matter in predicting the adoption of new media such as the Internet (Hargittai, 1999). In fact, the introduction of new information and communication technology requires a heavy investment that most developing countries can neither raise nor commit (Maherzi, 1997). Furthermore, mass-media spending by consumers and advertisers is determined by the general state of the economy. Any change in the level of the economy causes a parallel change in spending on mass media (McCombs, 1972). In essence, studies have shown that national economic factors such as income are closely related to media penetration (Islam, 2002).

International Business Factors. Although media systems had been primarily national before the 1990s, a global commercial media market had emerged by the beginning of the 21st century (McChesney, 1998). A more open economy and greater interconnectedness with the outside world are expected to drive people's demands for more transnational media content. It was suggested that even over and above other political, economic, and geographic factors, penetration of newspapers and number of personal computers, Internet hosts, and telephone lines increased with more economic openness (Yang & Shanahan, 2003).

A global, open trade environment not only builds demand for transnational media products, but also exposes firms at various markets to competition, new technology, and trading partnerships. Empirical studies covering more than 110 countries have shown that measures of institutional effectiveness are significantly related to openness in international trade. In addition, access to foreign media can create demand for institutional change and enable access to information on issues not illustrated by local media. Open information exchange and open trade also create demand for market-supporting media institutions. Studies have found that competition in the provision of information significantly increases the impact of the media on the quality of various institutions (World Bank, 2002). Carrington and Nelson (2002) pointed to the importance of foreign investment in assisting new-media companies with getting started in developing countries. Bell (1999) summarized the importance of a global communication market succinctly, suggesting that access to the revolution in communications is fueled by the desire of a nation to become a part of the world's market economic order.

Social/Consumer Factors.   Economic factors play a significant role in shaping a country's media systems, but disparities in media penetration exist even for countries with similar incomes. For instance, whereas the United Kingdom had an average newspaper circulation of 331 per 1,000 inhabitants, Italy averaged 104 (Dyck & Zingales, 2002). It is evident that the social and consumer characteristics of a nation also influence the nature of its media markets.

Research has found that a country's human development level, as measured by variables such as literacy rate, education, and life expectancy, is correlated with its level of Internet connectivity (Hargittai, 1999; International Telecommunications Union, 1997). By nature, literacy is essential for the development of print media (Demers, 2002). For example, print media outlets have multiplied to meet a growing readership associated with rising literacy rates in the Middle East (Ayish, 2001). Political economists have also pointed out that in media markets where contents are accessible by price, consumption of that content would be significantly governed by poverty rates or the distribution of household incomes in that country (Golding & Murdock, 1991). For example, Chad, Ethiopia, and Zambia, all low-income countries, vary widely in terms of media penetration because of such social factors. The social aspects also impacted Botswana and Thailand, which have similar levels of gross national product (GNP) per capita, but differ markedly in the distribution of television sets (Islam, 2002).

Structural differentiation brought about largely by urbanization and industrialization in a country also has important consequences for its media markets. As social systems become more differentiated, needs for information increase, which in turn helps promote growth in the number and variety of media (Demers, 2002).

Finally, sociodemographic variables such as age, income, education, and occupation indirectly influence media adoption (Dyck & Zingales,

2002; Vishwanath & Goldhaber, 2003). For instance, residents of Hong Kong who were younger, better educated, or single or had fewer children tended to have a higher evaluation of life quality than their counterparts in different countries, and the higher evaluation of their life quality significantly correlated with the number of new-media technologies they owned (Wei & Leung, 1998).

Technological Factors.   Technology and related infrastructure also limit the scale of media development and market competition (Islam, 2002). For instance, telecommunications technology leads to the creation of at least one leading sector of an economy and accelerates diffusion of other technologies, thus allowing faster catch-up for less developed countries in many aspects, including media development (Maddock, 1997). The close connection between information technology and media systems is significant as info-rich countries like Sweden, the United States, and Australia are not ahead just in terms of new-media systems such as the Internet but also in the distribution of other media like newspaper readership, radio, and television sets (Carrington & Nelson, 2002).

The relationship between technology and media is reciprocal. Technological innovations provide a driving force for economic and infrastructure development, which increase the diversity and diffusion speed of media systems. The advancement of media systems could then enable social change in a country, which in turn affects the process of technological innovation (Bijker, Hughes, & Pinch, 1987; Edge, 1995; Powell, 1987).

Cultural Factors.   Tradition or culture may also affect how people perceive different media: Some cultures may be less television bound or less print bound than others at similar levels of economic development (Islam, 2002). To a certain extent, mass media reflect the degree of social integration by delivering information of general interest to a large population of society as well as by exposing an audience to unfamiliar people and information. In fact, the proliferation of media systems and content may point to a society of many competing social and cultural interests (Lievrouw, 2001). For instance, the more languages that are spoken in a country, the more fragmented the newspaper market.

Another dimension of national culture might be revealed by a country's religious environment. In their modern manifestations, the world's religions continue to be woven into the fabric of daily life for billions of individuals through the advent of nationalism, mass culture and mass politics, and most recently the electronic mass media (Singh, 2000). For many of the world's geographically dispersed peoples, as well as for those living in media-intense environments, religious beliefs are frequently sustained via mass-media channels such as television, radio, film, and the Internet (Singh, 2000). Cultural characteristics, as manifested in a nation's religious multiplicity and intensity, are likely to affect the demand as well as supply of media in that nation.

Political Factors.　It is intuitive that a country's political environment is relevant to its media development. World Bank (2002) suggested that one of the main factors that makes a country's media more effective in producing better social, political, and economic outcomes is a political system that ensures media independence. Information or communication industries also tend to develop faster in democratic societies, which foster freer information flows (World Bank, 2002). Djankov, McLiesh, Nenova, and Schleifer (2002) pointed out that government ownership of the media is often higher in countries that are poorer, that have more autocratic regimes, and where overall state ownership in the economy is higher.

It is clear that government policies can improve media access. For example, removing entry barriers for new media firms or investing in building media infrastructure will improve media markets. Studies have found that, to advance the adoption of information and communication technologies, a climate of democratic freedoms, security of property rights, and a low level of government distortions are essential (Rodriguez & Wilson, 2000).

There seems to be a direct connection between the characteristics of a media environment and the political control of media ownership. Studies have concluded that the more newspapers the government controls, the less credible the newspapers are, the less they will be read, and the harder it would be for competitors to enter the market (Dyck & Zingales, 2002). Poor countries with interventionist and nondemocratic governments also exhibit higher state ownership of the media (Djankov et al., 2002). Countries that are rated as more democratic have a higher level of news media penetration as measured by newspaper and television ownership (Besley, Burgess, & Prat, 2002). Since the 1970s, many governments have liberalized the communication industry by introducing private competitors in broadcasting and telecommunications. Supporters contend that liberalization lowers prices, expands services, and generally speeds up the process of innovation (Besley et al., 2002).

The importance of political environment is magnified by its relationship with technology in the case of leapfrogging development, in which certain countries are able to skip generations of intermediate technology and adopt the new alternatives. The chief barrier to leapfrogging is government policy in developing countries ("Tele-Haves and Have-Nots," 1996). In essence, a leapfrog move to DVD (skipping VCR) or broadband (skipping narrowband) would have to be stimulated by appropriate governmental policies.

Supporting Industry Factors.　Finally, complementary, supporting industrial factors such as the advertising market can also impact the role of media in a country. A more robust economy provides more sources for advertising revenue, thus offering more opportunities for media companies to expand into new markets and/or formats (Carrington & Nelson, 2002; McCombs, 1972). For instance, in a changing media environment, Lee (1998) found that the Russian newspaper industry tends to depend on advertising revenue for survival.

Comparison of Media Markets and Their Determinants

Using "nation" as the unit of analysis, Chan-Olmsted and Oba (2004) examined 98 media markets in eight world regions with data from sources like the Freedom House Index, the Frazer Institute's world economic freedom reports, the United Nations Development Programme's (UNDP) Human Development Index (HDI), the World Advertising Research Center's regional marketing pocket books and global media cost comparison report, ZenithOptimedia's market and media fact books and its regional television reports, and the International Telecommunications Union (ITU). They assessed the condition of individual media markets by looking at the degree of media multiplicity (i.e., the breadth of the market), media diffusion (i.e., the depth of the market), and media openness (i.e., the degree of commercialization, competition, and access to foreign content). Their results indicate that the multifaceted nature and potential of a media market is best reflected by the composite availability of media options (breadth), the degree of diffusion of the available media (depth), and the system-based opportunities a country offers to a variety of firms in that media market (openness).

Specifically, the availability of mass media such as newspapers, books, radio, television, cinema, and Internet servers in a country was used to measure the breadth or multiplicity of a media market. The reaches of newspaper, magazine, radio, TV, cinema, and the Internet were assessed to indicate the depth or diffusion of a media market. The penetration rates of the Internet, satellite TV, cable TV, and digital TV were scrutinized to investigate the degree of media diffusion for newer media. Three aspects of market opportunities—commercialism, internationalism, and competitiveness—which were measured by commercial-radio reach, commercial TV's weekly hours of transmission, number of imported films per 100,000 individuals, and the level of competition for newspapers and television stations in each country, were examined to assess the degree of market openness in a media market. Because digitization is the foundation of most new-media systems, the Digital Access Index (DAI)—the first global index to rank information and communication technology (ICT) access in 178 economies developed by the ITU—was used as a proxy for assessing the new-media market potential. Finally, to address the drivers that might shape a country's media environment, Chan-Olmsted and Oba (2004) also reviewed the relationship between the aforementioned media measures and the economic and IB environment, the social/consumer and cultural environment, the technological and political environment, and the supporting industrial environment.

It was found that whereas social and cultural factors such as the urbanization, employment, religion, and ethnic characteristics of a country did not contribute to its media system multiplicity, some social factors like life quality and education impacted the arrays of media outlets available. The economic productivity, technology, and political/civil rights profiles of a country also played a significant role in this regard. Certain environmental factors seemed to affect media multiplicity differently depending on media types. For example, IB, intellectual-property rights protection, and business regulations were relevant only to the media multiplicity of cinema and books. Environmental factors such as economic productivity, IB, consumer characteristics, and technological factors also impacted mostly print and Internet media diffusion. Surprisingly, religion and ethnic characteristics played a minimal role in shaping media openness in a nation. Whereas IB, technology, and intellectual-property rights protection affected both transnational content and print competitiveness, life quality, education, and political/civil rights seemed to affect mostly print competitiveness. Finally, economic factors influenced newspaper competitiveness, and state media ownerships affected the degree of media commercialism in a country (Chan-Olmsted & Oba, 2004).

When all environmental factors were reviewed simultaneously to assess their relative roles in affecting media multiplicity, diffusion, and openness, Chan-Olmsted and Oba (2004) found that a country's technical infrastructure, advertising industry, and degree of civil-rights protection enhanced most significantly the multiplicity of its media markets. However, another set of factors comes into the picture when media diffusion is considered. In this case, intellectual-property rights protection, ICT expenditures, and religious diversity became most critical. In a sense, general political and industrial systems and infrastructure seem to contribute to increasing the supply of media (breadth of media systems), whereas specific policy factors and societal diversity matter more in increasing the demand for media (depth of media systems). The role of intellectual-property rights protection continues to be significant in promoting media openness. The degree of international trading rights also logically plays a role in impacting media openness. Interestingly, the general economic condition of a country is not a dominant force for enhancing its media multiplicity, diffusion, or openness. On the other hand, a country's infrastructure, state media ownership, advertising industry, and business regulatory environment influence the overall development of its media markets. Finally, though economic productivity, private media ownership (i.e., less state media ownership), international trading rights, and supporting telecom and advertising industries seem to set the stage for new-media development, media market characteristics such as content production capacity and visual-media availability also seem to influence the potential of growth of new media. In fact, media openness and multiplicity matter more than diffusion in advancing the development of digital media.

The environmental forces discussed thus far are essential to the examination of media as business entities in individual countries because these factors influence not only the development of an important economic sector but also the parameters in which global media conglomerates may diversify geographically. The different sets of factors that were found to affect different aspects of media markets point to the complexity associated with the study of transnational or global media economics and the need to examine media markets from multiple perspectives. We now address the global media markets from the perspective of media firms, specifically regarding how the leading media conglomerates have expanded worldwide and the consequences of such expansion strategies.

DIVERSIFICATION STRATEGY
OF GLOBAL MEDIA CONGLOMERATES

Scholars have suggested that the development of global media conglomerates is driven primarily by the privatization of television in many European and Asian markets, deregulation of media ownership, increasing parallel lifestyles in many metropolises across the globe, saturating demands for many media products in the United States, and the advance of new communications technologies (Chan-Olmsted & Albarran, 1998; Hollifield, 2001; McChesney, 1999). To capitalize on the potential of growth abroad, U.S.-based firms such as Time Warner operate in more than 60 countries. Multinational industrial giants such as Bertelsmann and Vivendi Universal (before the sale of Universal) turned to the communication sectors by acquiring U.S.-based media companies and even divested some industrial assets into separate publicly traded companies (Goldsmith, 2000). There is also evidence of oligopolistic, interdependent behavior because we have seen many strategic alliances between the same leading media conglomerates.

Chan-Olmsted and Chang (2003) investigated both product and geographic diversification strategies for leading global media conglomerates in terms of their relatedness, extent, and mode and explored the existence of strategic preferences for related product and geographic diversification and complementary distribution–content alignment. Using a case study approach, they analyzed Sony, AOL Time Warner (now Time Warner), Bertelsmann, Vivendi (before the sale of Universal), News Corp., Disney, and Viacom, the top seven global media conglomerates based on their overall revenues in 2001.

Product and Geographic Diversification of Leading Global Media Conglomerates

Chan-Olmsted and Chang (2003) found that there was a range of product and international diversification among the leading conglomerates (see Fig. 9.3). In terms of product diversification, the European Vivendi (with Universal) and Bertelsmann had the most diversity, whereas Viacom and News Corp. were the least diversified. In regard to interna-

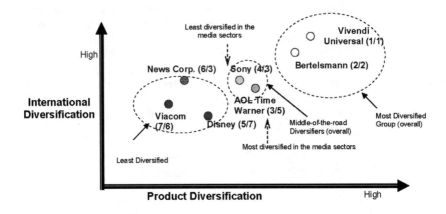

FIG. 9.3. Relative international product diversification of global media conglomerates. The first number in parenthesis is the conglomerate's product-diversity ranking, whereas the second is its geographic-diversity ranking.

tional diversification, partially due to the importance of the North American media markets, the most geographically diversified companies were non-U.S. corporations such as Vivendi, Bertelsmann, Sony, and News Corp. (before moving its headquarters to the United States). In fact, AOL Time Warner (now Time Warner) was the only U.S.-based company that was aggressively competing with the European conglomerates in Western Europe in addition to North America. Nevertheless, most likely because of the significance of the North American market, the less diversified conglomerates (e.g., Disney and Viacom) that have concentrated on developing businesses in their own region still attained a relatively good performance. As for the notion of related geographic diversification, it was concluded that the uneven distribution of M&A activities between regions from 1990 to 2000 was consistent with the proposition that regional experience and relationships are best realized in "related" international diversification.

In terms of the interaction between product and geographic diversification, the study did not find an inverse relationship between product and international diversification. In fact, the most geographically diversified conglomerates also had the widest product diversity. Nevertheless, the most internationally diversified conglomerates tended to have more content-based core products (i.e., the products that contribute the highest percentage of revenues). It is likely that the diversification of "distribution/outlets" products generally involves more risks and investment than the "content" products. In a sense, the type of core products a conglomerate has in the global media market moderates the degree of interaction between product and international diversification. Chan-Olmsted and Chang's (2003) study also points to the necessity of owning North

American media assets, especially those of content properties; the importance of allying with partners that improve content accessibility globally; and the need to explore the new media opportunities via alliances with international media facilitators, distributors, and content producers. There was an observable oligopolistic behavior between the leading conglomerates as these competitors frequently become collaborators for business ventures in a less certain market environment.

Diversification Over Time and Its Effect on Performance

To systematically investigate the relationship between diversification and performance, Jung and Chan-Olmsted (in press) studied the top 25 media companies longitudinally over a 12-year (1991–2002) period. It was found that these leading media firms had diversified their business operations continuously into multiple media sectors and expanded their foreign operations into many world regions over time. The trend was most evident between 1999 and 2002 because of the mega-mergers such as AOL-Time Warner (2000), Vivendi-Seagram (2002), Clear Channel-AMFM (1999), Tribune-Times Mirror (20002), Viacom-CBS (1999), and Gannett-Central Newspapers (2000), in addition to Disney's, Bertelsmann's, and Cox Enterprise's diversification into other strategically important content media sectors. The extent of international diversification also continued to rise throughout the period investigated, similar to that of product diversification. Jung and Chan-Olmsted asserted that the average number of total international units was 13 in 1991 and 63 in 2002, indicating the firms increased their business units in foreign countries by almost five times for the period. The average number of countries in which the firms had foreign subsidiaries increased from 5 to 12 for the period. Nevertheless, despite the move toward more international diversification, several firms such as Cablevision, Charter, Echostar, Belo, and Meredith had mostly focused their businesses in domestic markets. These firms were mainly involved in the distribution business, specifically, local cable operations and television stations. Thus, it was more difficult for them to expand into foreign territories.

As for the relationship between diversification and performance, Jung and Chan-Olmsted (in press) found that a firm's direction (related degree) of product diversification has an inverted-U curvilinear relationship with financial performance (as measured by return on sales [ROS] and return on assets [ROA]). Specifically, their empirical study concluded that a media firm's performance increased as it shifted from concentrated business strategy to related diversification, but the firm's performance decreased as it moved from related diversification toward unrelated diversification. It seems that the combinations of related cross-media ownership that yielded the most significant economic efficiencies were those that facilitate sharing of common content or a common distribution infrastructure and expertise (George, Joll, & Lynk, 1992). Jung and Chan-Olmsted also discovered that media firms with more focused businesses and highly diversified firms outperformed modestly diversified firms in regard to "cash flow" performance measurement. It is plausible that, because most media businesses are in technology-driven sectors (Rizzuto & Wirth, 2002), an initial move to diversify creates a substantial drain on their cash reserves. More diversified media conglomerates, on the other hand, might be able to cross-subsidize their cash-strained business units with the cash-rich units and enjoy the benefits of scope economies through better distribution and marketing efficiency, thus improving their cash flow standing. Note that, because more diversified firms are typically bigger firms that also generate more revenues, the degree of diversification is logically positively related to a firm's cash-related performance measures.

In terms of international diversification, the same study found that a media firm improved its performance (as measured by ROA and ROS) as it diversified into international markets. However, after a threshold point, performance was inversely related to international diversification. The inverted-U curvilinear relationship between the direction of international diversification and firm performance is reasonable as extensive geographic dispersion increases coordination, distribution, and management costs (Porter, 1990). Moreover, the uncertainties caused from cultural differences work negatively in the IB setting. In particular, because media products are very subjective to cultural preferences, diversification into a related area would be a more effective way to exploit the full benefits of globalization. Conversely, the unrelated international diversification might increase coordination costs due to uncertain business environments. Similar to the product diversification finding, the direction of the relationship shifted to a U-shaped model based on cash flow measures like earnings before interest, taxes, depreciation, and amortization (EBITDA). That is, a media firm's performance was inversely related to international diversification, but beyond a certain point, the relationship becomes positive. Again, it is plausible that a media firm's initial attempt to expand to more countries produces a significant drain on its cash reserve. As it learns how to market its product across borders more efficiently, its cash flow standing might improve with market expansion and more experience in cost control.

It seems that performance is related to diversification in a nonlinear manner. Media firms with related diversified businesses are more profitable than undiversified firms or diversified firms with unrelated businesses. In other words, managerial efficiency and profitability, as measured by return ratios, decrease with unrelated product diversification, reflecting the fact that market investors devalue overly diversified media conglomerates with nonsynergistic asset holdings (Ferrari, Harper, Ubinas, Wolf, & Zeisser, 2002). In essence, while related business and regional diversification was more effective in building the financial health of media firms, extensive diversification may still be used as a strategic move to acquire a certain competitive position (e.g., better cash flow or presence in a critical sector), and the latter approach might be equally important as we enter the technology-driven era of digital media that are highly dependent on cash resources.

Top 10 Global Media Conglomerates and Their Holdings

Since the aforementioned major media conglomerate studies, News Corp. has successfully acquired an MVPD distribution system through its merger with DirecTV and moved its headquarters from Australia to the United States, AOL Time Warner has been restructured as the new "Time Warner," and NBC has become a vertically integrated broadcast network, just like all of its competitors, with the addition of Universal. Table 9.1 details the top 10 global media conglomerates and their media holdings. Time Warner continues to be the leading conglomerate among its peers with an emphasis in branded content and MVPD business. It has a relatively lesser presence in the broadcast sector. Nevertheless, though Time Warner is comparably weaker in the market of broadcast networks, it more than made up its strategic competitiveness with its content production properties in the television sector. The number two conglomerate, News Corp., is very competitive in both broadcast and MVPD markets, in both branded television/film and print content, and in many regions of the world. Its strategic emphasis, however, is different from that of Time Warner in that it rests on the wireless MVPD platform. The following two U.S.-based conglomerates, Disney and Viacom, are very similar in their holdings as well as total revenue size. Both conglomerates have strong broadcast properties, MVPD brands, and successful production resources. The rest of the six media conglomerates are significantly smaller than the top four firms discussed thus far and have comparatively fewer media holdings. Whereas Vivendi and Comcast focus on the MVPD sectors, Bertelsmann centers its holdings in the broadcast, TV/film production, and print sectors. NBC is relatively diversified into broadcast, MVPC, and TV/film production businesses, though with a more modest number of holdings in each area. Finally, Sony's strength seems to be in the content production and music sectors, whereas Cox has more presence in broadcast and MVPD distribution businesses, along with its print holdings. It is evident that the majority of the top global media conglomerates have invested heavily in developing MVPD and content production assets. The competencies of producing attractive content, owning branded MVPD products, and/or having access to MVPD distribution systems seem to be essential for most global media conglomerates.

FINAL THOUGHTS

Because of many inherent characteristics as discussed in chapter 3, media firms are likely to expand into different product and geographic markets. In a way, the decision is not whether to diversify but to what

TABLE 9.1

Top Ten Global Media Conglomerates 2004

Rank	Company	Sales (In mil., 2003)	Broadcast Networks/Stations	MVPDs	TV/Film Production/Distribution	Print	Other
1	Time Warner	$39,565.0	The WB Network	Time Warner Cable Bright House HBO TBS CNN Cartoon Network TNT Court TV Cinemax	Warner Bros. Pictures Warner Bros. Studios Warner Bros. Television Warner Bros. Animation Telepictures Production Castle Rock Ent. Turner Entertainment New Line Cinema Fine Line Features	Time Inc. Warner Books Little, Brown, & Co.	America Online Warner Bros. Records The Atlantic Recording Warner Home Video
2	News Corp. /DirecTV	$31,080.2[a]	Fox Network Fox Stations Group Fox Sports Radio Networks Chris-Craft Industries Sky Radio	DirecTV PanAm Sat Fox Sports Net Fox Movie Channel Fox News Channel FX National Geographic Channel Speed Channel British Sky Broadcasting China Network Fox Sports Australia Phoenix Satellite Tele. Sky Italia Sky Latin America Sky PerfecTV Japan STAR Cine Canal	20th Century Fox Film Fox Television Studios 20th Century Fox Television Twentieth Television Blue Sky Studios Fox 2000 Pictures	Harper Collins Publishers TV Guide New York Post The Sun The Sunday Times The Times News International Daily Telegraph Herald Sun Post-Courier Sunday Herald Sun Sunday Times The Advertiser The Australian The Courier Mail The Mercury The Sunday Telegraph Weekly Times	Fox Music

	Company	Revenue	Broadcasting/Radio	Cable Networks	Film/TV Production	Publishing	Other
3	Walt Disney Co.	$27,061.0	ABC Network ABC Stations Group ABC Radio Radio Disney ESPN Radio	ABC Family The Disney Ch. ESPN A&E The History Ch. Lifetime E! Entertainment Fox Kids Europe Fox Kids Latin America SOAPnet Toon Disney	Walt Disney Pictures Walt Disney Television Walt Disney Animation Touchstone Films Buena Vista Pictures Miramax Films Platinum Dunes Productions	Disney Publishing	Buena Vista Music B.V. Home Entertainment
4	Viacom	$26,585.0	CBS Network UPN Network Viacom Stations Gr. CBS Radio Infinity Broadcasting Corp.	MTV BET Nickelodeon Nick at Nite CMT VH1 Spike TV Comedy Central Showtime The Movie Channel FLIX	Paramount Pictures Paramount Tele. CBS Productions CBS Television City King World Prod. Spelling Television Viacom Productions Big Ticket Television DNA Productions United Cinemas International United Int'l Pictures	Simon & Schuster The Free Press	Blockbuster Viacom Outdoor Famous Music Publishing Famous Players
5	Vivendi	$19,940.0		CANAL+ Group			Universal Music Group Vivendi Univ. Games
6	Comcast Corp.	$18,348.0		Comcast Cable Comcast SportsNet E! Entertainment Golf Network Outdoor Life Network Style QVC			

TABLE 9.1 continued

	Company	Revenue	Broadcast	Cable	Film/Production	Publishing	Music
7	Bertelsmann	$14,980.0	RTL Group		FremantleMedia SPORTFIVE TeamWork UFA Film	Random House Group Waterbrook Press Gruner + Jahr Group Direct Group	Sony BMG Music
8	NBC Universal	$14,433.0	NBC Network NBC Stations Group Telemundo Network Telemundo Stations Group PAX TV Network	CNBC MSNBC Bravo USA Sci-Fi Trio	Universal Pictures Universal Studios Universal Television NBC Studios NBC Entertainment		Universal Studios Home Video
9	Sony	$11,919.6[b]		Game Show Network AXN Animax Japan	Columbia Pictures TriStar Sony Pictures Television Sony Pictures Anima.		Sony BMG Music
10	Cox Comm.	$10,700.0	Cox TV Stations Group Cox Radio Stations Group	Cox Communications		Cox Newspapers Trader Publishing	

Note. From "100 Leading" (2004), "Who Owns What" (2004), Hoover's Online (2004), and OneSource (2004).

[a]Total of $20,959.0 million for News Corporation and $10,121.2 million for DirecTV.

[b]Total of film-, television-, and music-related sales.

degree and into which target market. Various media sources have identified up to 50 conglomerates that have actively pursued a diversification strategy in the global media marketplace ("Global Top 50," 2001). To examine the strategic behavior of this group of media firms systematically, the next step is to devise a framework of analysis that identifies the factors that impact such market behavior for the quantitative phase of empirical investigation. We now suggest a list of systematic determinants that reflect the characteristics of the industry in its choice of product and geographic diversification (see Fig. 9.4).

As found in the industrial economics perspective of diversification, the external environment shapes the strategic behavior of a firm. In the case of diversification for a media corporation, the general environment of a target country such as its regulatory, economic, technological, cultural, and social (e.g., education) environment influences not only the attractiveness and characteristics of the media industries in that country but also another set of important country-specific external factors—the communications/media environment such as a country's communications/media infrastructure (e.g., Internet connectivity and broadcast facilities) and demand for multimedia products (e.g., cable programming and Internet usage). These environmental factors also directly impact the attractiveness of each media industry in that country. Continuing with the industry economics theory of diversification, a media conglomerate's decision to enter a specific industry is likely to be determined by its target industry's basic characteristics such as market size, growth rate, profitability, and competition, as well as the factors of product/geographical relatedness and content–distribution complementary alignment as discussed previously.

Adopting a resource-based view of strategic management (Lockett & Thompson, 2001), we propose that, in addition to the aforementioned external factors, many internal resource determinants such as financial performance and stability, assets/complimentary assets, management teams, marketing systems, and related strategic alliances, which have been established to impact corporate diversification in previous literature (Chatterjee & Wernerfelt, 1991), also affect a conglomerate's diversification decision. Many other firm-specific resources and capabilities relevant to the media products are likely to shape a conglomerate's preferences in both product and geographic diversification as well. The specific internal factors might include a media firm's existing strategic networks with other related media product firms, its proprietary "content" products, its dependency on the core product (content vs. distribution), and its branded properties (e.g., MTV). Knowledge-based resources such as access to content production "talents" (e.g., writers, actors, producers, etc.) and the capability of transferring or repurposing content products for different media outlets as well as the availability of a multistream revenue system would also determine the degree of geographic diversity and the extent, directions, and mode of product diversification. As suggested by previous studies that stress the flexibility of

198

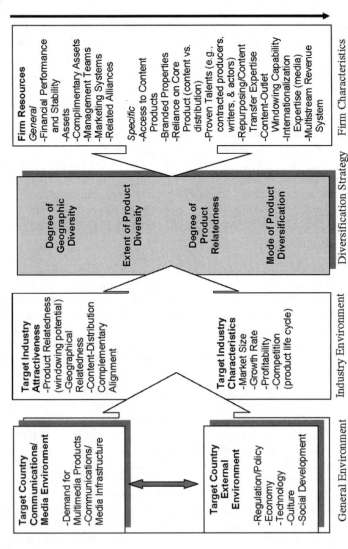

FIG. 9.4. Analytical framework: Factors influencing global media conglomerates' diversification strategy.

knowledge-based resources in coping with changing and uncertain environments (Miller & Shamsie, 1996), we also believe that the knowledge-based resources of media conglomerates would be more critical in determining the effectiveness (i.e., performance) of their international product diversification strategy.

In summary, the media-specific characteristics such as the complementary nature of content and distribution and the windowing process for media content products play a role in shaping the conglomerates' diversification strategies. Because the global media market entered a period of economic and technological uncertainty in the early 2000s, media firms are faced with an increasing need to be less reliant on traditional advertising revenues and to develop additional revenue opportunities in new-media systems. We believe that the trend toward global conglomeration will continue because global media conglomerates are in a more competitive position compared to nondiversified media firms. Global media conglomerates often have the resources to exploit content products via the repurposing process for distribution in multiple platforms under different ad or fee structures, to perform cross-platform marketing with complementary distribution systems, and to be well positioned to deliver products in the developing broadband spectrum with their diverse holdings and partnerships.

REFERENCES

Ayish, M. I. (2001). The changing face of Arab communications: Media survival in the information age. In K. Hafez (Ed.), *Mass media, politics, and society in the Middle East*. Cresskill, NJ: Hampton Press.

Bell, S. (1999). Impact of the global media revolution. *Usa Today Magazine, 127*(2646), 28–31.

Besley, T., Burgess, R., & Prat, A. (2002). Mass media and political accountability. In The World Bank (Ed.), *The right to tell: The role of mass media in economic development* (pp. 45–60). Washington, DC: The World Bank.

Bijker, W. E., Hughes, T. P., & Pinch, T. J. (1987). *The social construction of technological systems: New directions in the sociology and history of technology.* Cambridge, MA: MIT Press.

Carrington, T., & Nelson, M. (2002). Media in transition: The hegemony of economics. In The World Bank (Ed.), *The right to tell: The role of mass media in economic development* (pp. 225–248). Washington, DC: The World Bank.

Chan-Olmsted, S. M., & Albarran, A. B. (1998). The global media economic patterns and issues. In A. B. Albarran & S. M. Chan-Olmsted (Eds.), *Global media economics: Commercialization, concentration and integration of world media markets* (331–339). Ames, IA: Iowa State University Press.

Chan-Olmsted, S. M., & Chang, B. (2003). Diversification strategy of global media conglomerates: Examining its patterns and drivers. *Journal of Media Economics, 16*(4), 213–233.

Chan-Olmsted, S. M., & Oba, G. (2004, August). *The world media landscape: A comprehensive examination of media markets and their determinants in 98 countries.* Paper presented at the meeting of the Media Management and Economics Division of the Association for Education in Journalism & Mass Communication, Toronto, Canada.

Chatterjee, S., & Wernerfelt, B. (1991). The link between resources and type of diversification: Theory and evidence. *Strategic Management Journal, 12*(1), 33–48.

Croteau, D., & Hoynes, W. (2001). *The business of media: Corporate media and the public interest.* Thousand Oaks, CA: Sage.

Daniels, J., & Radebaugh, L. (1998). *International business: Environments & operations* (8th ed.). Reading, MA: Addison-Wesley.

Daniels, J. D., & Radebaugh, L. H. (2003). *International business: Environments & operations* (10th ed.). Reading, MA: Addison-Wesley.

Davis, C., & Craft, S. (2000). New media synergy: Emergence of institutional conflicts of interest. *Journal of Mass Media Ethics, 15*(4), 219–231.

Davis, S. (1999). Space jam: Media conglomerates build the entertainment city. *European Journal of Communication, 14*(4), 435–459.

Demers, D. P. (1999). *Global media: Menace or messiah?* Cresskill, NJ: Hampton Press.

Demers, D. (2002). *Global media: Menace or messiah?* (Rev. ed.). Cresskill, NJ: Hampton Press.

Djankov, S., McLiesh, C., Nenova, T., & Schleifer, A. (2002). Media ownership and prosperity. In The World Bank (Ed.), *The right to tell: The role of mass media in economic development* (pp. 114–166). Washington, DC: The World Bank.

Dyck, A., & Zingales, L. (2002). The corporate governance role of media. In The World Bank (Ed.), *The right to tell: The role of mass media in economic development* (pp. 107–140). Washington, DC: The World Bank.

Edge, D. (1995). The social shaping of technology. In N. Heap, R. Thomas, G. Einon, R. Mason, & H. Mackay (Eds.), *Information technology and society* (pp. 14–32). London: Sage.

Ferrari, B. T., Harper, N. W. C., Ubinas, L. A., Wolf, M. J., & Zeisser, M. P. (2002). *More restructuring ahead for media and entertainment.* Retrieved October 12, 2004 from http://www.corporatefinance.mckinsey.com/_downloadsknowledge/mof/2002_no6/viewpointmedia_entertainment.pdf

George, K., Joll, C., & Lynk, E. (1992). *Industrial organization* (4th ed.). London: Routledge.

Gershon, R. A. (1997). *The transnational media corporation: Global messages and free market competition.* Mahwah, NJ: Lawrence Erlbaum Associates.

Global top 50. (2001, August 27). *Advertising Age,* p. 24.

Golding, P., & Murdock, G. (1991). Culture, communications, and political economy. In J. Curran & M. Gurevitch (Eds.), *Mass media and society* (pp. 15–32). London: Edward Arnold.

Goldsmith, J. (2000, December 17). Congloms & showbiz: an uneasy alliance. *Variety, 381*(4), 3.

Gooderham, P., & Nordhaug, O. (2003). *International management: Cross boundary challenges.* London: Blackwell.

Hargittai, E. (1999). Weaving the Western web: Explaining differences in Internet connectivity among OECD countries. *Telecommunications Policy, 23*(10/11), 701–718.

Hollifield, C. A. (2001). Crossing borders: Media management research in a transnational market environment. *Journal of Media Economics, 14*(3), 133–146.

Hoover's Online. (2004). Hoover's Online. Available from http://premium.hoovers.comsubscribe/

International Telecommunication Union. (1997). *Challenges to the network: Telecoms and the Internet.* Retrieved October 15, 2004 from http://www.itu.int/ITU-D/ict/publications/inet/1997

Islam, R. (2002). Into the looking glass: What the media tell and why—an overview. In The World Bank (Ed.), *The right to tell: The role of mass media in economic development* (pp. 1–26). Washington, DC: The World Bank.

Jung, J., & Chan-Olmsted, S. M. (in press). Global media diversification strategy and performance: Assessing the relationship between dual diversification and firm performance in media industries. *Journal of Media Economics*.

Lee, S. (1998). The political economy of the Russian newspaper industry. *Journal of Media Economics, 11*(2), 57–71.

Lievrouw, L. A. (2001). New media and the "pluralization of life-worlds": A role for information in social differentiation. *New Media & Society, 3*(1), 7–28.

Lockett, A., & Thompson, S. (2001). The resource-based view and economics. *Journal of Management, 27*(6), 723–755.

Maddock, R. (1997). Telecommunications and economic development. In D. Lamberton (Ed.), *The new research frontiers of communication policy* (pp. 159–175). Amsterdam: Elsevier.

Maherzi, L. (1997). *World communication report: The media and the challenge of the new technologies.* Paris: UNESCO Publishing.

Mandel-Campbell, A. (1998, October 5). Argentina's massive media consolidation. *Advertising Age*, p. 4.

McChesney, R. W. (1998). The political economy of global media. *Media Development, 45*(4), 3–8.

McChesney, R. W. (1999, November 29). The new global media. *The Nation*, pp. 11–15.

McCombs, M. E. (1972). Mass media in the marketplace. *Journalism Monograph, 24.*

Miller, D., & Shamsie, J. (1996). The resource-based view of the firm in two environments: The Hollywood firm studios from 1936 to 1965. *Academy of Management Journal, 39*(3), 519–543.

100 leading media companies. (2004, August 23). *Advertising Age*, p. S4.

OneSource. (2004). *OneSource Online Business Information.* Available from http://www.onesource.com/

Parker, J. (2000). The CBS-Viacom merger: Impact on journalism. *Federal Communications Law Journal, 52*(3), 519–530.

Porter, M. E. (1990). *Competitive advantage of nations.* New York: The Free Press.

Powell, W. W. (1987). Review essay: Explaining technological change. *American Journal of Sociology, 93*(1), 185–197.

Rizzuto, R., & Wirth, M. (2002). The economics of video on demand: A simulation analysis. *Journal of Media Economics, 15*(3), 209–225.

Rodriguez, F., & Wilson, E. J. (2000). *Are poor countries losing the information revolution?* Retrieved December 17, 2004 from http://www.infodev.orglibrary/WorkingPapers/wilsonrodriguez.doc

Rogers, E. M. (1995). *Diffusion of innovations* (4th ed.). New York: The Free Press.

Shearer, B. (2000). AOL/Time Warner sparks speculation on the future of media. *Mergers & Acquisitions, 35*(3), 16–17.

Singh, A. (2000). Preface: World religions and media culture. *Polygraph: An International Journal of Culture & Politics, 12*, 3–11.

Smith, A. (1991). *The age of behemoths: The globalization of mass media firms.* New York: Priority Press.

Teinowitz, I. (2001, July 23). Senate eyes media mergers. *Advertising Age*, p. 31.

Tele-haves and have-nots. (1996). *The Economist, 339*(7966), 19–20.

United Nations Development Programme. (1999). *Human development report 1999.* New York: Oxford University Press.

Vishwanath, A., & Goldhaber, G. M. (2003). An examination of the factors contributing to adoption decisions among late-diffused technology products. *New Media & Society, 5*(4), 547–572.

Wei, R., & Leung, L. (1998). Owning and using new media technology as predictors of quality of life. *Telematics and Informatics, 15*(4), 237–251.

Wellstone, P. D. (2000). Growing media consolidation must be examined to preserve our democracy. *Federal Communications Law Journal, 52*(3), 551–554.

Who owns what. (2004). Columbia University's Graduate School of Journalism, *Columbia Journalism Review*. Retrieved December 17, 2004 from http://www.cjr.org/tools/owners/

World Bank. (2002). *The right to tell: The role of mass media in economic development*. Washington, DC: Author.

Yang, F., & Shanahan, J. (2003). Economic openness and media penetration. *Communication Research, 30*(5), 557–573.

Chapter 10

Conclusions

Going beyond general management functions in media organizations, this book zooms in on a specific area of media management and economics studies that tackles the subjects of media strategy and branding in the context of an emerging digital media marketplace. Asserting that media products have certain inherently unique characteristics that necessitate the revision of some generic management concepts derived from nonmedia industries, this book reviews relevant business frameworks and concepts for the analysis of media markets and applies these tools in discussions of strategy and competition in electronic media industries such as broadcast television, multichannel media, and broadband communications. Because the process of strategy formulation and implementation is fundamentally a firm's alignment of its internal resources with the changing environment to develop competitive advantages, the magnitude of the challenge or opportunity depends on the major trends that have shaped and are forming the competitive arena of today's media markets. In this final chapter, we begin with an overview of the developments expected to continuously mold the competitive landscape in the aforementioned industries, followed by discussions of the essential theories and paradigms that ground this track of study, critical issues in the methods of investigation, and interesting strategic and brand media management topics waiting to be explored.

TRENDS IN MEDIA INDUSTRIES: OPPORTUNITIES AND CHALLENGES

Driven mostly by technological advances, various trends are fundamentally changing how media audiences consume media and how media firms might attain competitive advantages. We begin with a discussion of the major shift in media consumer behavior, which basically defines the strategic parameters of all media firms.

Increase of Audience "Control"

The most significant development in audience consumption of media products in the 2000s has been the tip of balance regarding "control." Gone are the days when broadcast stations enjoyed captive audiences who sat through advertising or planned their schedules around a favorite show. Today's audiences, especially the younger ones, are becoming accustomed to the idea of "control" in what and how they watch, listen, or read. Amid the availability of electronic offerings such as MP3 players, DVDs, PVRs, and VODs, media consumers are increasingly demanding about issues like the timing, pricing, and even portability of media use. Commercials are skipped with a PVR, individual songs and videos are downloaded from the Internet, and favorite programs are delivered on demand. The implications of the increase in audience control are staggering. Most significantly, the traditional advertising formats for electronic media need to be reexamined, the business models upon which most media firms have operated are in need of revamping or diversifying, and conventional program-scheduling strategies are losing relevance. Finally, all media firms have to contemplate how to internalize new technology and be responsive to the new media audience and their need for "control" without overextending their resources.

Digital Conversion and Convergence

The arrival of new digital communication technologies have facilitated the delivery of digital signals via various platforms, improved audiovisual quality, brought forth more content options, and made interactivity possible and even demanded. The progression to a digital media environment also fuels the convergence of computing, networks, and media, further enriching consumers' media experience as well as expectations. The trend toward digital conversion and convergence also has significant implications. There is first the challenge of conversion costs in both hardware and software as well as the marketing of new digital products. There are also the challenges and opportunities of developing services that will take advantage of the multicasting, interactivity, and other ETV functions enabled by the new digital environment.

The Internet–Broadband Revolution

The Internet is now a ubiquitous medium that notably expands the variety and flexibility of traditional electronic media. The continuous growth of broadband deployment further boosts this new medium's role in revolutionizing the existing media landscape. The developments of streaming media (i.e., Internet delivery of audio and video content), online communities, VoIP networks, and PC-based ETV functions mean that the Internet, with its broadband distribution system, is now an attractive sector in which to develop or acquire resources. Although the opportunities presented by the broadband Internet go beyond marketing and possibly include new revenue potentials, the challenges remain to find a healthy mix of off-line and online ventures that improve the overall strategic position of a media corporation.

Globalization, Consolidations, and Alliances

As discussed earlier, media industries today are infused by digital technologies and converging platforms. The changing, complex environment promotes the necessities of being less reliant on traditional business models, developing attractive new-media services, competing multilaterally, and finding ways to spread risk and share resources. Very often, the strategic answer to cultivating these conditions for media firms is to diversify, acquire, collaborate, and internationalize. Though consolidation, alliance formation, and globalization might present an effective approach to gain competitive advantages in a short run, the biggest challenge for today's media firms contemplating these strategies is to find their optimal level of expansion because excessive international diversification, partnerships, and mergers and acquisitions might not only dilute their core competencies but also create bureaucracies that are less responsive to a changing media environment.

FOUNDATION OF INVESTIGATION: THEORIES AND PARADIGMS

It is our belief that the studies of media strategies would rely on a multiplicity of theories and paradigms. The brand management constructs such as brand knowledge, brand equity, and brand extension offer a rich tradition for the application of media-branding practices. Both the RBV- and IO-based approaches to strategic management provide solid frameworks for analyses of media firms' strategic behavior and performances. Notions such as value chains and strategic entrepreneurship present an excellent basis for explaining strategic postures and preferences regarding new-media investments. Diversification and strategic networks theories help elucidate the drivers for many popular media market phenomena and the relationship between such strategies and performance. Because the process of theory construction typically includes stages such as the identification of relevant constructs, the development of hypotheses about relationships, and the profferment of explanations for the relationships (Eisenhardt, 1989), a good understanding of relevant marketing and strategic management paradigms and theories provides the basic building blocks of propositions that we can integrate with established mass-communication theories to examine media-specific characteristics. For example, Chan-Olmsted (2006) proposes a theoretical framework for exploring the factors that shape the technology adoption decision and process for media firms. The analytical framework addresses the adoption of new media technologies through the integration of various theoretical perspectives such as entrepreneurship, strategic networks, and innovation adoption. Eight sets of antecedent variables in firm characteristics (e.g., size and organizational traits), media technology characteristics (e.g., newness and compatibility), perceived strategic value, alternatives available, strategic networks, market conditions, competition, and media regulation and policy are proposed to influence a media firm's decision of whether, how much, and/or when to invest in the commercialization of a new media technology. We believe that a focus on simple descriptions of media firms' strategic behavior would limit the explanatory and thus the predictive power of the investigations. Approaching media strategy research with both conceptually sound assumptions and theory-driven empirical studies would not only offer a more reliable, pragmatic assessment of media firm conduct with meaningful managerial implications but also provide a stronger linkage to past observations and thus contribute more substantially to the body of literature in media management and economics. In essence, the fluidity of media industries, due to the continuous changes in communication technology, creative development, and audience preferences, requires media management and economics scholars to constantly introduce, incorporate, and test new paradigms.

METHODS OF INQUIRY

Because of the lack of large data sets concerning media firms and the difficulty of analyzing media conglomerates with their nonstandardized reporting of financial data from different business units, most studies of media strategy have utilized the case study method of inquiry or based their analyses on secondary data sources. Hollifield and Coffey (2006), in their analysis of media management and economics literature, found that single case study was the most frequently adopted qualitative research method, followed by comparative case study; interview; historical methods; essays; legal, regulatory, and policy analysis; and field-participant observation, respectively. The adoption of qualitative investigations might be partially explained by the challenging tasks of developing ways to empirically test the resource-based view of a firm because valuable resources, by nature, are less observable (Godfrey & Hill, 1995). In fact, the definition for resources and capabilities that create sustainable competitive advantages (i.e., valuable, rare, not substitutable, and imperfectly imitable) presents great difficulties in strategy measurement and thus causality examination. Due to such limitations, in-depth case studies that review a firm or a group of firms in their market context and incorporate both archival and interview data present a more reasonable approach of examination. In regard to quantitative research methods, Beam (2006) noted that almost 60% of the primarily quantitative articles published in main media management and economics journals were analyses of data not collected specifically for the research project for which they were being used. Because of the availability of general industry or country data (e.g., total advertising revenues and GDP), use of secondary data to explore the relationship between exogenous determinants and strategic choice is common. However, the RBV approach continues to pose challenges in the measurement of intangible resources. The use of many proxy variables such as awards (e.g., Emmys) and salaries (e.g., CEO's compensation) as measures of intangible resources has been criticized as questionable to validly represent various underlying constructs (Godfrey & Hill, 1995) and should be employed with caution. In fact, many researchers have identified "construct measurement" in strategic management research as a significant problem, suggesting that too little attention is given to the reliability and validity of many indicators (proxies) used in strategy studies (Hitt, Boyd, & Li, 2004).

As the studies of media management and economics progress, we believe that it is essential to utilize larger data sets to test theory and apply multivariate statistical tools in advancing media strategy research. It might even be fruitful to combine quantitative examinations like questionnaires and qualitative investigations like interviews to increase the validity and reliability of their measures (Henderson & Cockburn, 1994). Because of the multiplicity of methods needed to identify, measure, and understand firm characteristics, strategy might be best researched as a dynamic or evolutionary phenomenon and empirically approached with a combination of longitudinal, in-depth case studies and other quantitative measures. In terms of the application of statistical techniques, due to the complexity of strategic behavior, it might also be productive to go beyond the typical multivariate statistics like regression and cluster analyses and explore various sophisticated tools such as panel data analysis, multinomial logit analysis, conjoint analysis, structural equation modeling, and multidimensional scaling. Hitt, Gimeno, and Hoskisson (1998) specifically suggested that strategic management scholars should make greater use of longitudinal designs and panel data methodologies, dynamic analytical models, and more sophisticated statistical tools like structural equation modeling.

TOPICS OF EXPLORATION

It is often useful to anticipate the course of an ongoing research agenda by first assessing the answers to the fundamental question of "What highlights the presumptions and boundaries of the field?" (Rumelt, Schendel, & Teece, 1996). A specific list of questions might be "How do a certain group of media firms behave?" "Why are these media firms different?" and "What determines media firm success or failure?" Operationally, one might investigate the empirical patterns of media firms, propose theoretical assumptions to explain the observed behavioral patterns and potential consequences, and empirically examine the implications of these strategic patterns. In essence, the three comprehensive areas of investigation are (a) the effects of the environment on media strategy, (b) the dynamic adaptation of media strategy to environment, and (c) the effects of media strategy on performance. The following list identifies some examples that address various aspects of these topics:

- *Application of "value chains" in the context of media industries.* This type of study would provide an excellent architecture for systematically understanding the sources of buyer value and even approaches to differentiation strategy.
- *Application of media taxonomy.* Such a study could help us identify specific business strategies (e.g., sales force management) within each media firm type (e.g., prospectors versus defenders). It can also be used to systematically depict different corporate strategies of media conglomerates.
- *Application of strategic entrepreneurship.* This strand of study would offer insightful examinations of new online or digital media venture patterns and the drivers and implications of different new-media strategies.
- *Investigation of innovation adoption of media firms.* Innovation is an integral strategy in today's technology driven media industry. Because innovations influence the market environment in which media firms operate, studies like this would help firms develop market response models to adapt to the changes brought about by relevant communications innovations.
- *Application of brand management concepts.* One might study media brand extension practices, both horizontally and vertically, as MVPD channel capacity continues to increase and consumers are faced with a proliferated media environment. One might examine the conditions in which a brand extension such as a new cable network is effective (e.g., perception of fit, risk of cannibalization, etc.). One might also investigate ways to measure brand equity in media businesses. As competition heats up among media firms in an increasingly fragmented and converging marketplace, the nourishing of brand equity, sensible extension of successful brands, and thoughtful management of the brand portfolio present excellent strategic avenues for media firms to create competitive advantages and eventually superior financial returns.
- *Studies of media consumption behavior.* As discussed earlier, technological forces, along with other exogenous factors, are changing consumers' consumption and expectations of media products. Research of media consumption, especially from a brand management perspective, provides critical insight for understanding media firms' marketing strategy. For example, one might apply the concept of brand consideration sets to explain how heteroge-

neous audiences with different programming tastes choose new programs, considering programming as products with uncertain attributes. Studies in the consumer goods industry have shown that a multiproduct firm's portfolio of products affects consumer purchase decisions about each of the firm's products due to consumer loyalty from the information set consumers use to evaluate the profile of multiproduct firms (Anand & Shachar, 2004). Another area of media consumer studies might be the investigation of the effects of corporate ownership on consumption choices.

- *Reexamination of programming strategy.* Various management theories might be applied to explain an important business strategy of electronic media organizations—programming selection and scheduling. For example, a finance portfolio selection theory was used to explain network program selection behavior (Litman, Shrikhande, & Ahn, 2000).

- *Analyses of mergers, acquisitions, and divestiture.* As the trend of media conglomeration continues, one might examine the patterns of M&A, divestitures, and their implications. Various issues have been pointed out as potential problems for the strategies of mergers and acquisitions. Hitt, Ireland, and Hoskisson (2001) specifically identified seven pitfalls to watch for: integration difficulties, inadequate evaluation of target firms, large or extraordinary debt, inability to achieve synergy, overdiversification, excessive focus on acquisitions by management, and oversize corporations. It would be interesting to empirically investigate not only the patterns of media M&A but also the challenges and consequences of different M&A scenarios.

FINAL THOUGHTS

From the oldest incumbent broadcasters to the newest Internet entrants, the electronic media industries today are fluid, dynamic, and filled with firms of different resources, capabilities, and thus strategic preferences. Because of the embedded nature of media in our daily lives, their pervasive influence on a society, and the largely intangible consumption of these products, we often fail to regard the media suppliers as institutions that still need to develop competitive advantages and deliver healthy financial returns. Subsequently, the emphasis on media strategy studies has been somewhat limited amid the substantial environmental changes in media industries during the past decade. It is our assertion that with the growing multiplicity of product offerings, programming sources, and distribution platforms, the media industries present an ideal arena for strategic competition and thus a fertile setting for media strategy studies. Vertical integration, international diversification, joint-venture alliances, brand extensions, innovation management, corporate entrepreneurship, and many more market behaviors are ripe for the empirical testing of strategic and brand management and other economics theories in a media context. Finally, as digital technologies continue to converge the presentations of media contents and induce the conglomeration of media firms, a multifaceted approach to strategy research (i.e., multiple time periods, methods, and units) might offer the most productive outcome for this journey. It is my hope that this book will serve as a springboard for an exciting new area of scholarship and for the pragmatic applications of examining media institutions as dynamic market competitors in a fascinating economic sector.

REFERENCES

Anand, B., & Shachar, R. (2004). Multi-product firms, information, and loyalty. *Journal of Marketing Research, 41*(2), 135–150.

Beam, R. A. (2006). Quantitative methods in media management and economics. In S. M. Chan-Olmsted, A. Albarran, & M. Wirth (Eds.), *Handbook of media management and economics* (pp. 523–550). Mahwah, NJ: Lawrence Erlbaum Associates.

Chan-Olmsted, S. M. (2006). Issues in media management and technology. In S. M. Chan-Olmsted, A. Albarran, & M. Wirth (Eds.), *Handbook of media management and economics* (pp. 251–274). Mahwah, NJ: Lawrence Erlbaum Associates.

Eisenhardt, K. M. (1989). Agency theory: An assessment and review. *Academy of Management Review, 14*(1), 57–74.

Godfrey, P. C., & Hill, C. W. (1995). The problem of unobservables in strategic management research. *Strategic Management Journal, 16*(7), 519–535.

Henderson, R., & Cockburn, I. (1994). Measuring competence? Exploring firm effects in pharmaceutical research. *Strategic Management Journal, 15*(special issue), 63–84.

Hitt, M. A., Boyd, B., & Li, D. (2004). The state of strategic management research and a vision of the future. In Ketchen, Jr. D. (Ed.), *Research methodology in strategy and management* (Vol. 1, pp. 1-31). Oxford, England: Elsevier.

Hitt, M. A., Gimeno, J., & Hoskisson, R. E. (1998). Current and future research methods in strategic management, *Organizational Research Methods, 1*(1), 6–44.

Hitt, M. A., Ireland, R. D., & Hoskisson, R. E. (2001). *Strategic management: Competitiveness and globalization* (4th ed.). Cincinnati, OH: South-Western College.

Hollifield, C. A., & Coffey, A. J. (2006). Qualitative research in media management and economics. In S. M. Chan-Olmsted, A. Albarran, & M. Wirth (Eds.), Handbook of media management and economics (pp. 571–598). Mahwah, NJ: Lawrence Erlbaum Associates.

Litman, B. R., Shrikhande, S., & Ahn, H. (2000). A portfolio theory approach to network program selection. *Journal of Media Economics, 13*(2), 57–79.

Rumelt, R. P., Schendel, D. E., & Teece, D. T. (1996). Fundamental issues in strategy. In R. P. Rumelt, D. E. Schendel, & D. T. Teece (Eds.), *Fundamental issues in strategy: A research agenda* (pp. 9–47). Cambridge, MA: Harvard Business School Press.

Author Index

211

Subject Index